Catherine Eddy at age 15

*"The happiest period of all humanity in the Western World
in ten centuries was the twenty-five years before the First Word War"
Herbert Hoover, "Memoirs"*

*"... in those pre-1914 days when it was bliss to be alive
(and the world was never the same again)"
A.L. Rowse, "Glimpses of the Great"*

Corner of my mother's bedroom —
1601 Michigan Ave. —— Where I was born

An American Girl Travels into the Twentieth Century

THE CHRONICLE OF
CATHERINE EDDY BEVERIDGE

Albert J. Beveridge III
and
Susan Radomsky

HAMILTON BOOKS

A member of
The Rowman & Littlefield Publishing Group ·
Lanham · Boulder · New York · Toronto · Oxford

Copyright © 2005 by Hamilton Books
4501 Forbes Boulevard, Suite 200
Lanham, Maryland 20706

Hamilton Books Acquisitions Department (301) 459-3366

PO Box 317
Oxford OX2 9RU, UK

Library of Congress Control Number: 2005931847
ISBN 0-7618-3335-8 (alk. paper)

    The paper used in this publication meets the minimum require-
ments of American National Standard for Information Sciences—
Permanence of Paper for Printed Library Materials,

ANSI Z39.48—1984

Produced in association with
Salsgiver Coveney Associates Inc.

Portrait of Catherine in Paris in 1899 by Lucien Levy-Dhurmer (1865-1953), entitled Pandora's Box.

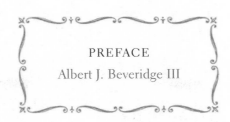

PREFACE

Albert J. Beveridge III

The diary that forms the core of this book was kept by my grandmother during the years 1902–1908 when she was a young woman engaged in the serious business of finding a husband. It is likely that the original diary covered a considerably longer period, but in the 1940s she decided to put her "papers" in order, and as a result she edited her handwritten daily entries from the period of her life that she considered the most interesting and exciting into an integrated narrative. To the written material she added photographs and memorabilia. The final product consisted of three three-ring binders that have been deposited in the Newberry Library in Chicago. We have made no changes to the final typewritten pages except as noted at the end of the diary.

She never revealed, insofar as I have been able to determine, her motive or purpose in editing her original handwritten record. She prepared only one copy, which came to me as part of her estate without instructions of any sort. In some ways, this was out of character since my grandmother usually left precise instructions as to the disposition of any objects I or my siblings received. She would even go so far as to tell us what pieces of furniture would look good

together so that she could guide our tastes from beyond the grave. Whatever her reasons may have been, we decided to seek a publisher after lending the original diary to a number of friends who read it with pleasure and urged us to make it available to a wider audience.

This book would not have been possible without the generosity and dedicated help of many persons. Susan Radomsky deserves special praise. She contributed much of the historical research and was the author of "Catherine's Family." Karen Salsgiver has been a talented designer and a creative editor. My assistant, Delores Cooper, has been indefatigable in helping prepare the manuscript.

I owe thanks to my brother, Franklin, and especially to my sister, Elissa, who has been generous beyond the bonds of family responsibility. And I would be remiss if I did not also give special recognition to my wife, Madzy, who established a special attachment to my grandmother, urged me for many years to have the diary published, and has been a sympathetic critic and counselor during the years it has taken to prepare the manuscript.

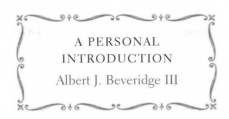

The young girl you meet in the pages of this book is not the person I knew as a boy growing up. Catherine Eddy may have been a shy and diffident young lady; Mrs. Albert J. Beveridge was a formidable matriarch. I cannot recall the first time I became conscious of her as an individual, any more than I can remember when my father or mother appeared to me as personalities—and probably for many of the same reasons. She was omnipresent. I grew up in Indianapolis, where my parents' house was contiguous to my grandmother's. At that time it was evident to me that "Baba" (a name that she loathed, which was mercifully replaced with "Nonna" after my sister married a Florentine doctor) was the center of our family universe. Her position in the community, as the widow of a celebrated Indiana senator, and in the family gave her a natural base from which to exercise her leadership talents, and she did. I believe that the first words I recall from my youth were my mother saying, "Mrs. Beveridge would like…" or "Mrs. Beveridge has asked…" The requests issued from a woman with a very firm view of the world.

In all matters important to my character as a grown-up—education, deportment, health, appearance, intellectual development, artistic sensibility, and responsibility—she dominated; my parents followed. In all matters important to my life as a young boy—athletics, friends, games, and relationships with girls—she had little interest or influence, except the right to veto. She was not cold—quite the contrary—but she was intimidating. Indeed, it was not until 1961, when she was eighty and I was in my second year of law school (after two years as a junior army officer), that I was able to break her intractable grip on my life. A trivial social incident was the occasion of a strong disagreement between us. I did not apologize or repent. I was banished for about six months, then restored to grace as if nothing had happened.

As might be expected, however, Nonna prevailed in the end. After my marriage to a lovely and enchanting Dutch woman, of whom Nonna resoundingly approved, we assumed the position previously occupied by my parents. (They had meanwhile divorced, and shortly after my marriage my father had died.) Her campaign began with the furnishing of our first house, which she not only directed but, to our relief, substantially paid for. It continued with the offer of a summer cottage just below her

Opposite: Catherine and Albert with Albert, Jr.

magnificent beaux arts stone mansion in Beverly Farms, Massachusetts, where she lived during the summer, an offer which we again gratefully accepted.

Nonna was in the habit of giving Sunday lunches—a custom that, happily, has ceased in most families. As a young lawyer commuting to Massachusetts from Washington, I wanted to spend Sundays playing tennis or golf, or sailing—anything but languishing away at a formal lunch. And so the veiled struggle would begin. Every Monday morning my wife would call Nonna, thank her enthusiastically for the previous day's lunch, and explain that, if she were planning a lunch for next Sunday and we were to be invited, we (unfortunately) could not come because "Albert [who was five hundred miles away] had made plans for golf, tennis, sailing, picnics," etc. "Of course; I understand," would be the reply. Then on Friday would come the inevitable call: "My dear, I'm having a few people in for lunch Sunday and I'm counting on you and Albert to be there…." When I arrived in Boston from Washington, the first thing I would hear would be, "Guess what?" I didn't have to guess. After expressing my frustration I would hear, "Okay, if you feel so strongly about it, you call Nonna and settle it with her yourself." I never did call.

Not only in social matters was her influence dominant. She, like many grandparents, strongly shaped the cultural values of her grandchildren. All her life she was a Europhile, as is evident from the papers, artwork, furniture, and clothing she left behind. Her love of Europe was, however, highly selective. In music, it meant European conductors and the European repertoire, with the exception of John Alden Carpenter—the sole American composer I recall that she liked.

(I believe he was a personal friend.) As for the visual arts, she was under the influence of her lifelong friend Frederic Clay Bartlett, and his tastes were definitely Continental. He had studied art as a young man in Munich and had assembled one of the great early private American collections of post-Impressionist painting. Her reading was equally Continental in flavor. I cannot recall one American work of fiction she read during the period I knew her. In addition to the serious works mentioned below, light modern European fiction, such as Juan Jiménez's *Platero and I*, the stories of Don Camillo by Giovanni Guareschi, or a Lawrence Durrell tale pleased her, as did any work that argued that the works of Shakespeare were written by someone other than Shakespeare, and hopefully by the Earl of Oxford. She must have purchased dozens of copies of Dorothy and Charlton Ogburn's *This Star of England*, which propounded this theory, to give to friends. A quick way to make her take favorable notice of you was to mention the earl admiringly.

Although I did not realize it at the time, I suspect that her undying love of Europe was fueled by nostalgia for her youth and the world revealed in the pages of this diary. The buildings, languages, smells, and tastes of the Continent revived the memory of her young, happy days. She once told me that when she was driven to downtown Indianapolis (she never learned to drive) she would close her eyes and imagine she were on the Champs Élysées. She exerted all her influence to make sure that her grandchildren traveled throughout Europe and learned at least one European language. As a result, two of them married Europeans, and to her delight one of them, my sister, settled permanently in Florence, Italy.

Political Europe she either ignored or disdained, with the exception of Switzerland, where beginning in 1953 until the end of her life, she spent her summers, outside Zurich. Politically, she was very much an American, with distinct midwestern Republican values. A copy of the *Chicago Tribune* was in the front hall, and, in the evenings, if we had enjoyed a family dinner, we listened to Fulton Lewis Jr. and Lowell Thomas on the radio. Among politicians, she respected the conservative Robert Taft— that is, until John Kennedy was elected, at which point she transferred her remaining political enthusiasm to him. I suspect her shift in allegiance owed less to Kennedy's programmatic initiatives than to the favorable mention of her husband, the senator, in *Profiles in Courage*, and to his good sense in marrying Jackie.

How did she exercise her influence? There was, of course, a financial dimension. She didn't provide an allowance, except perhaps to my sister in the first few years after her marriage, but she always provided funds for education, a trip to

Europe, or concerts and operas. Above all her force was moral. In women she admired intelligence, wit, and joie de vivre, and she was not unaffected by physical beauty. In men she admired accomplishment. Effort was commendable, but it merited no praise unless it led to accomplishment. For my father and me, who carried the senator's name, accomplishment meant something the senator would have viewed with pride. For me the burden was supportable; for my father I am afraid it was not, for he never came close to realizing his natural talents.

Nonna was extremely interested in our education— both within and outside school. She saw to it that we went to the Herron Art Institute (today the Indianapolis Museum of Art) and encouraged an occasional concert when we were young. She was shocked at my meager vocabulary, so at the age of ten I was required to learn a word a day. The original wordbook is still in my possession, and the first two words are "politician" and "statesman." You can imagine in which category my grandfather, the senator, fell.

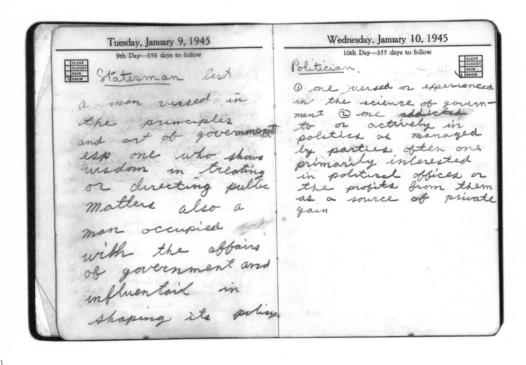

After we reached our mid-teens, nothing was held back. We were given many trips to Europe, where our objectives might include journeying to Bayreuth to view the rejuvenated Wagner festival of Wieland Wager or stopping in Basel for a Hodler exhibition.

But what was she like? She was of moderate height, about 5 feet 7 inches, and even though I was not particularly conscious of her physical beauty as a boy, I must have been subconsciously aware of what the photographs in this book reveal. Nonna also had an unforgettable crystalline laugh. It was spontaneous, girlish, unrestrained. It resounded through the whole house, like Melba's high C, which, according to Mary Garden, "came floating over the auditorium like a star and passed us and went out into the infinitude." It was beautiful. The laugh never changed. Even in her eighties, it remained unaffected, a youthful peal full of joy. One physical feature she retained her entire life was her glorious hair. When I was little, I would sometimes be admitted when she was engaged in her daily ritual of putting it up. She would be seated before a mirror with her hair falling behind her to the floor. First, there was vigorous brushing—which would last perhaps fifteen minutes, during which time she would converse—followed by braiding, usually with the help of her personal maid. Finally, the braids would be set on the back of her head—not, regrettably, on the top as they had been when she was a girl.

Then, if it were the summer—and that is the time of the year that I recall her best—she would be visited by the gardener, who let her know what vegetables were ready and the state of the cutting garden and the rest of the property.

He was followed by the cook, who went over the menu for the day and beyond. Since every member had been in service for at least a decade, these visits were businesslike but affectionate. Then, frequently, her attention would turn to me for a round of self-improvement. This might entail picking up marbles with my toes to improve my flat feet (worthless) or the word-of-the-day exercise to improve my vocabulary (more successful). Then she would turn her attention to her friends either on the telephone or by mail.

She was definitely reserved, except with good friends, and to many she was intimidating as well. I believe this was in part the result of natural shyness and in part the consequence of disappointments she had experienced in life. Widowed at the age of forty-six, she became estranged from her daughter, who married against her wishes. Her son, whom she came to realize was an incurable alcoholic, was a great disappointment. But once you broke through her reserve, a world opened to you. Perhaps the best indication of her personality is the close bond she established with her grandchildren's spouses. The two who knew her—one an Italian doctor, the other a young Dutch girl—developed an instant, intense, and permanent attachment to her. Why? Perhaps, as Europeans about to marry Americans, they found an understanding and appreciation of their backgrounds that gave them confidence and comfort. In any event, the attachment was real and immediate.

Considering her privileged upbringing and social position, Nonna was remarkably unself-centered. She liked to have her way, but, as I recall, it was generally for the perceived benefit of a family member or friend. She spent a great deal of time maintaining her friendships, which were many, varied, and of long standing. Some of those friendships, with people you will meet in the following pages, such as Frederic Bartlett or Adelaide Hamilton, lasted from childhood to old age. My grandmother also made friends with men, and occasionally women, whom she considered important to her well-being. More than once she told me that while all friendships were important, three were essential: "You should always make friends with your doctor, lawyer, and banker [by which she meant financial advisor]—and if you are so inclined your pastor, too." Correspondence and telephone calls were important, as was continued socializing and entertaining. Those Sunday lunches were essential to her.

Entertaining was no casual matter. Offering the best food was extremely important. Since my grandmother had a vegetable garden, tended by a professional gardener, the vegetables she served were determined by the season and the prevailing weather. She then chose the meat or fish to complement the vegetables. None of her dishes were simple. They were usually copied from a restaurant she had visited—never, but *never* from another hostess, since good recipes were trade secrets not to be passed about. If she found a good dish, she noted the basic ingredients for her own cook to work on. After she was satisfied that the dish was substantially ready, she and her cook then went to the restaurant for a meal to review the seasoning and presentation. The efficacy of these proceedings led to their gradual extinction, for toward the end of her life, the food at her table was so far superior to that at most restaurants that there was seldom any reason to eat out.

Her table was as sumptuous as the food. There were usually between sixteen and twenty-four guests at a single elliptical table. If you dropped by at about ten in the morning on a Sunday, you would find one of the staff—she did not have a butler, which she considered ostentatious—hanging a weighted cord from the chandelier to make sure the table was centered. The porcelain settings were spectacular, mostly Meissen, but occasionally Sevres, Old Zurich, or Nymphenburg. The best pieces are in the Art Institute of Chicago. In one respect she was well ahead of her time. There was never a cigarette holder or an ashtray, either on the table or, indeed, anywhere in the house. She loathed smoking, undoubtedly because she associated it with her husband's emphysema. Occasionally guests who were unaware of her aversion would light a cigarette in the living room over coffee after lunch. Then the scene, which I saw repeated often, always with amusement, would begin. What to do with the match? That was not so difficult because once it was dead it could be hidden. The ash was another matter. It would grow and grow to alarming lengths and always to the discomfort of the smoker, until my grandmother would say, "Esther, I believe X needs an ashtray."

Nonna's style of living required more than a little domestic help. When I was growing up, her household included a cook, a pantry maid who also did general housework, a personal maid, a chauffeur, and a gardener with a helper. At times this full-time staff would be supplemented by a seamstress, a laundress, and additional help for large social occasions. None of the staff were servants, however; they were members of the family, treated as valuable parts of a vibrant social organization. A personal maid like Esther

Bjorkman could become a close friend. Every one of the household staff I knew had worked for my grandmother for twenty or more years. A few retired with modest pensions she provided, as did the three servants who outlived her. Most, however, died in service, because the household had become their family.

Although social life was very important, so was the life of the mind. My grandmother was always a voracious reader. She was not particularly interested in novels during the period I knew her, although she had been fond of Edith Wharton's and Henry James's works as a young woman. She read biography and history and was interested in topical nonfiction like Rachel Carson's *Silent Spring*. Above all, toward the end of her life she became passionate about the works of Teilhard de Chardin and Sainte-Beuve, that she read in French. She never completed Sainte-Beuve's *Causerie du Lundi*, but she had read large portions of it before her death. In addition, she never lost her interest in current events. Reading was not for her a solitary or purely personal activity. Discussing books and reading aloud, even after we children had learned to read ourselves, were important activities in our household.

No portrait of Catherine would be complete without mentioning the animals that surrounded her. During my youth, there were dachshunds: she had up to fourteen, and no less than ten, at any one time. There were one or two favorites who were constantly with her, but the pack itself was a constant presence. Alarm clocks were superfluous in her house, since the dogs were walked at 6:30 a.m. Even a young man with an unlimited need and desire for sleep could not fail to awake when a pack of yelping hounds was released under his window at that time.

As I look back on the time I spent with her, I believe the one constant in her life was her desire that my brother, sister, and I be worthy of the family heritage. She spent a great deal of time investigating that heritage through genealogical study and by collecting anything that related to the family's past. She also kept copious records of the family's possessions, believing that succeeding generations had a responsibility to see that they were treated properly, and, if sold or given away, disposed of in a manner that would have been approved by the former owners. She also indoctrinated the family, especially the males, in their responsibility to live up to their forebears—the senator above all. That may sound forbidding; actually it was not. It made the past very much part of the present, though.

I cannot close this brief recollection without mentioning some of the persons you will meet in the pages of Catherine's chronicle whom I had the good fortune to know. Foremost was the artist Frederic Clay Bartlett, whom Catherine had knew from an early age. Frederic, who owned a farm in Essex, Massachusetts, attended virtually all my grandmother's Sunday lunches until he died in 1953. He also hosted "picnics" in a Bavarian *Jagdschlösschen* ("hunting lodge") that he had constructed on his farm. The lodge was modeled on François Cuvilliés' splendid Amalienburg near Munich, where Frederic had studied as a young man. To call a meal taken in such surroundings a picnic is a gross understatement. The *Jagdschlösschen* had about four rooms and a lovely terrace with a view toward Ipswich Bay. The large central room had mirrors on three sides with the fourth exposed to the water. It was decorated in *faux marbre* in Napoleonic style and was graced with a copy of David's famous portrait of Napoleon on horseback that Frederic had copied. Frederic had spent three years building and decorating it as an anniversary gift to his third wife, Evelyn Fortune Lilly, whom he had married in 1931.

The *Jagdschlösschen* replaced a fine old enclosed gazebo, a single room decorated with imitation Currier and Ives panels, which Frederic had designed and constructed some years before. Building and decorating whimsical spaces or redecorating rooms for friends was one of Frederic's chief occupations throughout his life. He completely redid my grandmother's dining room and terrace room in Beverly Farms. The dining room was done in severely classical style, *faux marbre* again, with *trompe l'oeil* columns and two huge real vitrines to hold her porcelain collection. The terrace room had a large Bavarian *Kocheloffen* set in a false niche below a mural frieze depicting the jungle with vines, monkeys, parrots, and similar creatures. Over each of the two entrances my grandmother's two favorite dachshunds were painted in profile.

What I recall most about Frederic is that as early as I can remember he treated me as a contemporary. He would say things like, "You know, Albert, martinis should be stone cold when served, and drunk quickly." This when I was about thirteen or fourteen. Or, "A pity [A] didn't live longer, he could have done so much," or "Why don't you convince your grandmother to build near us in Fort Lauderdale?" when I was perhaps fifteen. Actually, she did, but in no part due to me. Frederic was a gentle man of understated worldliness who always raised the gaiety of any gathering.

I also sometimes saw Adelaide Hamilton, my grandmother's childhood friend, who was married to the noted Chicago orthopedic surgeon Ned Ryerson. Adelaide was tall, slim, and very gentle. She seemed so delicate she could blow away. She had no children and seemed puzzled by me as a teenager. She was also a bit in awe of Catherine, her more energetic and peripatetic friend. Ned, Adelaide's husband, was gregarious and curious. He was always advocating excursions around Florida (where I usually saw them during my spring vacations), fishing trips, or anything that would break up the daily routine. Catherine was in the habit of making gifts to friends (she once gave a lovely small Berthe Morisot portrait to Frederic), and Adelaide had been the recipient of her generosity. In her will, Adelaide returned to our family any object that Catherine had given her or Ned.

I also met Katherine Dexter, whose marriage to Stanley McCormick, that tragic figure, became the subject of a T. C. Boyle novel, *Riven Rock*. Katherine, who never divorced Stanley, used to spend the summer in a beautiful chateau, Pragins, on the shore of Lake Geneva. I visited her twice there in the summer. She and a companion rattled around the twenty or more rooms, occasionally entertaining odd guests like me, who slept in beds surrounded by mosquito netting (in Switzerland!). The chateau now belongs to the United States and is used by official delegates visiting Geneva.

All of these individuals I knew in old age. What is wonderful about the stories you will read and the photographs you will see is that in them the same persons are in their youth — full of expectancy and enthusiasm, and ever so good-looking.

THE CHRONICLE OF CATHERINE EDDY BEVERIDGE

1902

Opposite, Catherine Eddy circa 1902

INTRODUCTION

⌒ 1902

IN A WAY CATHERINE'S WHOLE LIFE had been a preparation for her European journey. Tall and slender, and with an astonishingly bright coronet of thick, braided blond hair, she was a young woman of considerable cultivation and beauty. Her character and manners had been shaped by her mother, Abby Spencer Eddy, and her maternal aunt, Delia Spencer Caton. Abby and Delia, the daughters of Franklin Fayette Spencer, were prominent social leaders. The family fortune derived from hardware— specifically, from the great Chicago wholesale firm of Hibbard, Spencer & Bartlett, of which their father had been a founder. Delia had further increased her wealth by marrying Arthur J. Caton, the son of a leading jurist who had controlled the state's first profitable telegraph company.

Delia, who was childless, was deeply attached to Catherine and Abby. Abby had only a daughter and a son; it was understood that her children would inherit Delia's fortune one day. Abby and Delia had carefully superintended Catherine's upbringing, seeing her as the instrument of a potentially brilliant marriage that would affirm and augment the social position of the family. The Spencers and Catons were wealthy, but to marry Catherine to a European aristocrat would bring them to the apex of distinction. Toward this end, Abby and Delia not only instilled in Catherine their own highly refined sense of the feminine arts, but placed her under the care of a succession of distinguished ciceroni and tutors. Though Catherine had never attended school, except

for the briefest periods, she had all the polish and refinement that young ladies coveted: garbed in the latest Parisian fashions, she was well traveled and well read, an unflappable dancer and charming conversationalist, who was fluent in several languages. She was thought by some to have inspired the character, Nanda Brookenham, in Henry James's novel *The Awkward Age*.[1]

Catherine's account of 1902 begins in excitement and uncertainty as she embarks on a momentous trans-Atlantic journey. Just before Christmas, Catherine had learned that she was to be presented at the imperial courts of Berlin and St. Petersburg. Her home at 1601 South Michigan Avenue, in the Prairie Avenue district of Chicago, had been abuzz with preparations for her trip abroad. This was scarcely Catherine's first European odyssey. At twenty-one, she, like many of her Chicago friends, had spent a good part of every year since childhood on the Continent, traveling with her family. These presentations, however, represented a coveted form of recognition from Europe's ruling families. Yet even this fact could not quite dispel the regret Catherine felt at leaving Chicago. A twinge of doubt assailed her as she celebrated New Year's Day on the north side with a party of her friends, at the home of Mrs. Eleanor Patterson, whose family owned the *Chicago Tribune*.

Such was Catherine as she set out to be presented at the imperial courts of Berlin and St. Petersburg. She does not say how these presen-

---

[1] Details of Catherine's background and family life are given in the essay "Catherine's Family," on page 188.

tations were arranged, but they were almost certainly owing to the initiative of her brother, Spencer, a rising young diplomat who enjoyed a warm relationship with Secretary of State John Hay. Spencer had gotten his start in diplomacy by persuading Hay to take him on as private secretary in 1897, when Hay was appointed ambassador to England. In May 1898, Catherine had been presented at the Court of St. James, though she was then only sixteen years old and had not yet come out in the United States. In an unpublished account of that experience, Catherine deemed her juvenile presentation to have been unwise but explained that her mother couldn't resist the idea of having Catherine presented at court during a select diplomatic reception, when just a few guests mingled with the royal family. In addition to the thrill of the experience itself, the right sort of presentation could bring a young woman to the attention of desirable European suitors; because the presentation was written up in the papers, it also added to her prestige at home. Catherine's presentations at Berlin and St. Petersburg testify to Spencer's continuing warm relationship with Hay as well as to the power of his friendships with members of the Russian imperial family.

Catherine's first stop en route to Berlin was Paris, where she consulted with her mother's dressmakers, made the arrangements necessary for her trip, and joined other members of her traveling party. This included two other American girls—Elsie Porter and Ruth Snyder— who were also to be presented at court—along with their servants and family members, most of whom Catherine knew. Elsie, who was one of Catherine's close friends, was a resident of Paris, where her father, General Horace Porter, was American ambassador. Catherine had

known the Porters for some years, and it was under General Porter's protection that she and her maid, Jenny, were traveling. Catherine knew Ruth Snyder, who was the niece of Charlemagne Tower, American ambassador to Russia, from summering at Manchester, Massachusetts. Ruth was traveling with her mother, born Emma Pauline Tower, and her stepfather, Mr. Reilly. (Ruth later married into an aristocratic Belgian family, becoming the Countess Camille de Borchgrave in 1907.) Thus all three girls being presented were from affluent families with strong diplomatic connections. In addition, the families were Republicans, as Ambassadors Porter and Tower, along with Ambassador Andrew Dickson White, their counterpart in Berlin, had received their appointments from McKinley.

Though the presentation of Americans at European courts had gone on for more than a century, to be presented at Berlin or St. Petersburg was a rarity. Germany, which had only recently emerged as a world power, was still an autocratic, inward-looking country, whose rituals served mainly to perpetuate an esprit de corps among its own nobility. The experience of participating in a court ritual and being personally acknowledged by the sovereign was rare, a privilege that few of the sovereign's own subjects enjoyed. Elsie, who in 1907 wrote an account of the trip that we quote in the following pages, noted that the inhabitants of Berlin lined the streets at night to watch her carriage pass as it carried her to her brief appearance before the kaiser. She speculated that the Germans' decision to allow a few American girls to be presented at Berlin was a political gesture intended to warm relations with the United States. Indeed, the event was one of several occurring around that time that tended to encourage the United States to view the Germans favorably. Not only were these diplomatic families treated to a flattering reception at the German court, but the kaiser's handsome young brother, Prince Henry, soon toured the United States, at which time President Roosevelt's daughter, Alice, was given the honor of christening the kaiser's new yacht.

St. Petersburg, where the imperial family had ruled for three hundred years, was an even more esoteric society. The privilege accorded Catherine and her American friends may be gauged by the caliber of the other women presented, for Consuelo, Duchess of Marlborough, and Millicent, Duchess of Sutherland, were among the most eminent members of the English aristocracy. Russia's opulent, hermetic court, separated from the other courts of Europe by what was, until the advent of the railroad, an almost inconquerable distance, nonetheless enjoyed a curious intimacy with the other European courts, a consequence of the growth of an international elite and intermarriage among sovereignty. The Countess of Warwick deemed Queen Victoria's "idea of making Europe one huge family, by marriage, one of the most dangerous that ever entered a queenly head." Yet Victoria's goal was being practically accomplished, as the web of familial connections among the world's leading powers proliferated. Around the court circles of Europe a surprisingly well-integrated and compact international society was forming. Having gained entrée into one part of this society through her brother's diplomatic connections, Catherine moved in its various parts comfortably.

Whereas Catherine's time in Berlin was relatively brief, her stay in Petersburg was richer and more varied, thanks to the attention of the Grand Duchess Vladimir, a powerful member of the imperial family. On leaving Petersburg, Catherine passed again briefly through Paris and bid good-bye to her friend Elsie. She then proceeded to England, spending a weekend with Lord and Lady Elcho, who, with Prime Minister Arthur Balfour and others, made up the Edwardian social circle known as "the Souls." In late February, Catherine sailed for the States, returning home to enjoy the coming of spring with her Chicago friends, her days an idyll of feasting, riding, and theatergoing.

In mid-May, Catherine again embarked for Europe, this time in the company of her mother, her aunt Delia, and Jenny and Thérèse, their respective maids. Like other members of their social circle, many of whom they would see abroad, the Eddys and Mrs. Caton were headed for the pleasure spots of Europe. After two months spent mostly in Paris and Aix (where her mother was staying for the sake of her health), Catherine set off with her former tutor, Miss Moewis, for a two-week visit to Constantinople, where Spencer was attached to the American embassy. As Catherine's account suggests, under Constantinople's gaiety lay anxiety, uncertainty, and the threat of violence. Though the aging sultan, Abdul Hamid II, continued to rule, the authority of his government had drastically waned, casting doubt on the future of his empire. Representatives of the European powers were on the spot, seeking variously to shore up the sultan's government, monitor events, and exploit opportunities in the case of turmoil. Meanwhile, the pleasures of the place and a wave of prosperity had made Constantinople stylish and agreeable. The advent of autumn dictated a return to the States, where Catherine gaily participated in the fall social season.

The C

VOLUME LXI.—NO. 20.

TO BE PRESENTED AT THE GERMAN COURT.

MISS CATHERINE EDDY

Miss Catherine Eddy, daughter of Mr. and Mrs. Augustus N. Eddy of Chicago, will be presented to the Emperor and Empress of Germany tomorrow at Berlin. She is a member of the party of General Horace Porter, the United States Ambassador to France, and is now in the German capital. Later the party will go on to St. Petersburg. Spencer Eddy, Miss Eddy's brother, is first secretary of the United States legation at Constantinople.

On New Year's Day, 1902, I lunched at Mrs. Robert Patterson's. That evening my mother gave a dinner for me of twenty-eight, at three tables, and afterwards a little dance. There was some misgiving in my heart about leaving so soon to go abroad. I was having a good time, and Europe seemed very far away. The next day Joe Patterson[2] and Helen[3] were at the station to say goodbye. Mamma was in tears, and left before the train started. My father went with me to New York.

On January 4 Jenny[4] and I sailed for France. We landed in Cherbourg on the 10th, and went at once to the Embassy in the Rue de Ville Juste. General Porter, the Ambassador, had rented the hotel that had housed the Spitzer collection, which was now in the Louvre. Some of it, however, had been left in the great salle d'Armes, where the receptions of the Embassy took place. General Porter had been aide-de-camp to General Grant, and had been present in the room at Appomattox when Lee surrendered. He had been a shrewd business man, a conventional politician, and a warm supporter of McKinley, who had rewarded him with the Paris post. Mrs. Porter was small, with a pretty head of white hair, and little fine hands and feet. She was almost fanatically religious, absorbed in keeping Sunday undefiled, and with little interest in her duties as Ambassadress. Elsie loved her father, but was constantly irritated by her mother's religious obsession and the difficulty of running the Embassy properly. Elsie and I were all excitement at the prospect of the wonderful trip we were to make, but poor Mrs. Porter was only worried and flustered, and reluctant to go.

[2] Joe Patterson was one of the hundreds of remarkable figures who peopled Catherine's life during these years. He and many others are profiled for present-day readers in the section entitled "Dramatis Personae" (page 221).

[3] Helen Birch, Catherine's second cousin, was also one of her dearest friends.

[4] Jenny Byrne was Catherine's personal maid and companion, a domestic position without modern analogue. Jenny was responsible for helping Catherine with her dress, hair, and general appearance, but far more as well. Since no young lady of Catherine's class could venture out alone, even on the most insignificant errand, Jenny was her constant companion and chaperone. Catherine was close to her mother and to friends including Adelaide Hamilton and Helen Birch, and would confide even her most secret thoughts to them. Jenny, however, knew Catherine's thoughts first and did much to steady her unsure young charge.

Jenny Byrne with Pierrot

General Horace Porter

I had only a week in which to order my dresses for Berlin and St. Petersburg. Unfortunately, in my diary I say very little about them, and even in turning the pages of my little book I cannot quite remember the dress I wore to court in St. Petersburg. All I say is that it was made of cloth of silver. I think that my mother had written ahead to Mme. Dévie, and that some preparation had already been made. My court train for Berlin was the old court train I had worn in England, but the dress was new.[5] Jenny and I had busy days going from Worth to Paquin, where my mother's beautiful vendeuse, Mme. Louise, made what was really the prettiest dress I had.[6] We would lunch at Colombin's, and go from fitting to fitting. My blue velvet evening cloak, half lined with ermine, and my evening dresses were packed at Worth's and the trunk sent to the Embassy. I can

[5] In 1898, Catherine had been presented at the Court of St. James (see Catherine's Family"). Though Catherine's memory is hazy on this point, Elsie recalls that at Berlin Catherine wore a white satin dress with a long train trimmed in rosebuds and tulle. "Her bright gold hair [was] done in high braids like a crown around her head. She was very beautiful. Her Opera cloak was in royal blue velvet edged with white fox." Elsie's dress was also white satin, "embroidered in roses and gold and tiny green leaves"; the train was of "white panné, embroidered in gold wreaths and edged with white fox." Mrs. Porter's dress was of "silver brocade, trimmed with old point de l'Aiguillé lace, with a train of darker grey velvet, magnificently embroidered in paillettes and edged with sable." Their dresses and trains were so voluminous that "each lady took up one side of a carriage."

[6] The houses of couture founded by Charles Frédéric Worth (1825–95) and Isadore Paquin (ca. 1862–1907) were considered the best in Paris. A vendeuse was a skilled and discriminating artisan who oversaw the creation of her client's clothes and shaped the client's reputation for beauty over the years.

Elsie Porter at court

[7] The need to secure passports underscored the novelty of the journey. They were normally not required for European travel. The Russians, however, insisted on them, a measure that struck some as sinister.

[8] Catherine's brother.

[9] Countess Therese Brockdorff was one of three powerful ladies-in-waiting. She was the cousin of German chancellor von Bülow, who described her as extremely attractive and "intense." Her apartments lay within the imperial palace. As Mistress of the Robes, she was the arbiter of manners at court. Visiting her at the opening of the court was obligatory, a duty levied on Germans and foreigners alike.

not understand how it was all accomplished in that short space of time. Reynolds Hitt, who was to go with us to Russia, came one afternoon with our passports for us to sign.[7] The Grand Duke Michael sent me a telegram from Cannes. I think he wished my visit in St. Petersburg to be a very happy one. Finally we left Paris on the afternoon of January 17. General and Mrs. Porter, Elsie and Tante Marie (her maid), Jenny and myself, Reynolds Hitt, Mr. and Mrs. Reilly and Mrs. Reilly's daughter, Ruth Snyder. Mrs. Reilly was the sister of Charlemagne Tower, our Ambassador to Russia.

We arrived in Berlin early the next morning. We were met by Mr. Jackson and Dodge of the Embassy. Jackson said, "Where is Spencer?[8] We hoped you would bring him with you." We drove to the old Kaiserhof Hotel, where an apartment had been reserved for us. That afternoon, dressed in our best, we went with Mrs. White, the Ambassadress, to call on the Mistress of the Robes, Countess Brockdorff.[9] The drawing room was filled with "officers in smart uniforms, and many German ladies with their young daughters who were to be presented at the court—fair girls, very shy and simply dressed, with their hands thrust in little muffs." I wore my black velvet afternoon dress with a lace collar. With it I wore a black velvet hat with a little ruffle of the ecru lace falling over the brim. It sounds odd for a winter afternoon, but in reality it was one of the prettiest dresses I ever wore. I had a huge white fox muff. That evening we went to the Winter Garden.

The next day we lunched with the Ambassador and Mrs. White. I sat next to Reynolds Hitt. He was to sit next to me many times in the days to come. He was the son of the Congressman from Illinois, and his mother was, in her day, one of the great hostesses of Washington. He was a very pleasant fellow, with soft brown eyes, and charming manners. At this time he was second secretary of the Embassy in Paris. His principal duty now, beside acting as secretary to General Porter, was to look after Elsie and me, and I shall always remember his kindness and the good times we had together.

The next evening we went with the Ambassador and Mrs. White to the opera—The Meistersinger. Afterward we had supper, and I sat next to the Ambassador, a great honor for so young a girl. Andrew White was then seventy years old. He had been appointed to Germany in 1897, the year that General Porter had gone to Paris. He had been President of Cornell University, and had an interesting and varied life. He had been Minister to Russia, and was now our first Ambassador to Germany. Both he and Mrs. White were very kind to me in the few days that I spent in Berlin.

The next day we were presented at court. I wrote in my diary, "Begin to dress early in the afternoon. Only just ready in time, thanks to Ruth [Snyder] and Miss Perkins, who came in to see me." I drove to the palace with Mrs. White. Evidently Elsie and her mother drove together. Of all the royal palaces that I have visited as a tourist I have never seen one, to my mind, as beautiful and distinguished as the old Schloss in Berlin. The imperial family lived there very little, spending almost all their time in Potsdam, and some of the rooms, perhaps for that reason, had undergone almost no change from the time of Frederick the Great. Almost the first thing I noticed were the marvelous parquetry floors, so brilliantly polished that they reflected the lights from the great crystal chandeliers above us. The members of the Diplomatic Corps, with a few young women who were to be presented, assembled in one of those beautiful rooms. As I stood there with my train over my arm I felt very shivery, and a little frightened. Just at that moment footmen came in, bearing trays with cups of steaming tea. Never had anything tasted as comforting to me. Finally the time came for us to place ourselves in position to enter the throne room, which is known as the Rittersaal. Of our group Mrs. White, of course, came first, then Mrs. Porter, then Elsie and then myself. We were given the train of the person ahead of us in order to straighten it as we went in. I held the end of Elsie's train in my hand and dropped it at the door of the room adjoining the throne room. When I entered the Rittersaal I made a deep reverence, as I had been told to do in England, and afterwards I was complimented for doing so.

The Rittersaal was splendid and ornate in the heavy Baroque style. The throne was almost directly ahead of us as we entered, quite unlike London, where we had entered from the side. The Emperor and Empress stood on a raised platform. The Emperor, to whom I curtsied first, stood very stiffly, and, as I said in my diary, "a little pompous", with his hands on the hilt of his sword, which he held directly in front of him. The Empress had great presence. She was very erect, with quite a beautiful figure for the time. Her hair was almost white. She wore a lavender brocade dress with a train, as I remember it, of either purple or a deeper shade of mauve. After I had curtsied to her and turned to back out of the room I saw that she had turned her head to follow me. I think that the way I wore my hair had caught her attention. We made our way to the famous Marmor Saal, where a great buffet table was set with supper. It was superb in that magnificent setting. I wrote in my diary that the Marchesi Imperiali was the most beautiful person there. I can remember her even after all these years. She was the Italian Ambassadress. We left shortly afterwards and drove to the hotel, where Elsie and I detached our trains and went to the Jacksons' for a supper and dance.

The Jacksons were at that time the most popular and beloved diplomats in the American service. Although he was afterward Minister to Greece, it is in Berlin where he will always be remembered. They were hospitable and friendly, and all smart Berlin crowded to their parties. That particular evening I shall never forget. Some of the other girls who had been presented at court were way-wise and went home from the palace, not only to leave their trains, but to change their dresses. The tulle or lace with which most court dresses were trimmed could not be used in dancing with officers, as I soon learned, to my dismay. The beautiful tulle flounces on my white satin dress were soon torn to shreds by the officers' spurs, and I remember leaving little mounds of white in the corners of the room where we danced. Fortunately, the dress was beautiful with or without tulle flounces, and it did not affect my good time. I danced every moment. The Prince zu Wied asked me for a waltz, and I had supper with a handsome young Prince de Ligne.

The next day Miss Perkins came to lunch with me in the hotel. She had now become one of the most distinguished botanists in the world. She had received her doctor's degree in the University of Heidelberg, and so highly did the government think of her original work that several rooms in the Berlin Botanical Museum had been set aside for her use. She had two or three young scientists as her assistants. It was a pleasure to see her, and some years later my mother and I went to visit her in her laboratory and were taken through the beautiful botanical gardens connected with the Museum.

[10] Marquis de Noailles.

That afternoon Elsie and I went with Mr. Jackson and General Porter to the Reichstag. "We sat in the diplomatic box, and Mr. Jackson pointed out the celebrities. I wrote in my diary, "we had the good fortune to hear von Bülow speak; also Prince Herbert Bismarck, Barth and Bebel."

That evening the Whites gave a dinner for General and Mrs. Porter. The French Ambassador[10] was there, and was very kind and complimentary to me. Also "a very nice French secretary, who talked to me while the men smoked."

The next morning we started on our journey to St. Petersburg. I was very sorry to leave Berlin. Mr. Jackson was at the station to see us off, and told me that I had been a great success at his party. He brought me a bouquet from Mrs. White, and a little note saying that she was sorry to have me go. Mr. and Mrs. Reilly and Ruth were with us, so that we were a numerous party. Late in the afternoon we arrived at the Russian frontier. In those days it was the policy of the government to put very large men in the custom houses as officials and porters to greet the traveller's eye. Their beautiful Russian costumes made them appear even taller. Because of our diplomatic passports we were treated with great consideration, and hot, steaming tea in tall glasses, the first I had ever seen, was brought in to the Russian train, for on the frontier all German trains stopped and the Russian railroad, with its wider gauge, began. We went early to bed. I looked out of the window. "There was snow everywhere, and dreary wastes of night and whiteness. The sparks from the wood-burning engine flew by the window."

The following morning, January 24, I awoke to find the train speeding through snow-laden woods. Every twig outlined. "Occasionally we passed a clustering village and towering church. Then came vast stretches of plain. We arrived at St. Petersburg at 3:30. Mr. Tower, the Ambassador, met us with Morgan, the second secretary, and Riddle, the third. Tea at the hotel, and after dinner a visit from Mrs. Tower, who says nice things to me. Our invitations for the court ball are given us; also one from the Princess Cantacuzène."

The next day—I quote from my diary—"lunch at the Towers'. Only Americans, but I am delighted with Mrs. Slocum and her husband, the military attaché. The Crown Prince of Siam called afterward

11 The German resort the Eddys frequented annually.

12 Catherine's aunt, Delia Spencer Caton, later Mrs. Marshall Field.

and stayed nearly forty minutes. We could not leave until he rose to go. Then to the Italian Embassy (in), English (out), and French (in), where Mme. de Montebello asked me to come after dinner on the 29th. I signed the Grand Duchess Vladimir's book. In the evening we dine at the hotel and afterward Elsie and I go to the opera with Morgan. The Belloselskys in our box. Supper afterward with Mrs. Slocum as chaperone."

Then came Sunday, and we went to the Cathedral of St. Isaac's to hear the singing. In the afternoon we drove in troikas out to the islands where the Belloselskys had a house. Princess Belloselsky, before her marriage, was Susan Whittier of New York. She had been a friend of Spencer's, and, as a little girl, I had often seen her in Schwalbach.[11] Her mother, Mrs. Whittier, was a friend of Aunt Delia's.[12] She was then, in 1902, at the height of her beauty and charm. Her father-in-law, old Prince Belloselsky, was the ranking nobleman of Russia. After the imperial family he took precedence. The marriage had been a lovematch, as she was not an heiress. I can remember, when her engagement was announced, hearing my mother tell of the presents that Prince and Princess Belloselsky had sent her. She had been asked whether she wished a coat lined with sable, or with silver fox. The Russians always wore their magnificent furs as a lining, to give added warmth in their rigorous climate.

That afternoon when we had tea with her she wore a pink teagown. After all these years I have a distinct memory of her radiant beauty. Later that afternoon we went to call on Baroness Luttwitz, who had also been an American. That evening Elsie and I were very sad, as Mrs. Porter had not permitted us to go to the ballet because of her deep feeling about Sunday. We missed seeing the incomparable Russian ballet at its very best.

The following afternoon we called on Mrs. Tower, who was in, and then drove to see the Fortress of St. Peter and Paul, and Peter the Great's house. We returned to the hotel about 4:15, and there I found awaiting me a command from the Grand Duchess Vladimir for five o'clock that afternoon! Never did I fly in and out of a dress more quickly. Reynolds Hitt kindly had a carriage waiting for me, and I reached the palace at ten minutes past five.

The Grand Duchess Vladimir was the daughter of a Grand Duke of Mecklinburg-Schwerin. She had married the Grand Duke

Vladimir, who was the uncle of the present Czar. As the Czar's eldest uncle, he was very close to the throne. The Grand Duchess was
a friend of Spencer's, and I had already been presented to her in
Paris. In appearance she was very distinguished with dark hair and
eyes. She dressed well—many of her dresses came from Worth—
and was famous for her fabulous jewels. She ruled St. Petersburg
society, had become very Russian in her feelings and tastes, and was
far more popular than the beautiful young Empress. She received
me most cordially, and complimented me on my dress—my black
velvet. I had had time to hang around my neck Aunt Dell's silver
Psyche, with the enameled wings, that had been made by Lalique
himself. This interested her very much. Before I left she asked me
if I would not like to see her drawing rooms. I shall never forget
what she called her "winter garden". It was a vitrine, all glass and
crystal. On the shelves were little pots of jeweled flowers—cornflowers
made of sapphires, with emerald leaves; roses, forget-me-nots,
daisies—all of jewels; little diamond wheelbarrows and watering
pots. These precious objects had all been made by Fabergé, the
great Russian goldsmith. She kept me forty minutes.

Delia's Psyche, *made by
the jeweler Lalique*

That evening we dined with Prince and Princess Cantacuzène. Cantacuzène did not have the great position of Belloselsky, but his marriage to Julia Grant had increased his position at court. Because of General Porter's devotion to her grandfather, she was eager to do all she could to make the General's visit a pleasant one. After dinner we went to a dance at our own Embassy. I had a good time, so I relate in my diary, and danced mostly with Graham (oblivion has swallowed him. I remember nothing about him) and Prince Fürstenberg.

The next day was Tuesday, January 28—the day of the court ball, when we were to be presented to the Empress. According to the Russian calendar it was January 15. The day began with the news that Mrs. Porter would be unable to go to court. She was not feeling well, but nevertheless wished to go out to take the air! It required all our persuasion to keep her in her room because, of course, only serious illness would prevent anyone attending such an important function as a court ball. Reynolds Hitt rushed from hotel to Embassy, and from Embassy to hotel, for it really was a disturbing matter for the Ambassador and Mrs. Tower. The General went, of course, resplendent in his uniform, but without his decorations that had been left by mistake in Paris!

Presentations at court in Russia were made at a ball, and not at a drawing room, as in Germany and England. We therefore required no trains to our dresses. I wore my silver gown, but was not, according to my diary, altogether satisfied with my appearance. "The ball was a most wonderful, never-to-be-forgotten sight." The vast ball room where we assembled was glittering with lights from great crystal chandeliers. Its dimensions were enormous. At this first court ball of the season nearly three thousand guests were invited. As we were assembling with the Diplomatic Corps, young Russian girls were being presented to the Empress in a different part of the palace. The presentations of the Diplomatic Corps were made to the Empress by Mme. de Montebello, the French Ambassadress. We stood in groups—the French, the German, the American, and so on. In the Diplomatic Corps the presentations are not numerous, but in our American group there were three young girls—Elsie, Ruth Snyder and myself. The gentlemen of the Diplomatic Corps stood across the ballroom, awaiting the arrival of the Emperor.

Two women were presented by the British Embassy that night—the very tall Duchesses of Marlborough and Sutherland.[13]

At a signal everything became quiet, and the doors were thrown open and the Emperor and Empress entered. The Emperor was very undersized, with a pointed beard like King George of England, whom he greatly resembled. He wore a simple Russian uniform. Beside him stood the Empress, so fabulously beautiful that no Princess in a fairy tale could ever have been conceived as lovely. She was dressed all in white, with a great diamond tiara in the Russian manner. She advanced to the left, where the ladies of the Diplomatic Corps awaited her, and the Emperor moved to the right. Mme. de Montebello was the doyenne of the Corps, and made the first reverence to the Empress. Then the presentations began. To every person presented to her she said a few words. When Elsie curtsied to her she said, "I am so sorry to hear that your mother is not well. Will you tell her how much I regret it? I hope you will both come to the next court ball." When it came my turn, and she extended her hand, I remember that it was icy cold. I suppose that this great ceremonial was an ordeal to one as shy as she was supposed by nature to have been. She spoke to me for a minute or two. She asked me if I found the climate of St. Petersburg trying—had I been ice hilling yet—and she hoped that I would have a pleasant visit in Russia. After the presentations the dancing began.

The Grand Duchess Vladimir was there, and an equerry took me to her. She spoke to me for several moments. She wore a cloth of gold dress. Her diamond crown had little openings all around it, and in each opening hung an enormous sapphire.[14] I suppose that in no other place in the world at any time have such jewels been seen as at the great court balls in Russia. "The supper was a Veronese picture of unparalleled beauty and sumptuousness." I sat next to Morgan, the secretary of our Embassy, and as it happened, our table was just opposite that of the Empress. The imperial family sat on one side only of a long table that was on a raised dias. The Emperor did not sit down at supper, but circulated among his guests. The splendid liveries of the footmen dated from the time of Catherine the Great—white satin knee breeches, buckles on their shoes, and red coats elaborately befrogged with gold braid and tassels. The supper itself was extraordinarily good, with every delicacy. I remember with

[13] The American-born Consuelo Vanderbilt and Lady Millicent Fanny St. Clair-Erskine.

[14] The tiara later entered the possession of the British royal family; the queen of England is the current owner.

[15] Carl Gerhard von Heidenstam.

[16] The daughters of Sir Charles Stewart Scott (1838–1924), British ambassador to St. Petersburg (1989–1904).

a little gasp the fresh asparagus served to that great throng in the dead of a Russian winter. It was over all too soon, and we were waiting for our carriages at the diplomatic entrance, ready to go back to the hotel.

The following afternoon we had tea at Baroness Luttwitz's, where I met a great many very nice young men and had a good time. In the evening Elsie and her parents went to the French Embassy to dine. Ruth Snyder and I had dinner at the hotel, upstairs in the apartment, and afterward went on to the Montebellos' for the dance.

I was not altogether neglectful of sightseeing in St. Petersburg, for the next day I went with Jenny and a courier to the Hermitage Gallery. That afternoon there was a tea at Mr. Morgan's (the Secretary) where I had a pleasant talk with the young Swedish Secretary of the Legation,[15] who had taken a fancy to me, and who did so much to give me a good time. There were also two young daughters of the British Ambassador who were very friendly,[16] and of whom I saw something at all the parties.

Friday afternoon I went with Reynolds Hitt to Fabergé's shop. There we saw the two English Duchesses making their purchases. The elder Cartier learned his trade from Fabergé, who was the supreme creator of the objets de luxe of that period. That same afternoon we went in a troika as far as the Gulf of Finland, and came back through snow tinted pink and blue by the setting sun. After dinner that evening came the best time of all. We went in sleighs to the English Club, which was situated on one of the islands. We coasted for hours in that icy air. As St. Petersburg is very flat, the coasting is artificial on ice hills, or very long toboggan slides. The sport at that time was to go down in what they called busses. One man kneeling on a little sled would prepare to go down backwards. He would extend his two arms, each of which would be grasped by another man facing forward. Between the two men would be a girl with her arms around their necks; behind these three would cling three more, and usually the bus would go down with six or seven persons. The man who went backward would guide the bus by looking up at the light at the top of the ice hill. The slide was very long and very exciting. It was really a dangerous sport, and very few Russian girls were allowed to do it. But the English Embassy was there in force, and my young Swedish friend, Col. and Mrs. Slocum, and many others. There was some danger of freezing our noses, but happily we escaped. Afterwards there was a hot supper at the Club, and more coasting. We raced home by starlight in troikas—it was early morning. Never had I had such fun!

The next evening there was a musicale at the American Embassy, and I had a pleasant talk with the Duchess of Marlborough. I wore my blue forget-me-not dress that had been made at Paquin's and that everyone greatly admired. On Sunday I went to the English church with Elsie. As we walked home the congregation poured out of St. Isaac's, and bells in all directions were ringing. In the afternoon we went to the Nevsky Monastery to hear the chanting. Monday we made another visit to Fabergé's, and I lunched alone with Mrs. Slocum, who gave me the delicious Russian pancake with caviar and sour cream. I went with her to the British Embassy, and stayed for more than an hour playing ping-pong with the young secretaries. On our way back we stopped and signed the Grand Duchess's book. At Mrs. Slocum's suggestion I telegraphed Spencer, who was in Cannes at the Grand Duke Michael's, and asked if anything could be done about procuring an invitation for me to the court ball the next evening. General Porter had returned to Paris, but because of Mrs. Porter's illness the day of the first court ball, she and Elsie had been asked to this second ball—a much smaller party for only a very limited number of guests. Naturally I had not been included, but it was nevertheless very disappointing to me, and I hoped that perhaps through Spencer's friendship with the Grand Duchess Vladimir something might be done.

However, the morning dawned with no invitation, but a telegram came from Spencer saying that he was trying. At last I decided to go ice hilling with the Scotts, the daughters of the British Ambassador.

"I went with them in their sleigh, very smart, and we tobogganed all afternoon. I returned about five and took a bath—no invitation—at 6:15 it comes. I dash into my pink dress and go with Elsie and Mrs. Porter. Words cannot tell my happiness." I have a very distinct memory of this pink ball gown, one of the most beautiful dresses I ever had. It was heavy pink satin. The skirt flared out at the bottom with tulle ruffles as only Worth could make them, held by pink camellias. It was very becoming, and I felt much happier about my appearance than I had the evening of the first court ball. What a good time I had! "Dance every minute and dance the mazurka with the Swedish

Secretary and take supper with him in the wonderful palm garden, amidst fountains and flowers and hidden music." The suppers of these more intimate court balls were famous. They took place in the palm garden. Around each palm tree was built a table. The walls of the room were wainscotted with panels of fresh hyacinths—purple, white and pink—and the air was heavy with the perfume from these flowers. The Empress was dressed in pale blue satin, and looked even more beautiful than on the night of the first ball. We saw the Emperor passing from table to table. We were instructed not to rise as he went by. Of course, he only stopped to chat with important guests. I had a wonderful time. Evidently the Grand Duchess Vladimir had told her equerries to keep me dancing, for no sooner had one Russian been presented and asked me to dance, than up would come another. Some of the officers were Cossacks, with beautiful skirts to their coats. No girl could possibly have had a gayer evening. We reached the hotel at 4 A.M., and before I went to bed I wrote a note of thanks to the Grand Duchess, to whom I owed one of the most thrilling experiences of my life.

Alas—the next day we were to leave. My Swedish secretary and Morgan and the Secretaries of our Embassy were at the station. Mrs. Slocum had asked me to stay on for a few days longer with

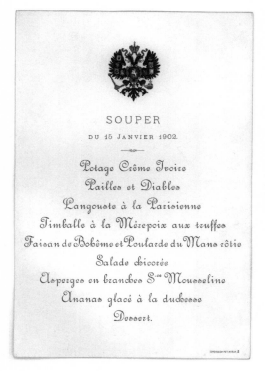

Invitation and menu for the court ball of 15 January 1902

Tuesday, February 4

No invitation but telegrams from Spencer saying he was buying. At last decided to go ice hilling with the Scotts. Go with them in their sleigh (very smart) & ice hill all afternoon. Return about 5 & take bath — No invitation — At six 15 it comes !!!!! I dash into pink dress & go. Words can not tell happiness. Dance every minute & dance mazurka with Swedish Sec & take supper with him in wonderful palm garden amidst fountains & flowers & hidden music. Afterwards dance with Garcia(!!!) Dance also with officers. Come home 4 A.M. & write thanks to H. I. H.

her, but it was not possible to do so. At Berlin Mrs. Porter left us, and Elsie and I continued on to Paris.

I was met at the station by Spencer, and we drove together to the Elysée Palace Hotel, where we were to be for three or four days. I had much to hear about the Stone case that Spencer had negotiated so successfully in Constantinople.[17] He had just come to Paris from Cannes, and I heard all the latest news of the Grand Duke Michael and Countess Torby and Villa Kazbeck; also, there was some question of Spencer's being transferred to Russia, and that seemed at the moment to be hanging in the balance. Then followed two busy days shopping and packing, and saying goodbye to my dear Elsie.

We left Paris for London on February 10, and arrived in time to dress and go to the play. A telegram was awaiting us from Lady Elcho, saying that she expected us the next day at Stanway. Mary Elcho was a dear friend of Spencer's. She was one of the most interesting

[17] The sensational abduction of Miss Ellen Stone is detailed in the "Dramatis Personae."

women of her time. Arthur Balfour had been in love with her for many years, and it was said that because of her he never married. She was one of the group that called themselves "Souls." She was a sister of George Wyndham, the Secretary for Ireland, and shortly before I knew her Sargent had painted his great portrait of the three Wyndham sisters. She was very beautiful, with dark eyes, and extremely slender. Her husband afterward became the Earl of Wemyss. She had a large family of children, and at the time of my visit was expecting another baby.

Spencer and I started for Gloucestershire after lunch. We arrived at Ivesham about 4 o'clock, and drove ten miles in a fly to Stanway. It was my first English visit, and I remember my little feeling of dismay that we were not met properly by a carriage or trap. In those days the perpetual visitors who went from one country house to another were often expected to find their own way from the station to the house they were to visit.

Stanway is one of the famous houses of England—Elizabethan, but with a wing built by Inigo Jones. The village church is almost a part of the house, and this whole group of buildings is indescribably mellow and picturesque. We were greeted by Lord Elcho, who asked me to pour tea for him. A little later Lady Elcho came in. That evening we dined alone, and afterward played games. There was no central heating in the house, but coal fires burning in every fireplace. The drawing room and the morning room were kept very warm, and you were expected to only open the door enough to squeeze in and shut it quickly behind you, lest any cold air should enter. I remember dressing that night with Jenny holding my chemise and petticoat by the fire.

The next day I drove Lord Elcho in the dogcart to Millet's studio in Broadway. Spencer and Lady Elcho followed in another trap. Broadway was a beautiful old village, and Millet's house had been a monastery, built in the 14th century. We saw in his studio his large half-finished picture of King Edward VII's proclamation. The drawing room of the house had been the refectory, and high on the wall was an *oeil de Boeuf* that opened on an organ loft. As we were having tea, who should come in but Mary Anderson and her husband, Mr. de Navarro. They were devout Catholics, and as the day was Ash Wednesday, they had little streaks of ashes on their foreheads.

Later they went up to the organ loft and sang old Gregorian chants for us. That afternoon made a never-to-be-forgotten impression upon me. Later Millet came to dine at Stanway. Years afterward he went down on the Titanic.

The next day I played with the Elcho children in the nursery, and walked in the park with Cynthia and her governess. There were some friends to dine, and we played a French alphabet game—whatever that might have been. That night we said goodbye to Lady Elcho, as we were leaving early in the morning. Back in London, we went to see Sherlock Holmes, with Gillette, and I rightly thought it a wonderful play.

The following Sunday we sailed for America on the *Kronprinz Wilhelm*. Mrs. Moreton Frewen and Mr. Allison Armour and his brother we found waiting for the tender in Southampton, but the principal passenger was Prince Henry of Prussia, who was on his way to make a visit of state to America. One of his aides-de-camp named von Egidy did much to make the voyage pleasant.

Arthur Caton's coachman, John Mooney, and groom, Michael Dunn.

On Sunday, February 23, when we reached New York we were kept on board until Prince Henry had landed amid much ceremony on the dock. Finally we disembarked and found mamma waiting for us. How glad I was to see her! We drove to the Holland House, where she and Aunt Dell were staying, and the rest of the day I spent telling them both of my experiences of the past few weeks. On the 27th we reached Chicago, where my father and uncle Arthur[18] met us, and Pierrot[19] gave us a rapturous welcome. I had been away exactly eight weeks!

Spencer followed us home in a few days, and stayed until March 14, when he returned to Europe.

I took up life as I had left it—dinners and luncheons and the theatre, which seemed to play so much more important a part in our life of that day.

On March 3 Prince Henry came to Chicago. Uncle Arthur's carriage, with Mooney and Mike on the box, escorted him from the station to the Auditorium, where that evening a great ball was given in his honor. My mother wore a beautiful gray satin Empire dress, made at Worth's, with red velvet puffed sleeves. She and Aunt Dell

[18] Arthur Caton, husband of Catherine's aunt Delia.

[19] Mrs. Eddy's beloved and affectionate little dog.

In honor of
His Royal Highness Prince Henry of Prussia
The City of Chicago
requests the presence of
Miss Katherine Eddy
at a Ball to be given
on Monday evening, the third of March
at ten o'clock
The Auditorium

The invitation to Chicago's great ball in honor or Prince Henry, and opposite, John McCutcheon's cartoon comment on the visit from "The Cartoons that made Prince Henry Famous" drawn by John T. McCutcheon and printed in the Chicago Record-Herald. Collection Newberry Library.

were presented to Prince Henry, who came back to mamma to say a nice word about Spencer. I danced with the young aide-de-camp whom I had met on the boat.

Mrs. Meynell, the English poet, came to Chicago to stop with Mrs. MacVeagh. I was invited to the dinner in her honor, and had a little talk with her afterward. Helen was in Florida,[20] and most of my time was spent with Cissy Patterson or Adelaide.[21] The Farquhars, the Herbert Stones, Clive Runnells, Redmond Stephens, Joe Patterson (who soon was to announce his engagement to Alice Higinbotham), and Medill McCormick I saw constantly. Helen came home, and much of our time was spent together. My mare, Duchess, I kept on the north side, and I rode three or four mornings a week. The opera came to Chicago. It was still the golden age of the Metropolitan, with Emma Eames, Calvé, Schumann-Heink, Ternina. One evening an opera by Paderewski, called "Manru," was sung. It was a complete failure.

In April we planned a surprise party for Aunt Dell. We were to dine at Medill's house, and go on afterward to Calumet Avenue. For some reason Adelaide and I decided that we would all dress as Greeks. There were many protests, but our costumes proved to be a great success. From Medill's we went to our house, where everyone assembled. I presume that there had been other dinners that evening. Mamma wore a domino in the shape of a champagne bot-tle, with a Veuve Cliquot label on it. Then we all drove over to Aunt Dell's. Needless to say, she was not at all surprised, and every prepa-

[20] In the late 1890s, Helen's father, Hugh Taylor Birch, had begun buying Florida real estate. By the time of his death, he owned much of Fort Lauderdale's beachfront property, two hundred acres of which he gave to the state.

[21] Adelaide Hamilton, one of Catherine's dearest friends.

SUGGESTION FOR PRINCE HENRY'S ENTERTAINMENT—WHY NOT MAKE THE AUDITORIUM BALL A COSTUME EVENT TO ILLUSTRATE LIFE IN THE WEST?

ration had been made for the party. She was dressed in her mother's purple velvet dress that had been worn at her own wedding, and her hair was powdered. Uncle Arthur wore a high stock, and carried a gold-headed cane. When we burst into the house, there they sat by the fire in the library with Dickey, the little Skye Terrier, and Trilby, the parrot, on a perch beside them. To all of us who knew how rare were such domestic scenes with Aunt Delia and Uncle Arthur, it was very funny. We danced and had supper, and Medill made a wonderful speech.

On April 28 we saw Frederic's new house for the first time.[22] He had returned from Germany with Dora, and had begun his work as a mural painter in Chicago. Mr. Bartlett wished him to live on the south side near him, and to please his father the house had been built on the corner of 29th and Prairie Avenue. It made a very great impression on all Chicago, and I think no one appreciated it more than my mother. It showed the influence of his years in Munich. As I look back upon it, it still remains one of the most charming houses I have ever seen. It became quite famous at the time, and Mrs. Gardner[23] made a trip from Boston solely to see it. There was the great studio, the little classic room in the modern manner of Stuck, the beautiful library and best of all, the dining room, made from an old panelled room and painted chalk-white. The butler, a young German, wore a livery of Bavarian blue. I have never forgotten the table, painted by Frederic, and the lovely Nymphenburg porcelain, and the delicious Sunday luncheons!

The great event of the spring was a dinner given for me by Medill McCormick in his mother's house on Cass Street. The hall and dining room were transformed into a restaurant, with little tables and palm trees. Cigarettes were peddled, and flower girls walked through with their trays. A band played. And finally, in burst newsboys calling "Extra! Extra!" A special edition of *The Tribune* had been printed, with my picture on the front page, and the news that I was about to sail for Europe. Another picture was of Marian Farquhar, whose husband was a Scotchman, with the caption, "The Princess of Wales." The rest of the paper was devoted to quips and gossip about everyone present. My copy of the little paper is lost. What would I give to see it after all these years!

[22] Catherine's lifelong friend, Frederic Clay Bartlett. At the time, he was married to the artist Dora Tripp Bartlett (1879–1917).

[23] Isabella Stewart Gardner (1839–1924) of Boston.

Four days later mamma, Aunt Dell and I, with Jenny, Therese and little Pierrot, sailed for Europe, and arrived in Paris on May 26. There I found Elsie and Ruth Snyder, Reynolds Hitt, the Munns and Cousin Mollie. Helen evidently was not there—perhaps she was in England with Cousin Ella.[24] We were at the Ritz on the Place Vendome—I think the only time we ever stopped there. There was a dance at the Embassy, and drives and walks in the Bois with my mother and Pierrot.

One Sunday afternoon I went with Cousin Mollie to hear *Pelléas et Mélisande*. I was greatly impressed by the music, which was then so new, and by the beautiful young American woman who sang the title role—Mary Garden. At the entre acte Cousin Mollie took me behind the scenes to the prima donna's dressing room. It was my first and only experience of the kind. I remember her vividly, sitting before her dressing table with a gigantic golden braid hanging down on either side. Cousin Mollie had been very kind to her, and had contributed something toward her musical education.

Cousin Mollie

Mlle. Cognier[25] would come almost everyday and we would do errands together. Occasionally mamma and Aunt Dell would give a dinner. Charles Walker was in Paris with his new motor. I said in my diary—"splendid run and quite gay at Armenonville." Today Armenonville is hardly ten minutes from the Ritz. Sometimes we went to Bagatelle to see the polo.

On Mrs. Porter's days at home I would go to the Embassy. One evening I dined with Helen Hay (who was now Mrs. Payne Whitney) and her husband, and Reynolds Hitt. My mother and I went, as always, to see the new pictures—the salon, the Arts Décoratifs, the Champs de Mars.

One Saturday we went to Chantilly, and had lunch at the Grand Condé, saw the Chateau, and drove through the forest after a rain "dripping and sweet-smelling." One Sunday I started out early with Mlle. Cognier, stopped for Carrie Louise Munn, and took the tram to Marly. From there we climbed the hill to Louvesienne, where we lunched in a garden full of roses. From there we walked to the foot of the hill in St. Germain, some seven or eight miles. Sun shining and birds singing. We passed nice looking villas and a large fair with

[24] Cousin Mollie was Catherine's mother's first cousin, Maria Root Birch; Cousin Ella was Mollie's sister, Ella Root Hurst.

[25] Mlle. Cognier, a paid companion or chaperone, had escorted Catherine around Paris over the years.

bands of music and merry-go-rounds at Marly le Roi. At St. Germain we had ices, and listened to military music—all this from my diary.

In the meantime mamma, Aunt Dell and I, with all the Munn family, made our plans to go to England to witness the festivities of the coronation of King Edward VII. Our rooms in the hotel were engaged, and a window to view the procession. We started for England on June 24, going early to the station to avoid the great crowds. We had a pleasant crossing and arrived at Dover, where we were met with the welcoming tea-baskets. When the train reached Dover proper we were startled by a guard, who thrust his head into the window and said, "Telegram from London, Ma'am. The King is ill and the coronation is postponed." The news proved to be only too true, and in London the decorations were already coming down.

The next morning we went to the Royal Academy, where we marvelled at two great portraits by Sargent, one of Lord Ribblesdale, and the other of the Duchess of Portland. Later in the day we went to the Wallace collection, which I had never seen before.

Friday we were back in Paris. Pierrot was almost beside himself with joy at seeing us again. Because of the English quarantine we had not been able to take him with us, and he had remained in Paris with Jenny.

On the first of July I left with mamma for Aix. Aunt Dell had gone the previous day to Carlsbad. We had never been in Aix before, and the beauty of the place was a great surprise to us. James Deering, who was a devoted friend of my mother's and Aunt Dell's, was there, and in the weeks to follow we dined or lunched together almost everyday. Alice Littleton was also in Aix with her parents, and often joined us in our pleasant excursions. We would have tea at Rumpelmeyer's, and dine in various restaurants around the lake. My mother started the cure, which occupied all her mornings. The weather was very warm, one unbearably hot day after another. Only on Mont Revard did we find cool breezes.

On July 10 I say in my diary, "After dinner Alice and her father come to say goodbye, and I give her my picture." It was really the beginning of our long friendship.

Day after day we lunched and dined with James Deering, sometimes going in a motor to a more distant point. On July 17 we all went "in an automobile to Chambery, where we had lunch. From there to Grenoble. The motion terrific. We have one of the fastest machines anywhere about these parts. Just escape killing dogs and chickens. In Grenoble the American Consul showed us the spot where Napoleon entered on the return from Elba. Back to Aix at lightning speed. From Chambery to Aix in twenty minutes!"

On July 24 we left for Geneva, where Miss Moewis met me. "As crazy as ever, with bonnet on one ear, but as kind-hearted as ever, and as excited. Take train to Lausanne and St. Trifou. There a carriage met us and we drove across the Rhone Valley, the rain beginning to fall. At last we reached Champery," where I was to spend a few days with her. Miss Moewis had a little apartment in a chalet in that delightful village. She had made it attractive with her own pretty things, and we had really a happy visit together.

I met my mother a few days later in Geneva, and the next day we started for Zurich, where we stayed at the Baur au Lac. I was to be often in the Baur au Lac in the years to come, and later with Albert and with my children, and it was always a romantic and beautiful spot to me.

The next day we went by train to Thusis, where we found a carriage and five horses awaiting us, and we began our drive over the Albula Pass to St. Moritz, "The road horribly seamed and scarred by the new railroad." It was ten o'clock before we reached our destination. For some reason we stayed at the Hotel Du Lac, which was in St. Moritz and not in the Dorf. It was bitterly cold. In our little sitting room was a green porcelain stove, and when James Deering joined us a few days later it became the object of his affection, for he hated the cold, and would stand by the hour embracing it.

A few days later Aunt Dell arrived from Carlsbad. Cissy Patterson was at the Dorf, and I made excursions with her and frequent visits to Konditorei, where we feasted on tea and cakes. Mrs. Slater and Miss Gwynn were there too, and a few other friends.

I had a great pleasure ahead of me. I was going to Constantinople to visit Spencer. Miss Moewis was to chaperone me.

"Frudy", as she was affectionately called, was Fraulein Elise von Roche Moewis. She came of old Prussian stock. Her father had been in Bismarck's cabinet. When she was still very young a brother

"Frudy" Moewis

43

in the army misbehaved, and contracted debts that, according to the military code of the time, had to be paid by the family, and Miss Moewis found herself obliged to do something to gain a living.

Sometime—just when I do not know—she studied archaeology in Rome with Professors Lanciani and Boni, and her studies of architecture and painting continued to be the interest and occupation of her life.

Her first contact with America was through the Remington family. She went with them to Egypt, and taught Jennie Remington, who was one of the great beauties of her day. Little by little she assumed all the responsibility of the Remington house in Cairo. Later she chaperoned Mary Leiter, Mrs. Remington's niece, who was to be Lady Curzon, superintended her studies, and traveled with her. A few other girls of the period spent winters with her in Vienna and elsewhere abroad.

She was no longer young when I first knew her. She was living in New York at the time, giving classes and lectures in archaeology. Mrs. Leiter spoke to my mother about her, and in the winter of 1898-1899 I spent two or three months with her in her little apartment on East 46th Street. We went to lectures at Columbia, and to concerts and the theatre, and for a few weeks we stayed with Mrs. Frederick Vanderbilt in the old Fifth Avenue house.[26] The next winter I went with her to Vienna for four months, and then to Rome for a fortnight of never-to-be-forgotten sightseeing.

She died in Vevey, where I went to see her shortly before her death.

Her originality of mind and character is written in her face. She was strong and energetic in body and mind, with a great sense of dignity and an integrity of spirit that I shall never forget. Her love of beauty, her ability to show the base from the pure in ancient sculpture and architecture, and her love of archaeic form made a lasting impression on my mind.

On August 18 I started on my way. Jenny went with me as far as Coire, where Miss Moewis met me. Frudy and I spent the day there visiting the Cathedral, the Museum and the "Curiosity Shops," and the next morning we left for Vienna. There we went to the Embassy for our passports, to the Turkish Consulate to have them visaed, and took the Orient Express to Constantinople at 6:45. We were on the train all

[26] This was the house at Fifth Avenue and Fortieth Street, which had been handed down from Mr. Vanderbilt's father, and before that from the commodore. The Frederick Vanderbilts lived there until 1914.

the next day, and the following morning arrived in Constantinople. Spencer met us, and we went in the launch to Therapia.

In the summer all the big embassies moved to this lovely spot, which lies between Constantinople and the Black Sea. Across the Bosporus was Asia, and I have never forgotten the thrill it gave me as I first looked at that distant shore.

Spencer had rented a little house for the season, but Miss Moewis and I stayed at the Palace Hotel, where the Ambassador and Mrs. Leishman and Marthe, their daughter, had been spending the summer.

The waters of the Bosporus are bluer than the Mediterranean. Villas and Embassies lined the shore. Back of the shore rise hills, for the most part barren, as was so much Turkish land in those days. That night Frudy and I dined with Spencer in his little house, and I saw for the first time the moon rising over the coast of Asia.

The two weeks that I spent in Therapia were very happy ones. Spencer's friends were young and gay, and gave me a very good time. Marthe Leishman, the Ambassador's daughter, was my age, and I liked her very much. Almost all the young secretaries of Embassy played polo. Arab or Maltese ponies could be had for very little, and the English Embassy had a vast stable where most of the ponies were quartered. The polo field, tradition said, had been the camping ground of Godfroie de Bouillon on his way to the crusades. In one corner there was an ancient cedar, under which he was said to have slept. The field was a little rough, but good polo was played there. Spencer had three or four ponies. The favorite was "Say When"; another was named "Now Then"; and I also remember "The Gentleman", which I was allowed to ride on days when no polo was to be played.

The day after our arrival Spencer and I rode with George Young, of the British Embassy, far up in the hills. It was the beginning of a friendship which has lasted to this day. At first he frightened me a little. He was supposed to be one of the coming young men of England, and at that time was codifying the Turkish law. He was the son of Sir George Young, the great Greek scholar, who owned Formosa, a famous old place on the Thames. That afternoon on our return we had tea with him in his rooms, looking down toward the Black Sea.

The next day we spent in Constantinople. Bertie McCormick, who was with his father in Constantinople, went with us on the launch. We saw the bazaar—the Prado—and after lunch went to the Treasury, which was opened especially for us. We saw the marvelous treasure of precious stones, and gold and silver. Turkish coffee was served to us in the Palace. Later we were shown through the Dolmabagche Palace, romantically situated on the shore.

I went with Frudy to see the great Mosque of St. Sophia, which she could show me with such intelligence and understanding, and the beautiful tomb of Alexander the Great in the Museum.

Evidently, from my diary, we rode almost every day, and the mornings were spent playing tennis. There was a young Prince Fürstenberg, Colloredo-Mannsfeld, Di Rossi, Herbert, the King's messenger,[27] Mr. and Mrs. Barker and Miss Woods, whose father held an important position in the Turkish service; but we rode the oftenest with George Young, and my mornings were mostly with Marthe Leishman.

One night we dined at the Minister's; another evening with George Young at the Embassy mess, where the table was set in the garden, and Mrs. Barker chaperoned us. I remember one afternoon when we went to the English cemetery, where the Crimean dead are buried.

August 29 we went to see the Selamlik. The diplomatic corps stood on a terrace over looking the drive where the Sultan passed on his way to the Mosque. The old Sultan, Abdul Hamid, was in constant fear for his life, and it was said that his place was often filled by a substitute.

Coffee was served to us in little jeweled cups, but we were glad to get back to the launch, where a good lunch was waiting for us. That same afternoon I went with Marthe in a caique to the Sweet Waters of Asia. This quiet waterway was the favorite resort of fashionable Turkish ladies, and there was a great turning-out of beautiful caiques. A caique is a long, elaborately carved rowboat, not like a gondola, but very distinctive of its kind. Some caiques had their own color schemes—pale blue, or pink or silver—and the oarsman would be dressed in the same color. The seat in the stern of the boat where the ladies sat, as if in a victoria, was covered with silk that trailed in the wake of the boat. The women themselves wore turbans and veils,

[27] Probably Aubrey Herbert (1880–1923).

all in the matching color. Marthe and I returned all the way to
Therapia in our caique, watching a glorious purple and yellow sunset.

One day we rode to Kelios, the lighthouse that the British government maintained at the entrance to the Black Sea. We lunched in
the open air, and came back in the launch through the narrowing
Symplegades. You remember in "Atlanta in Calydon," Swinburne's
beautiful verse —

> Who shall seek thee and bring
> And restore thee thy day,
> When the dove dipt her wing
> And the oars won their way
> Where the narrowing Symplegades whitened the
> Straits of Propontis with spray?

The next night we went out on the British boat, the Scout, to see
the illuminations. Coming back "an immense fire broke out on the
Asia shore. All the men go, and Marthe and I, having no one with
us, give up Mme. d'Arnoux's supper. I watch the fire, growing
greater every minute, from my balcony".

The day before I left, Spencer, George Young, Herbert and Miss
Woods and I went in the launch to the Asia shore, where we met
the ponies that had been ferried across in a flat boat. We rode ten or
twelve miles inland to a Polish village — a little settlement of Poles
that had remained on Turkish soil since the Crimean war. There we
had our picnic in a meadow, and after a long rest and pleasant talk,
started back to the shore and the waiting launch. The country
through which we passed — hill after hill — was wild and deserted
and supposedly frequented by brigands. The memory of Miss Stone
was still fresh in our minds, and added a considerable zest to our
ride. The young men all carried pistols. It seemed for a time that we
were lost, but finally George Young brought us safely out. The sun
had quite gone out of sight, and the sky had a gold and purple glow.

The next day I left, with a heavy heart. I was sorry to say goodbye to
Spencer. I had had one of the happiest fortnights of my life. Jenny
met me in Munich, and I parted from Frudy and started for Paris.

On September 20 I sailed for home, in Mr. Munn's care. I was
returning ahead of the family to be a bridesmaid for Alice Hay at
her marriage to Jimmy Wadsworth. Alice Littleton was on the boat

with her mother, and she shared my cabin with me. Mr. Littleton had died in Paris a few weeks previously, and the voyage, for them, was a very sad one.

On September 28 we landed in New York. My father came out on a tender, and it was an exciting moment when he climbed up on a rope ladder. We hurried to Boston, and from there I took a train to Newbury, N.H., where Alice and Jim met me at the station. There were more than twenty people staying in the house. The wedding was on the 30th, with many people coming up from Boston.

My father and I went to Washington for a few days before returning to Chicago. I had a whole month at home before my mother and Aunt Dell returned. It was still summer weather, and I enjoyed myself to the utmost, going to Lake Forest almost every day to ride. It was the first year of the hunt, and Mr. Arthur Aldis was the new Master. Duchess, my little mare, was transported to Lake Forest and kept in the Club stables. The first meet was on October 18. The M.F.H. said a few days later—"Take it all in all, Miss Eddy's mare is the best hunter out here". Needless to say, I was very happy.

I had a new admirer, Freddie McLaughlin, whose greatest interest was riding, and with whom I had the best of good times. It was a gay autumn for me. Never had I had such fun. Medill was engaged to Ruth Hanna, and there were many parties in their honor. Joe Patterson was married to Alice Higinbotham, and again there were lunches and dinners. From my diary, I dined out night after night. We hunted two or three times a week, and in that motorless day it involved me in endless trips by train to Lake Forest.

My mother returned the end of October, and the following month Helen and Cousin Mollie came back from Europe. Adelaide, my father and I drove to the 31st Street station and boarded their train as a surprise.

On November 12 we gave a dinner for Ruth Hanna and Medill. Thirty-two in all. "We danced afterwards. Very jolly, and a great success. The tables beautiful—all red roses."

Norman Williams, Uncle Arthur's nephew, was married to Joan Chalmers on December 3, and Adelaide, Helen, Cissy and I were among her many bridesmaids. On December 18 we gave a cotillion. There were forty-four to dinner, and more came in afterwards. And just before Christmas there was a wonderful ball given for Edith Blair's coming out. I danced the cotillion with Clive Runnells, and can remember to this day the good time I had. There was a cotillion at the young Marshall Field's the day after Christmas. Night after night we dined and danced, and danced the old year out on December 31.

Eddy home interior, Chicago

THE CHRONICLE OF CATHERINE EDDY BEVERIDGE

1903

Opposite: Adelaide Hamilton (left) and Catherine

INTRODUCTION

⤳ 1903 ⤳

CATHERINE'S ACCOUNT OF 1903 comprehends an array of activities that engaged the fancy of the rich, not just in Chicago, but globally. Country-house weekends, lavish dinner parties, hunt balls, fancy-dress balls, and cotillions, whether held in Chicago or Constantinople, were not just events but expressive media. What Thorstein Veblen had but recently termed "conspicuous consumption" was very much on display, coupled with a historical, even anthropological, consciousness that infused upper-class taste in dress, entertainments, and furnishings. The wealthy of Chicago and elsewhere—whether their money was new or not—were eager to adorn their lives with whatever was rare or exotic, and to connect themselves to the rich and famous of other times. We can discern this impulse in the historically and theatrically inspired dresses Catherine describes, in her mother's ornate, almost archaic table settings, and perhaps most of all in the costume, or fancy-dress, parties that were enjoying an international vogue at the time. Introduced into the United States by Alva Vanderbilt in 1883, the costume ball seemed to reach a global apogee around 1900, with London's famous Devonshire House ball in 1897 and Czar Nicholas's 1905 costume ball in St. Petersburg, where guests donned the heavy, bejeweled court dress of 1605 to celebrate the tercentennial of Romanov rule. Such occasions could be richly symbolic, as each guest looked into the past and chose a character with whom to identify. The making of costumes required historical awareness and skilled dressmakers, who labored to replicate archaic designs. The delight such costumes gave survives here in Catherine's descriptions of a beautiful silk dress made for her on the pattern of a famed eighteenth-century dancer's, as well as a lavish velvet gown that her mother had made, inspired by David's portrait of the French empress Josephine.

Catherine's life during this period was peopled by several noteworthy figures. The first was Katharine Dexter, a childhood friend whose marriage to Stanley McCormick (of the Chicago reaper family) Catherine was to witness the following year. Katharine and her mother, Josephine, widow of the late Wirt Dexter, exemplified a type of upper-class Chicagoan common at the time. The Dexters were an old New England family whose members had distinguished themselves as cabinet members and jurists since the Federalist age. Wirt Dexter himself had been born in Michigan, where his father had made a fortune in lumber. The son gravitated to Chicago to practice law, becoming instrumental in the rebuilding of the city after the 1871 fire. Having grown up in Chicago, Katharine moved to Boston with her mother around the turn of the century, after her father and her only brother,

Samuel, died. Thus the Dexters, like other families of Catherine's acquaintance, had strong ties to both Chicago and the East Coast and circulated comfortably in their interrelated societies.

Soon after Katharine married Stanley, he began exhibiting symptoms of dementia. His condition, later diagnosed as schizophrenia, had a profound effect on his brilliant and thoroughly modern wife. One of the first women to receive a degree in science from MIT, Katherine, who was also a pioneering advocate of birth control and a leader in the crusade for women's suffrage, used her scientific understanding and wealth to advance research into the causes of schizophrenia. Old-fashioned only on the point of virtue, she cared steadfastly for her husband until his death in 1947.

Also in 1903 we find the first mention of Marshall Field, a figure who loomed large in Catherine's family. Field was a sixty-nine-year-old widower. His two adult children lived mostly in Europe. The death of his wife, Nannie, in 1896, had ended an unhappy marriage. Mrs. Field died abroad, where she had spent much of her time since the 1870s. Her husband meanwhile lived "alone" in his massive Prairie Avenue house, attended by eleven servants. Mr. Field had been friends with Arthur and Delia Caton, his immediate neighbors to the rear, for decades. They traveled together, socialized together, and moved in the same social circles. Field's relationship with Delia was so intimate that the existence of a subterranean tunnel connecting their homes was rumored. In the following account, Catherine does not characterize or refer directly to the relationship

between her aunt and her neighbor. What she does write, however, points to a discreet arrangement among Arthur, Delia, and Mr. Field. For when, as in 1903, Mr. Field vacations in his private railroad car, both Arthur and Delia are among his party, whereas when Delia goes to Europe, Mr. Field also goes, while Arthur stays home. Thus, in both 1903 and 1904, Delia and Mr. Field, along with Catherine and Mrs. Eddy, travel quietly together in Europe. So often a haven for Americans seeking greater sexual freedom and privacy, Europe spared Delia, Mr. Field, and Arthur invasive scrutiny.

The Munn family also begins to appear more frequently in Catherine's story. At the head of this private, peripatetic, yet sociable clan was the elusive but fascinating Mrs. Munn. Born Carrie Louise Gurnee, she grew up in Illinois and married the young Joseph F. Armour, who was her brother-in-law until death carried off her sister Amelia. Carrie's joy at being Mrs. Armour was short-lived, however, for Joseph, who with his brothers was revolutionizing the meatpacking industry, died in 1881 in his late thirties. His will divided his estate among Carrie Louise and his brothers, after setting aside $100,000 to create the Amelia G. Armour Mission Church and School. (Renamed the Armour Institute, this was the nucleus from which the Illinois Institute of Technology grew.) Carrie sought to renounce her share of the estate on the ground that the union had produced no children, but instead the Armour brothers ceded their portions to her. In the end, she inherited $1.4 million, the entire residue of Joseph Armour's estate. Still a young woman, she remarried and had five children with her second husband, Charles Alexander Munn, a financier. Though associated with Chicago, the Munns lived mainly in Washington, D.C., and traveled in Europe extensively. Mr. Munn's death in 1903 did not change the family's style of living. The children later married into the Wanamaker, Pulitzer, Boardman, and Amory families. Mrs. Munn, wealth undiminished, lived into the 1920s.

Mrs. Munn's wealth and independence are at odds with our ideas of the unfree status of women at the beginning of the twentieth century, yet they are typical of the women in Catherine's story. Virtually all the women in her social set—including Mrs. Dexter, Mrs. Munn, Mrs. Slater, Cousin Mollie, and Cousin Ella, as well as Abby and Delia themselves—

were independently wealthy as a consequence of having inherited large fortunes from male relatives in the last decades of the nineteenth century. Although their wealth scarcely immunized them against misfortune, it enhanced their autonomy and affected dynamics within their families.

A final element to be noted is Catherine's admiration for Germany. Her fond descriptions of its landscape and picturesque towns, its flourishing arts and vibrant cities, capture the prestige that things German enjoyed in the years just prior to World War I. Catherine's unreconstructed admiration of the kaiser, Wagner, and Houston Stewart Chamberlain also bespeaks the powerful hold that nationalism and theories of racial dominance exercised among the thinking classes at the time.

Catherine at Ottowa

Eames MacVeagh, Mary Stone, Medill McCormick, Catherine, and Herbert Stone standing below , at Ottawa.

THE YEAR BEGAN with a luncheon at the Higinbothams. As I remember that winter, it was a very happy and gay one. My friendships were formed, what diffidence I may have had vanished, and I consequently had a very good time.

As I turn the pages of my little diary, the year starts with a chronicle of dinners and Sunday luncheons, endless long talks with Helen— and yet, I remember a certain restless discontent that may, for all I know, always accompany the last of adolescence.

On January 15 Aunt Delia gave a dinner for seventy-five. It was one of the famous parties of Chicago. I sat between Phillip Burne-Jones and Stanley McCormick. There were two long tables in the dining room, with the superb and elaborate decorations of the period. After dinner the men went downstairs to a deserted billiard room that had been put in order for the occasion, and the women upstairs to the large sitting room. While we were there a photograph was taken of us. In the foreground Helen, Adelaide and I are sitting together on the floor. We had all been told to come to the dinner wearing hats, or with powdered hair. My hat was of pink tulle, but in the old photograph not very effective.

When we went downstairs everything had been transformed with painted scenery of Moorish scenes and moonlight—Arabs in flowing burnooses were walking in "The Streets of Cairo," as the party was afterwards to be known. At the end of the library, completely transformed into this Moorish scene, had been built a stage, and on this appeared a continuous and delightful vaudeville—Russian dancers, trained animals, and last, the famous sextette from *Floradora*,[28] which was then playing in Chicago. As soon as the theatre had closed they were hurried to the house and made their appearance. They were encored and encored, and finally, instead of the professional men, appeared Eames MacVeagh, Marshall Field, Jr., and who else I cannot remember, dressed up in the gray coats of the men of the celebrated chorus. After that the dancing began in the big dining room, and lasted until four or five o'clock in the morning, when we had breakfast and went home. As I say in my diary, "the greatest possible success from start to finish."

The next day I started with mamma and Jenny for Boston, where we went to visit Mrs. Dexter and Katharine. Everything had been done

28 "Tell Me Pretty Maiden," from the 1899 smash hit.

for our pleasure, and nothing is clearer in my mind than the memory of that beautiful house, built by Arthur Little. Its perfect proportions gave the impression of a very large town house, which in reality it was not. Mrs. Dexter had the happy faculty of making a large room homelike and comfortable. In Schwalbach and our travels together, I can remember her sitting room in various hotels, always made attractive and liveable a few hours after her arrival.

I saw my friends in Boston—Olivia Thorndike, Eleo Sears, Clemence Crafts—and we lunched and dined every day. On the 20th we went to the Artists' Festival, a costume ball. I wore a dress that Miss Dodd[29] had copied from Lancret's portrait of Mlle. Camargo. Mamma wore her beautiful Empire dress that Worth had made several years before—heavy gray satin, with red velvet sleeves, a copy of a David portrait of the Empress Josephine. After the ball we went to Mrs. Montgomery Sears' for supper.

[29] Miss Dodd was *the* dressmaker at Marshall Field's.

The following day we drove out to see Mrs. Gardner's new house, which is now the Isabella Gardner Museum. She was there, and escorted us through room after room, explaining and commenting. To me it was "indescribably beautiful—the court yard, with its flowers and fountains, beyond all description." We had seen it in the process of building; now it was a revelation of beauty, both to my mother and to me. I wonder if at that time it was not less crowded than it now appears to our more critical eyes.

The last night of our visit we went to a hunt ball—the first I had ever seen. The men wore pink coats, and the beautiful tulle skirts of the period made a picture I have never forgotten. I danced the cotillion with Butler Ames, who sent me "a large bouquet of lilies-of-the-valley and two boxes of orchids." I had supper with Arthur Dixey, a charming boy I had met in Lenox two summers before. (He died a few years later in Korea, where he was Secretary to our Legation.) I danced until four-thirty, and said goodbye to Katharine and her mother that night, as we were leaving on the morning train for New York.

By February 1, I was back in Chicago, seeing Helen and Adelaide and various young men, going to concerts and parties, and reading Henry James from cover to cover. Almost every Sunday mamma had a luncheon. Mondays we went to call on the north side; Tuesdays mamma and Aunt Dell were at home.

I kept my mare, Duchess, in a stable on the north side near Lincoln Park. As I turn the pages of my diary I marvel how anything could have been accomplished with the interminable drive from the south side to the north side, and the north side to the south. In a brougham with a pair of horses it was a drive of at least twenty-five minutes to Lincoln Park. There was always the chance that Rush Street bridge would be open, and that again made a delay of from five to ten minutes. Backward and forward I seemed to go — to the park to ride, home to dress, out to lunch, back again, to the north side to dine, home again. In the evening Helen, Adelaide and I, who were often invited together, took turns in furnishing the carriage. But change was in the air that year, for in May I wrote, "go in Min Palmer's automobile to all the west side parks and boulevards — F. McLaughlin, Herbert and Mary; then to Saddle & Cycle to dine. Come back very fast in the moonlight."

On February 20, mamma, Aunt Dell and Uncle Arthur left for California in Mr. Field's private car. My father and I and little Pierrot were alone, but not for long, as on February 22 Alice Littleton arrived from Philadelphia for a two weeks' visit. We had a pleasant time together. James Deering, with whom we had had such good times in Aix the previous summer, was very attentive. We dined and lunched with him several times. And there were younger parties, with Adelaide, Clive Runnels, Howard Gillette, the Herbert Stones, Edith Blair, and Ned Ryerson, who was even then very devoted to Adelaide. We lunched one day with Frederic and Dora Bartlett in their beautiful house that Alice greatly admired.

So the days went on. On March 16, I wrote — "back to lunch. A cake for Adelaide, whose birthday it was. Then to north side to ride — Adelaide and myself. Beautiful gray day. Then back to house, dress, and go with Adelaide again to north side to call. Back again, dress, and to Cyrus McCormick's to dine, to meet the French Ambassador. I was the only girl there. Very pleasant. Mme. Jusserand was very complimentary, and said, 'the greatest pleasure of the evening has been watching your youthful face and beautiful gown.'"

As Spring drew nearer we began to go to the Saddle & Cycle Club, then in its prime. It was almost in the country, and directly on the lake, with a little line of silvery beach.

Spencer arrived from Europe on April 3, and my mother from California the next day. I wrote in my diary, "Pierrot immediately deserts me, and transfers his adoration to mamma."

Later in the month Mrs. Slater and Miss Gwynn came from Washington to visit Aunt Dell. There were great festivities in their honor. Mamma gave a dinner for twenty-two that was long remem-

bered. A pergola was built in the dining room, and hung with Japanese wisteria and small electric lights. Down the center of the table was a lake, bordered with maidenhair fern and narcissus. In the center of the lake was an old bronze holy water fount, with the papal arms, that had been converted into a fountain that played continuously. The four candelabra were the bisque figures of The Graces. The effect was very beautiful. Two days later there was a supper party in the same setting for Ethel Barrymore, to whom

Spencer was at that time very devoted. She had never looked more beautiful. The party was a great success. The Odells, Bruce Clarks, Nancy Coleman, Herbert Stones, Honoré Palmer, Eames, Helen, the Bartletts, etc. Afterwards we danced until three-thirty.

Aunt Dell opened the Ottawa house, and the weekend parties began—the Herbert Stones, Medill McCormick, Howard Gillette, Eames, the Bartletts. I shall always remember Dora Bartlett upstairs, sitting gossiping with us all—Helen, Aunt Dell, Mary Stone—and letting down her fabulous hair that swept the floor.

Those pleasant days at Ottawa, with the apple blossoms below the terrace and the parks behind the house coming into leaf! Some of the deer were still there, and Helen and I sometimes found little fawns just dropped by their mothers in the tender grass. Later on came the June roses, some of which had been brought from California by Judge and Mrs. Caton, and which always seemed to thrive in spite of little care or attention. The warm summer nights on the porch with the melancholy whistles of the trains going west across the plains . . . .

Aunt Dell kept up the traditions of the house, even to the lavish Caton breakfasts, and the Ottawa potatoes—sliced fried potatoes in rich cream. We drove through the parks in an old buckboard or a buggy, the deer scattering before us. In Judge Caton's time there had been three parks, the first devoted to domestic deer, the second to another species, and the third to elk. I remember as a little girl peeping through a small opening in the high stockade fence to see the elk leap a deep ravine. Long before these happy days in the Ottawa of 1903 the elk had been sold by Uncle Arthur to the zoo in Hamburg, Germany.

The 2nd of June we started on our way to Europe. I left the train at Poughkeepsie, where I was to spend a few days with Mrs. Vanderbilt at Hyde Park. There I met Emily Rogers, of whom I was to see something in the years to come, Mary Newbold, and some young Roosevelts, whose names I do not remember. The Vanderbilt house stood high above the Hudson. It had been built by Stanford White, and was heavy and uninteresting, but surrounded by the most beautiful trees I have ever seen in America.

Below left: Delia McGarry was in Catherine's grandmother Spencer's service, and later, her mother's. Delia is pictured here in front of the old bowling alley at Ottowa.

Below right: Carrie Louise Munn (left) and Catherine (right) playing tennis at Ottowa.

Mamma and little Pierrot and Uncle Arthur arrived in New York on the 14th. Aunt Dell joined us from Newport, where she had been with Mrs. Slater, and on the 16th we sailed. I was sorry to go, and felt blue and depressed.

We arrived at Cherbourg on the 22nd at 7 o'clock in the evening, and started on our long journey to Paris, where we arrived at 3:30 in the morning. We drove to the hotel in broad daylight, where we found fires burning and flowers from the Munns and from Elsie Porter to welcome us. We were in Paris only ten days. I had time for a few rides in the Bois with Mrs. Hensman. Mrs. Hensman was almost as celebrated as a riding teacher as was Howlett for driving lessons. She had a beautiful, slender, riding habit figure—I have never seen anyone look as well on a horse. Her stables were near the Bois.

There were fittings to attend to, but not as many as usual, as it was late in the season. The days were busy, and we were always ready for tea at Rumplemeyer's or Colombin's, where I can see my mother in my mind's eye in her beautiful tailored suit and pretty hat and veil, and little Pierrot on her lap. Every year we brought back tea from Colombin's, and my mother's Marion had learned to make their celebrated toasted buns.

On Sunday, June 28, I wrote in my diary, "in the afternoon go to drive with mamma—Jenny, too—to St. Cloud. On our way pass Santos-Dumont, just about to start up in his flying machine. We wait and see the plane rise up in the air, and he sails off to Paris."

On the 4th of July I started with Elsie Porter's devoted Tante Marie, and the dachshund, Waldina, to Dinard, where I was to spend three weeks with Elsie and her father. Mrs. Porter had died the previous winter. The General had rented a villa called "Bric-a-Brac," which hung on the very edge of the sea. It was pretty and quaint, with a little garden made in the rocks. The days passed quietly enough, with excursions and tennis, and hours on the beach. Charlie Munn came for a few days, and while he was there we went to St. Malo, where we visited Chateaubriand's tomb by the sea, and to Mont St. Michel. We lunched at Mme. Poulard's, and saw her make her famous omelet.

On the 27th I said goodbye to Elsie and her father, and left for Paris, accompanied by a courier maid. Even in 1903 it would not have been thought suitable for me to make the journey from Dinard to Paris alone, incredible as it seems. Mlle. Cognier was waiting for me at the station, and that evening I took the train to Mayence. I was going to Schwalbach to spend a short time with the Munns.[30] I was delighted to be in Schwalbach again, but a little sad to be there without my mother. My room was next to Mrs. Munn's in the Allee-Saal. Alice Littleton and her mother were at the Metropole.

I settled down happily enough. We played tennis and made excursions. Charlie and Gurnee went fishing in the Wisper Thal, and we would meet them and have supper at the Riesemuhle and drive home in the moonlight. One afternoon we drove again to Hohenstein, where we made tea and spent the afternoon.

On August 11 I met mamma and Aunt Dell in Berlin, where we stayed at the Bristol. I went with mamma to the old Schloss, where "I showed her just where I had put down my train and where I had curtsied to the Emperor and Empress." We went to Charlottenburg and to Potsdam, and through Sans Souci and the gardens. That evening we left for Munich, where we stayed at the Hotel De Russie. We arrived very early in the morning, and that same afternoon heard Nordica at the new Wagner Opera House in *Tristan and Isolde*. It is one of the great musical memories of my life.

The next day we lunched at the Künstler House,[31] which was new to us then, and seemed to have all the flavor of the Munich of that day. After lunch we went to see the "Secession" Austellung.[32] Apparently modern art made little impression on me, for later in the afternoon I compared it unfavorably to the pictures we saw in the Glass Palast, "the Lenbachs, Kaulbachs and Laszlos[33] — so many fine portraits." Much of our time was spent in antique shops or, as I called them then, "curiosity shops." Many of the things we love and enjoy in Indianapolis and Beverly Farms were bought in these shopping excursions.

Mr. Field joined us a few days later. He enjoyed sight-seeing, and shared my mother's enthusiasm and love for Munich. The day after his arrival we went to the National Museum, which was then new, and marked the beginning of a different era for museums.[34] For the

[30] The resort the Eddys favored was in the mountainous Taunus region of Germany, a few miles northwest of Weisbaden. It was known for its mud baths and mineral springs.

[31] A clubhouse for artists designed by architect Gabriel von Seidl (1848–1913). Completed in 1900, the Künstlerhaus was beautifully decorated inside and was considered an outstanding building of its kind.

[32] An art exhibition organized by the Munich Secession, an artists' association founded in 1892. Among its members were Franz von Stuck and Lovis Corinth. Unlike their counterparts in Berlin and Vienna, the Munich Secessionists enjoyed power within Munich's official art community but rejected the conventions that constrained their peers.

[33] Leading portraitists of the day: Franz von Lenbach (1836–1904); Friedrich Kaulbach (1822–1903); his son Friedrich August von Kaulbach (1850–1920); and Philip Alexius Laszlo de Lombos, known simply as Philip de Laszlo (1869–1937). The Hungarian-born Laszlo lived and worked mainly in England and was a naturalized British subject. He painted a full-length portrait of Delia, which is now in the Newberry Library in Chicago.

[34] The Bavarian National Museum, founded in 1855, had moved in 1900 to a new building designed by Gabriel Seidl. The rooms, which were chronologically arranged, were designed and ornamented to match the character of the objects that they contained. The ceilings of the rooms dated from the appropriate centuries. The museum also showcased "objects of industrial art" exhibited in rooms of a modern style.

first time we saw the installation of rooms arranged chronologically, so that beginning with the Middle Ages one would pass from room to room until the period of Louis Phillipe was reached. Architecturally the Museum made a great impression on Mr. Field, and we persuaded him to communicate with the architect, thinking that he might draft plans for the museum Mr. Field contemplated giving in Chicago. We were so interested that we also spent the next day there.

Marshall Field

We made the excursion to Hohen Schwangau, and to Neue Schwanstein, and back to the Alpen Rose, where we spent the night. The next day to Linderhof, with its enchanting gardens, and back to Munich that evening. We visited Franz Stuck's house, which I admired greatly. He, himself, was there, quite like his portrait, and showed us about. We went to the Residenz, with its lovely porcelains in their glorious settings, and "to a shop where mamma finally buys the little commode, and then to the Café Luitpold for lunch." That afternoon another opera, *The Rheingold*. There we met cousin Ella and her new husband, Theodore Byard. The next day to *The Walkurie*.

On August 27, with the American Consul we went to Lenbach's studio, where he and Mme. Lenbach received us. We asked him if he had the time to paint mamma's portrait, and he finally said yes, that he would do so, and asked her to come the next day at eleven o'clock. Afterward Mme. Lenbach took us through the wonderful house, all Italian Renaissance. It is now a Museum. That night, *Siegfried*.

The next day mamma had her first sitting. I can remember the excitement of her dressing. Her hair went up beautifully, and she looked very well. Lenbach admired her greatly, and took infinite interest in painting her portrait. It was one of his very last. Lenbach himself was tall, with a long beard. He used photography in painting his portraits, and for that has been severely criticized. He photographed his sitters from every possible angle, and in that way had a complete record and study of their heads; but that did not mean that he did not actually paint the portrait, for I saw him do that with my own eyes. Mme. Lenbach spoke excellent English, and I could speak German, so that together we interpreted satisfactorily, for my mother spoke almost no German. We were so thrilled by our successful and pleasant morning that that same afternoon I persuaded

Catherine's favorite photograph (above) and a portrait (above right) of Abby Eddy by Lenbach

[35] In 1934 Catherine traveled to Munich in a vain attempt to deter her daughter, Abby, from marrying a German, Franz Baum, whom Catherine saw as an opportunist. The only success of the trip was Catherine's acquisition of Fex, her favorite among the dozens of dachshunds she owned.

my mother to go to a photographer, where the picture was taken that I have always loved, and some other pictures holding little Pierrot. That evening *Götterdämmerung*, with Nordica. We had heard all the *Ring*.

During these days in Munich I had been hoping to go to Constantinople to see Spencer again, and had tried to persuade my father to come from America and go with me, but this he would not or could not do, and it was a great disappointment to me.

Mamma's portrait was progressing so favorably that Mr. Field decided to have his painted. This time I was the interpreter.

Almost every afternoon we had tea in the Hofgarten. On my ill-fated trip to Munich in 1934 I often walked through the Hofgarten with Fex.[35] The snow was on the ground, but I could visualize those pleasant afternoons thirty years before, with the band playing and my pretty mother sitting there under the trees with another little dog in her lap.

We were indefatigable sight-seers. To the Glyptothek, where we saw the Aegean marbles, to the library, where we saw old manuscripts—Dante's *Inferno*, with illustrations by Botticelli, with its beautiful ivory and jeweled covers—and often to the Pinakothek.

In the mornings I would walk with Mr. Field to the Lenbach studio. At first his portrait seemed to progress better than my mother's, but eventually hers proved to be much the finer picture.

One afternoon I went with Jenny and little Pierrot to the English garden to give him a walk. As our cab drew up to the curb I stupidly put little Pierrot out. A boy coming along on a bicycle between the curb and our cab ran over him. I was horror-stricken. We picked him up howling and the coachman whipped his horse and we went on the run to the nearest veterinarian. It turned out to be a new veterinary hospital, modern and beautifully equipped in every way. A young intern met us and took little Pierrot into a room to examine him. By that time his fright had subsided, and although they punched him and poked him, they could find nothing wrong with him, and I was able to bring him back to mamma alive. I wrote in my diary, "I did not tell mamma about it."

In the Glass Palast in the annual exhibition was a little painting by Hertling, of a snow scene near Munich. I often went in to look at it, and finally took my courage in my hands and asked the price. After some negotiations I secretly bought it and gave it to my mother the following Christmas. It now hangs over my bureau in Beverly Farms.

On September 9 we had a telegram from Spencer, saying that he had been appointed first secretary at St. Petersburg, and just before we left Munich a letter came saying that Mr. Leishman had cabled Washington that for the present he could not let Spencer go.

Finally we were ready to leave, and mamma and I started on our way to Karersee. The first night we stopped at Botzen, where the weather was very warm, and we regaled ourselves with figs, grapes, plums and peaches.

The next morning we left Botzen in the rain at 9 o'clock, driving in a landau. "After a bit we could put down the top, but the rain continued off and on all day. The pass is very beautiful, narrow in part, with deep gorges and mountain streams. Of course, the high mountains were hidden by the clouds. After luncheon at Welschnofen we began to climb again. It grew colder and colder, and little patches of snow grew larger and larger, until they covered the whole ground, with here and there a green bush showing through. The pine trees were heavy with snow. We arrived at Karersee at 3:30. Very nice, fresh, clean rooms, with German stoves. After tea, just before nightfall, a great mountain loomed out of the mist for a minute like a spirit.

Had table d'Hote downstairs. Very still and dark when I am in bed." But mamma was not well, and a few days later we decided to return to Munich. Pierrot was delighted to be back in his old haunts.

From Munich we went to Vienna. I had not been there since my winter with Miss Moewis, and it was fun to go about with mamma. The German Emperor was visiting the Emperor Franz Joseph, and all Vienna was en fete.

The end of September we were back in Paris. Flowers everywhere in our very cheerful apartment. We were there for five weeks before we sailed for home. It is difficult to describe to anyone in the age in which we live the importance that was attached to dressmaking in Paris every autumn. It was not alone my mother and aunt who accorded it so much attention, but all the women of the society of that day did just as they did. Their days were filled with various fittings and visits to shops; not only dresses were ordered, but everything that went to clothe the human form—underwear, stays, stockings, shoes, handkerchiefs, gloves, hairpins and combs for the hair. It was as if we were going to some distant land where shops were unknown, and where it was impossible to obtain any of the necessities of life. Even boxes of pins were bought at the Bon Marché. We would return sometimes, my mother and I, with sixteen or eighteen trunks. The dresses were laboriously and beautifully packed in trays. The greatest packer in Paris was Charles, of Goyard's.[36] He was so much in demand by ladies of fashion that his services would be engaged in the Spring to pack us for America in November. Jenny was taught to pack by him, and to the end of her days she never lost the art. The dresses would be folded with absolutely mathematical precision—every fold and pleat meeting exactly its corresponding fold. Endless tissue paper was used, and a complicated system of tapes held everything in place. The dresses would come to America in perfect condition, without a crease of any kind.

[36] Goyard, 223 Rue St. Honoré, specialized in *articles de voyage*.

Of course, all the time was not devoted to dressmaking. In the evening mamma and Aunt Dell would often dine out with friends in the great restaurants of that day—Voisin, Laurent, Henri, Marguery, Foyot, the Café de Paris, Paillard and The Tour d'Argent. As I grew older I sometimes dined or lunched with them, but in this particular year I had my own friends in Paris—Cissy Patterson, Bertha Coolidge, Alice Littleton, Martha Leishman, Mary Edwards, Elsie Porter, and a few—a very few—young men. Elsie and I drove one day with Alice Colburn in her motor to Chartres. I had been reading Huysmans' *Cathedral*, and looked forward to this, my first glimpse of Chartres, with eager anticipation. It took us nearly three hours to drive there in a blinding rain. The door of the motor was in the rear, and we faced each other on two benches. I think the motor must have been a Panhard. I have been in Chartres many times since then, but my first glimpse of the great church is something I shall never forget.

Spencer reached Paris from Constantinople a few days before we sailed November 11. He returned to America with us. Aunt Dell and Mrs. Slater had been in England, and we found them already on the Kaiser Wilhelm der Grosse when we went aboard at Cherbourg.

My father and Uncle Arthur met us in New York, and we went to the Waldorf. Always on landing our first dinner started with oysters and ended with a play, and that evening it was Ethel Barrymore in *Cousin Kate*.[37] The next day Spencer left for Washington. I was in New York for a few days longer and a night at Hyde Park, and with my father saw Spencer sail again for Europe and his new post in St. Petersburg on the 24th.

Adelaide Hamilton

Back in Chicago we found heavy snow and dull skies, but when I reached 1601 I found my little sitting room filled with the beautiful old Adam furniture that I loved so dearly. It was a complete and delightful surprise that my mother had planned for me.

There was a happy reunion with Adelaide and Helen, and for the rest of the year every page in my diary bears their names. Word came from Phoenix, Arizona, that Mr. Munn had died, and Aunt Dell arranged to have the funeral from her house. All the family

[37] The English comedy by Hubert Henry Davies had opened in New York on October 19, 1903.

arrived in Chicago—the five children, Mrs. Munn, the maids and tutor. They stayed with us and with Aunt Dell for a few days before going on to Washington.

As I read my diary, December seems a very gay month. I dined and lunched out almost every day. On the 19th Katharine Dexter arrived from Boston. It was a memorable visit for her, because it was then that Stanley McCormick fell in love with her. Alas! Perhaps it would have been better if she had never come! In all events, we had a gay time. On the 22nd Aunt Dell gave a large dinner—it must have been for fifty or sixty. I had the idea of asking everyone to dress in fancy costume as a surprise to Aunt Dell. I think I may have been influenced by wanting to show my lovely Lancret dress that had been made for the Boston ball. I arranged to have Katharine wear Aunt Dell's Spanish costume that had been copied from one Calvé wore in *Carmen*. It had been made by Doucet. Katharine, with her dark hair, looked her very best, and I think it must have been that night that Stanley completely lost his heart to her. Robert Allerton was dressed in a Bavarian officer's uniform—pale blue. We all came in the house by a back door and assembled upstairs. Aunt Dell thought it very strange that nobody was arriving, and she sent Churchill[38] repeatedly to see what was wrong, and if any carriages were driving up to the door. I had engaged a Hungarian band that was in great vogue that winter, and the first thing Aunt Dell and Uncle Arthur knew, the band began to play, and marched downstairs in their bright uniforms, and we all followed after. It was a great success, and we danced after dinner and had a late supper, with Medill making speeches.

On the 28th Hazel Martyn was married to Ned Trudeau, the son of the great doctor. I sat at the bride's table, between two nice ushers from out of town. That beautiful Hazel—little did she know what was in store for her!

Katharine left on December 30, and that same day occurred the tragic Iroquois Theatre fire. For a few moments late that afternoon Aunt Dell could not be accounted for, and we were frightened. She had not been near the theatre, and arrived safe and sound at the house, to my mother's great relief.

[38] One of the Catons' menservants.

HARPER'S WEEKLY

Vol. XLVII.   *New York, Saturday, January 17, 1903—Illustrated Section*   No. 2404

AMERICANS OF TO-MORROW

XXIII.—ALBERT J. BEVERIDGE, *AET. 40*

See page 9 —Editorial Section

1904

Opposite: Stanley McCormick, John Garrett, Katherine Dexter McCormick and Catherine, September 15, 1904.

In 1904, CATHERINE wintered in Washington, D.C., for the first time. Staying at the home of Mrs. Slater, a Newport socialite who was Delia's close friend, Catherine immediately joined a select company, attending a White House musicale and meeting the president on the very evening that she arrived. Many of her friends were in town for the winter. The Pattersons and Munns were on the spot, as were the politically important Hays, MacVeaghs, and Wadsworths, whom Catherine knew through her mother and Spencer.

It was a heady time to be in Washington. McKinley's assassination in 1901 had brought Theodore Roosevelt and his family into the White House, opening a new era in capital society. Whereas the austere McKinley and his frail wife had been strictly decorous, the young Roosevelts, with their brood of six children, were venturesome and fun. Glamour suffused the Washington scene, with Alice Roosevelt and other young women setting the tone. Meanwhile, the currents that were bringing younger, less conservative Republicans to the capital gave politics a momentous uncertainty.

Albert J. Beveridge was the young Republican who interested Catherine most; she soon managed to meet him at one of Mrs. Slater's parties. Beveridge was a handsome widower sometimes referred to as the "boy senator." At forty-two, he had already represented Indiana in the Senate for five years. Intelligent and hardworking, he was a rising star, a brilliant orator, known to be

ambitious for something higher. The memory of childhood hardship drove him forward. Transcending an impoverished rural upbringing, Albert had worked his way through college and, through cool and dauntless effort, quickly made a name for himself in public life. His energetic stumping style, his unwavering respect for the facts, and an amazing ability to write books and articles cogently outlining complex issues for the public had gained him many admirers. An exemplar of the new Progressive spirit in American politics, Beveridge had a reputation and prospects that could hardly have been brighter. Mrs. Eddy sniffed at his credentials, however, and frowned on him as a prospective suitor for her daughter. She saw a widower considerably older than Catherine, of meager wealth, whose social background was lackluster. His career was demanding and uncertain, and his politics, which were about to take a crusading turn, were disturbing. True, he had been featured on the cover of Harper's Weekly as one of America's "men of tomorrow" and was being talked of for the presidency, but that was scarcely enough to tip the scales in his favor.

Albert's debut in Catherine's life afforded her a fitful distraction from her mother's illness, for Abby had begun to suffer from the cancer that would kill her. Though the newspapers would attribute her death in 1909 to "stomach trouble," Abby was suffering from ovarian cancer. Letters she wrote Catherine in the final year of her life meditate on the powerful stigma then associated with cancer and on its terrible exactions in a period when surgery offered the only hope of recovery. Although, as a wealthy woman, Abby had access to the best care available, the understanding and treatment of cancer was not much different in 1902 than it had been at the beginning of the nineteenth century. Superstitions surrounded the disease. Many people believed that cancer's causes were moral, that its victims were people who were faithless or sinful. Although Abby indignantly rejected such insinuations, in the difficult years ahead she periodically turned for healing to the new religion of Christian Science at intervals when she doubted the efficacy, and feared the pain, of conventional treatment.

Despite undergoing a serious operation in February, Abby was well enough to depart with Catherine for their customary excursion to Europe in May. Five idyllic months followed: visits with Spencer and Mrs. Vanderbilt in France, sightseeing in Brussels, then six weeks in Schwalbach where Delia, Mr. Eddy, and the Munns all joined them. A month in the Italian Alps with Mr. Field was rounded out with a jaunt to Venice, where they met Helen Birch and Mrs. Slater. Then they turned back to Paris, with a stop in Geneva to witness the wedding of Stanley McCormick and Katherine Dexter. In November, as Catherine returned to the States with her mother and aunt, the current of pleasure ended abruptly, when in New York Arthur Caton died suddenly.

The death of Caton, at age fifty-three, is a matter Catherine might have written about more fully. From her account, we learn only that Caton had come from Chicago to New York to meet Delia, Catherine, and Abby on their arrival. Two days later, he lay ill at the Waldorf-Astoria, and by the end of that day, he had died. Catherine expresses no regret, nor does she venture to identify what carried off her relatively young and active uncle. Normally precise and liberal in her use of dates, Catherine forebears mentioning the date he died, which is almost impossible to infer from what she writes. Shame blankets the details of Arthur Caton's demise. Just weeks earlier, he had been in his glory, presiding over the fashionable Horse Show in Chicago's Washington Park and rising above stiff competition to carry off the four-in-hand prize.

Arthur's death and the family's muted response underscore the emptiness and estrangement of the Catons' marriage. Contemporaries wondered whether Caton had gone to New York to commit suicide. Arthur Meeker Jr., a novelist who grew up in Prairie Avenue and was a pallbearer at Caton's funeral, later wrote a roman à clef depicting the suicide of a cuckolded husband confronted with the public's knowledge of his wife's infidelity. Certainly, Arthur's situation was unenviable. Delia's independence from him and her relationship to Marshall Field threatened to bring on him the shame and disgrace associated with infidelity. The *Chicago Inter-Ocean*, which published the earliest account of Arthur's death, reported that the family's return to Chicago had been delayed because the New York coroner had mistakenly deemed his death a suicide. A later article in the *Chicago Tribune* attributed Arthur's death to peritonitis, whereas Augustus Eddy issued a statement on behalf of the family saying that Arthur had died of liver failure. Public attention swiftly turned to other matters, however, and Delia began a new era as a free woman.

Every New Year's day there was a luncheon, and this time at Ruth and Medill McCormick's. Medill had been married the previous June and they were living in a large house on the Lake Shore Drive. That afternoon Mrs. McCormick gave a tea for her new daughter-in-law.

Mrs. Gardner came to Chicago with the musician, Proctor, and there were many festivities among my mother's friends. I saw a great deal of Frederic and Dora, and Ruth and Medill. Almost every Sunday my mother gave a luncheon, and night after night I dined out, but on January 13 there is an interesting item in my diary, as follows: "Dine alone *en famille* and read rather late. Begin Beveridge's *Russian Advance*."[39] The book was at that time creating interest, and was very much talked about. It made a great impression on my mind.

Through all the pages of my diary there runs now a little note of anxiety about my mother's health. Aunt Dell and I tried to prevail upon her to go to New York to consult Dr. Tuttle, a celebrated surgeon of his day. We finally left on the 27th, and I wrote in my diary, "Decide to take Pierrot with us. Aunt Dell comes to cheer us a little."

We arrived in New York four and a half hours late. Robert Allerton met us at the hotel, and we hurriedly dressed to go with him to *Parsifal*. It was one of the first performances of the opera in America.[40] Ternina sang. We dined at the Waldorf, in the entr'acte, but my mother was too tired to return to the opera, and my father went with us.

The next morning I arose early and took the train to Washington on my visit to Mrs. Slater. That evening Mrs. Slater dined at the White House, and afterward I joined her there at a musicale. Busoni played. I was presented to the President,[41] and he spoke of Spencer with real enthusiasm. It made me very happy, and I sat up late that night writing Spencer all about it.

The next day Mrs. Slater said, "Is there anyone especially whom you would like to meet while you are here?" I answered promptly, "Yes, Senator Beveridge." She tossed her head a little and said, "That's what they all say. I don't know why everyone wants to meet Beveridge." I did not press the matter, but the next day—Sunday, January 31—in Mrs. Slater's beautiful drawing room, in walked my beloved Albert with Senator Allison. How little I realized that

[39] In 1901, Beveridge had gone on an extensive journey to familiarize himself with conditions in Russia, Japan, and Manchuria. He admired the strongmen of Russia and viewed Russia's policy toward Manchuria, which it had recently seized, as a model of how the United States should govern the Philippines. Though Albert took pains to meet Russians in all walks of life, he failed to appreciate the tensions soon to convulse Russian society. First published serially in the *Saturday Evening Post* from the autumn of 1901 to the spring of 1902, his travel memoirs were published in book form as *The Russian Advance* in 1903.

[40] *Parsifal* premiered in America at the Metropolitan Opera House on December 24, 1903. It was Wagner's wish that *Parsifal*, which had first been performed at Bayreuth in 1882, never be performed anywhere else. Bayreuth representatives had gone to court trying to prevent the Metropolitan production from opening.

[41] Theodore Roosevelt.

SENATOR ALBERT JEREMIAH BEVERIDGE, of Indiana, wears the toga with all the grace of a Roman senator. Having personally visited the Philippine Islands, he is recognized authority on matters affecting the Filipinos. Has a fine war record, having defeated the Texan Fire Eater, Joe Bailey, in a desperate encounter without removing his cigar from his mouth.

From "Around the Capital with Uncle Hank" by Thomas Fleming, Nutshell Publishing Co., 1902.

Destiny at that moment had decided my future! In the same company was Mr. Justice Holmes, who was to become my Albert's dear and devoted friend—but that afternoon we were all but strangers in that gathering.

Monday, with Alice and Jimmie Wadsworth, I lunched with Mr. and Mrs. Hay. Mr. Hay was now Secretary of State, and Jimmie and Alice were spending the winter in Washington. The only other guests were Mr. and Mrs. Root, who were leaving Washington that same afternoon. Mr. Root had just resigned as Secretary of War, and they were on their way to New York. That night I dined at the Wayne MacVeaghs', and afterwards went to a musicale at Mrs. Warder's. When we reached Mrs. Slater's house there was a telegram from New York, saying my mother was to have a slight operation. I packed my belongings, and lay awake most of the night in great distress of mind.

Mrs. Munn went with me to New York on the 8 o'clock train, and we hurried to the hotel, where Aunt Dell and my father awaited us. They told me that my mother was to have a very serious operation the following Thursday, and the next evening she went to the old Roosevelt Hospital. Mrs. Slater and Mrs. Dexter came on to be with me.

The operation did prove to be very serious, but Dr. Tuttle hoped for her permanent recovery, because of her perfect physique and general good health. With Jenny, I did what I could for my mother, and took care of little Pierrot. Mrs. Vanderbilt was in New York, and was very kind to me. I saw her almost every day. The Munns came and went.

My grandmother Eddy died on February 15, and my father left to go to Chicago.

I went to the opera occasionally, and heard *Parsifal* again. Mamma began to improve, and left the hospital on March 15. Ten days later we went to Lakewood to finish her recuperation. Helen came on from Chicago and spent some time with me. During all this time little Pierrot was our constant joy—the most faithful, cheerful, gay little dog, ready to romp in the park, or sleep at the foot of our beds—never stupid or dull. Sometimes when we were out with him my mother would walk on ahead, and I would hold the frantic little fellow in my arms. About a hundred feet away my mother would stop and call him, and I would let him go. It was like an arrow shot from a bow—a little white streak through the grass until he reached her, and then such a demonstration, as if the absence had been hours instead of seconds.

Emily Rogers came to spend a few days with me, and on April 4 we left for Washington, where my mother had rented Alice Hay's little apartment at Stoneleigh Court, a very large and new apartment house on Connecticut Avenue. We found the rooms flooded with sunshine, and flowers everywhere. MacGregor had come on from Chicago and made everything ready for us. I went off with Charlie Munn in the afternoon, and dined at the Hays'. Life was gayer for me, and I was once more with people of my own age.

Mamma was happy to be there. It was a liberation for her after all the dreary weeks of her illness. She was fond of Mrs. Slater, who was always devoted to her, and Mrs. Munn was one of her oldest and dearest friends.

A few days later I received a little note from Senator Beveridge, enclosing a card for the Senate gallery for the memorial session in honor of Senator Hanna. The next day I went with the Munns to the Senate, and found it very interesting, but it grew late and I could not wait to hear Beveridge speak. I wrote in my diary that I was very sorry.

Mamma began to go out to lunch and to see people in the apartment. My spirits rose, and I found myself very happy again.

On April 8 I dined at Mrs. Slater's. I wrote in my diary, "Eleo Sears, Alice Roosevelt, Josephine Boardman and Mrs. Bay Lodge, Senator Beveridge, Senator Kean, the Swedish Minister, Mr. Collier, Count Hoyos. Very nice. Beveridge never leaves my side for a minute. Quotes poetry and prose, and is really very interesting. When I come back mamma is awake, and I tell her about it."

The next day I met Albert again by chance at Mrs. Slater's. He lent me a book to read, and I spent that evening perusing it. Every moment was occupied. I went out to lunch and tea and dinner. Margaretta MacVeagh was very friendly. She was the center of a little group, among whom I particularly remember John Lodge and Marjorie Nott.

Mrs. Slater

One evening, April 13, I read in the newspaper of the fearful disaster to the Russian navy, and the Grand Duke Cyril's marvelous escape. The Grand Duke Cyril was the son of the Grand Duchess Vladimir, who had been so kind to me in St. Petersburg.

The next day Cissy Patterson was married to Count Gizycki, a Pole whom she had met the previous winter in Vienna, where her uncle, Mr. Robert McCormick, was Ambassador. She had only announced her engagement a few weeks previously, and Mrs. Patterson quite properly had done everything in her power to prevent the marriage. They were married in the Patterson house on DuPont Circle, by a Catholic priest. Afterwards at the wedding breakfast I sat at Cissy's table, between Bertie and John Lodge. Alice Longworth was at the table, and Josephine Peck, as well as Medill and Ruth. A little later Cissy went up to change her dress, and we waited and waited and waited—the time seemed interminable. It transpired that Gizycki had gone to the hotel to change, and never came back. He telephoned that he would meet Cissy at the train. Finally she drove off with her mother. Joe, white with rage, jumped on the box beside the coachman, with the evident intent of killing Gizycki when he should see him! Thus began her stormy married life that ended in divorce a few years later. She was an interesting, intelligent and charming girl, with far more sophistication than any of us possessed.

That same afternoon my Albert came to tea. I begin to be teased about my conquest. Albert sent me his debate with Senator Simmons, and kept me supplied with books which he sent me to read.

One day I went with Margaretta to lunch with Mr. Henry Adams. His house was next to Mr. Hay's, but facing Lafayette Square. It had been built by Richardson, but the large library and other evidences of a cultivated life redeemed the ugly features of the house. Mr. Adams always lunched at 12 o'clock. There was a little book kept downstairs, and if you were one of a group of privileged young people, you could write down your name as a luncheon guest for any day that you might select, unless the limited number had been reached. What that number was I do not remember. Mr. Adams, himself, never lunched away from home.

We stayed on in Washington until May, through all the beautiful season of forsythia and flowering trees, and almost unbroken sunshine; then we went out to Chicago. The house was full of flowers.

Delia McGarry[42] had a garland with "Welcome" in Gaelic in my mother's room, and Thérèse[43] a wonderful basket of lilacs.

The middle of May we left in a private car with Mr. Field to go to the St. Louis Exposition.[44] Mamma and my father, Aunt Dell and Uncle Arthur, Mr. Field and Mrs. Dibblee, his sister, and Mr. Bartlett, Frederic's father. The Exposition had only just opened. We dined one night with Governor Francis—a dinner for the French Ambassador,[45] in one of the new buildings of the Exposition. It was cold, and so draughty that the wind "blew my hair!" Afterwards we watched the beautiful illuminations and fireworks. We lunched and dined a few times in the German building, and saw the pictures, which was the principal interest for my mother and father. One day we went on a Mississippi steamboat that Secretary and Mrs. Hay had chartered. Mr. Henry Adams was with us. Going under a bridge the water was so high that the funnel of the steamboat was broken. It was my one and only trip on the Mississippi. We dined at Catlins'. I was to see Irene Catlin very often in the years to come.

On May 28 we started for New York, and sailed three days later. Spencer came to meet us at Cherbourg, and arrived in Paris, we went to the Elysée Palace Hotel. My mother seemed very well again, and we lunched and dined in various restaurants. It was the beautiful Paris of early summer. Mrs. Vanderbilt was there, and I saw her often.

The middle of June, Spencer, my mother and I went to Brussels. We spent the first day seeing pictures, and the following morning left early on our way to Bruges. I had read Rodenbach's *Histoire des Beguines*, and the old town was inexpressibly interesting to me. We saw the Memling pictures and the Van Eycks. That day is very clear in my memory after all these years.

June 18 was Spencer's birthday. We drove to Waterloo over cobble-stones all the way. It was not only Spencer's birthday, but the 89th anniversary of the famous battle. After luncheon we went over the field with an old guide to Huguemont and Belle Alliance. I thought it very gruesome. We went to Antwerp and to Louvain and to Ghent. Spencer left us to go back to St. Petersburg, and my mother and I went to Ardenne in the heart of the great forest. We stayed there only a few days, and returned to Brussels.

[42] Delia McGarry (b. 1865), one of the Eddys' veteran maids.

[43] Delia Caton's personal maid.

[44] The fair celebrated the centennial of the Louisiana Purchase. Henry Adams, whom Catherine mentions as being in attendance, was strongly interested in such expositions. Attending another such fair had opened to him the vision of modern times articulated in the *Education*, where he contrasts the attributes of the Dynamo and the Virgin.

[45] J. J. Jusserand, whom Catherine had met in Chicago the previous year.

Langenschwalbach.
1891
from steps of Evangelischen Kirche

Drawing of Schwalbach by
Augustus Eddy

On June 28 we left for Frankfort on our way to Schwalbach, where we arrived in time for a supper of brook trout and chicken. The next day was my birthday. I wrote in my diary, "after lunch we go to Schlangenbad, where I have a rose bath, as I have had on all my birthdays here." We were in the villa Grebert, and just outside my window was the rose garden, which even the Beverly Farms rose garden cannot efface from my memory.

Our life was very quiet. I took the cure, and walked over the beautiful and familiar countryside. The Munns arrived a few days later in their Winton car.[46] Our tennis began, and excursions for tea and sometimes supper at the Riesemuhle in the Wisperthal. Supper at the Allee-Saal was always outside the dining room on the broad gravel path that led to the Weinbrunnen. We had a table d'hote dinner at 1 o'clock, but our supper at night was a la carte. I remember the enormous German pancakes, and every night an incomparable compote of wild strawberries. My mother and I were on the first floor of the villa, and the Munn family on the second.

My father arrived from America on July 10. He and Aunt Delia had come to Europe together. Adelaide was in Nauheim with her family, and spent a few days with me. I returned the visit in Nauheim. On the 19th Elsie arrived to be with us for a fortnight.

[46] Alexander Winton (1860–1920) made the first automobiles offered for sale in the United States; introduced in 1898, they were for a time the nation's most popular automobiles. The car alluded to here may have been a buggy with a one- or two-cylinder engine.

Clockwise from top left: Schwalbach street, Augustus Eddy with Pierrot, Catherine

The summer of 1904 was one of the few times that my father was with us in Europe. Evidently the alarm over my mother's illness, and our insistence, had induced him to come over with Aunt Dell. As I read the pages of my diary, much that I had forgotten comes to my mind. My father rented a bicycle and went off on long excursions, even as far as the Rhine. Sometimes he would return long after dark. The Munns had their motor, and the Munn boys motorcycles. Both motor and cycles were constantly breaking down. It meant long waits by the side of the road for repairs and changing tires, which was one of the greatest obstacles in the motoring of that day. Whenever it did not rain we played tennis, and while Charlie, the eldest of the Munn children, was two years my junior, we were all congenial enough, and their young company and the sports we did together kept me in a happy atmosphere. I walked a great deal. The country was familiar to me, and I loved every foot of it.

The middle of August my mother and father and I left Schwalbach and went to Wurtzburg, and from there to Rothenburg. I wrote in my diary, "Find it quite as wonderful as we had expected. The town wall as it was in the Middle Ages, and the grouping of roofs and gables very picturesque. See the beautiful carvings in the Jacobskirche, and

Marshall Field, Delia Caton, Abby and Augustus Eddy

admire the Rathhaus and a delightful house with a courtyard. Take train back to Steinach, where we make tea while we wait for the train to Munich. We arrive a little before nine. Aunt Dell meets us, and I dash for the same bathtub as last year."

Twenty-nine years later, in the very depths of winter, I was to re-visit Rothenburg, this time with Frederic, Evelyn, Abby and Evie.[47] The snow was deep on the ground, and covered the roofs and the famous old fortified wall. We had come by motor from Nuremberg that bleak winter day, and we were cold and hungry. I shall never forget our delicious hot lunch and the gluhwein that Frederic had ordered for us.

[47] Frederic Bartlett and his third wife, Evelyn Fortune Bartlett; Abby, Catherine's daughter by Albert; and Evie, Evelyn Fortune's daughter by her first husband, Eli Lilly.

We were long enough in Munich to see the Secession Exhibition, and to go for coffee in the Hofgarten. Then we left for Toblach and the Dolomites. This was a new journey for us to make. We had never been there before. I wrote, "Leave Toblach about 10:15 and start on a most wonderful drive. The scenery finer than the Engadine. See the Monte Cristallo in all its glory. Wonder at the pink tops of the mountains. Lunch very late in Cortina. From there an hour and a half's drive brought us to the frontier, and just over the frontier to Borca." Three years later I was to spend my honeymoon there.

The hotel at Borca was new, and built on plain, modern lines that were very refreshing after the musty hotels in the Europe of that period. The bathrooms were superb, as only very fine Italian and German bathrooms can be. There were many balconies, and broad terraces. On one side was Mount Antelao, and on the other Mount Pelmo. We stayed there almost four weeks. The walks and excursions were endless. Mr. Field, who was with us, rented an Italian motor, and in it we made many excursions through the incomparably beautiful mountain passes. Mrs. Munn and all her children joined us there, so we were a very large party. Walden Myer, of Washington, a young clergyman, and his sister were staying at the hotel, and we saw something of them.

Spencer Eddy at Borca

Late in August, after a rainy day, there was snow on the mountain peaks, making the scenery more beautiful than before. We went often to Cortina for coffee at the famous Konditorei. At that time Cortina was still in Austrian territory, and benefitted by the delicious Austrian coffee, which was always served with whipped cream. The Munns and I had tennis every day, and sometimes the boys would go off with a guide chamois shooting. While we were there a letter came from Katharine Dexter, saying that she was shortly to be married to Stanley McCormick, and we made our plans accordingly to go to the wedding.

On September 9 we started for Venice. We went by motor to Belluno, and at Mestre a launch was waiting to take us to the Grand Hotel.

Catherine with Pierrot in the Piazza San Marco, Venice

Mrs. Slater and Miss Gwynn were there, and in a few days Helen came and I had two uninterrupted happy days with her. I took photographs of everyone on the Piazzo di San Marco feeding the pigeons, as you will see in turning the pages of this book. One afternoon she and I went together to the Lido and came back after tea in a beautiful sunset. Helen and Cousin Mollie were staying on in Venice, where Cousin Ella's husband, Theodore Byard, owned a little palace on one of the smaller canals. Nothing would have made me happier than to remain there with her, but we had to leave for Katharine Dexter's wedding.

We arrived in Geneva on September 14. Our trunks were lost—something that rarely happened to such experienced travelers as my mother and Jenny—but they came in time for the festivities.

The next day was her wedding. She was married in the beautiful Chapelle des Machabees, a part of the great cathedral of Geneva. First came the civil marriage—a very dignified ceremony in a beautiful room overlooking a garden. From there we walked to the chapel. They were married by Mr. Frothingham, a Unitarian clergyman of Boston. Afterwards there was a breakfast at the Beau Rivage. Stanley's best man was John Garrett, of Baltimore. He was afterwards to be second secretary in Berlin, and present at my wedding, too. I was to see him occasionally in the years to come, as he married Alice Warder, of Washington. After the luncheon I went to Katharine's room and helped her dress, and she and Stanley went off in his motor to Caux—where we ourselves had intended to go and couldn't go now. Mrs. Dexter was very sad, and felt herself alone, and mamma decided to stay on for a few days with her. Stanley and Katharine sent their car back from the foot of the mountain at Caux and in it we made excursions in all directions.

It is extraordinary to read of the number of tires we had. When a tire burst I call it a "panne" in my diary. It must have made motoring a very uncertain means of locomotion, for we thought nothing of a half hour's delay.

One day we took the funicular to Caux to see Katharine and Stanley, and a few days later went with Mrs. Dexter to Paris, where we stayed at the Elysée Palace Hotel. As usual, we were there some six or eight weeks before sailing for America.

It was the same autumnal Paris that I knew so well. My mother ordered for me at Worth's a very beautiful dress, copied from a Nattier portrait. It was pale blue taffeta, with superb sleeves, and from the shoulder was suspended a wreath of unbelievably lovely flowers that she had had made especially for the dress by Camille Marchais. Mme. Dévie was my mother's vendeuse, and when Aunt Dell heard about it she said to Mme. Bond, who took care of her, "I want you to make a dress even more beautiful for my niece. Now see which is the best." This other dress was also a copy of an old portrait. It was made of pink brocade, with a stiff bodice and bows lined with silver. Both of the dresses, as you know, are packed away in the attic at Beverly Farms.[48]

[48] Now among the collection of the Chicago Historical Society.

I remember a day when I went with my father to Fontainebleau and Barbizon. We went by train from the Gare de Lyons, with many changes before we reached the famous village, where we had lunch. I enjoyed these excursions with my father, whose knowledge of pictures and love of sight-seeing made him always a pleasant companion.

On October 11 I received a cable from Adelaide, telling me of her engagement to Ned Ryerson. It was a moment of great excitement to me. Ned was to become one of the most distinguished surgeons of his time, and their married life was destined to be supremely happy.

Elsie was in Paris, and Emily Rogers and Katharine and Stanley arrived from Switzerland. One day we motored with Mrs. Dexter to Chartres, where I took some photographs, and had the pleasure of showing the cathedral to my mother, who, strangely enough, had never seen it. Cousin Mollie and Helen were at the Hotel d'Albe, and I was looking forward to a happy time with Helen when word came that Cousin Ella was very ill in Venice, and Helen left at once to go to her.

On November 9 we started for Cherbourg. I wrote in my diary, "Trunks start very early and we go soon after. Mrs. Munn and Gladys at station. When we reached Cherbourg the rain was falling in sheets. Everyone crowded on tender like animals, and when about to start learned that the Kaiser der Grosse was four hours late, so we have to go back to Cherbourg and to a hotel—Mrs. Slater, Miss Gwynn, Aunt Dell, mamma and I—for something to eat, and shelter. Jenny and Thérèse stay on tender. Wind howls and blows. We have a funny little room and four candles. At last we go down to the wharf and finally sail, going on board about 12 o'clock. Hurry and unpack and get to bed. Rough at once." This was often the departure from Cherbourg of that period.

My father, who had preceded us home, and Uncle Arthur met us at the dock. Uncle Arthur looked so ill that we were shocked at his appearance.

Arthur Caton in 1904

My mother went to see Dr. Tuttle, who said her condition could not be better, so that I felt very happy and reassured. She left with my father the next day for Chicago, and I planned to stay at the Waldorf for a day or two with Aunt Dell. The next morning Michael, Uncle Arthur's faithful man, telephoned to my room that Uncle Arthur was very ill. I hurriedly telephoned Dr. Tuttle for a doctor, and he sent Dr. Lockwood, who came in half an hour. He said at once that Uncle Arthur's condition was very serious. A nurse arrived, and other doctors were called in consultation. Mrs. Slater was there, and Dr. Hall hurried to the hotel to be with Aunt Dell. Late that evening Uncle Arthur's condition grew worse, and a few minutes before 10 o'clock he died, very quietly and peacefully, without regaining consciousness.

The next day in a private car we went to Chicago. Mr. Bartlett came on board the train at Grand Crossing, and at the station my father, Mr. Robert Lincoln, Mr. Field, Norman Williams, and many others met us. Mamma was waiting at the house. That evening Mr. William McCormick, who had been one of Uncle Arthur's closest

friends and companions, asked to sit with him through the night.
The next day was the funeral. The ministers of the First and Second
Presbyterian Churches read the service. We went by train to Ottawa.
From the station we drove to the cemetery in my own grandmother's
old carriage. The sun was setting when we reached the Caton lot,
and the ground was covered with flowers. Poor Michael[49] was
unconsolable. He had hardly left Uncle Arthur's side for many
years, and loved him with true devotion.

[49] Arthur Caton's manservant.

Mrs. Slater went back to Washington, and Mrs. Frederick Eames,
whose husband had been Uncle Arthur's cousin, stayed on with
Aunt Dell. She was a charming person, and very pretty. Aunt Dell
has always been fond of her, and they had had in the past the best
of good times together.

Little Pierrot had an operation to remove a small growth on his head.
He came back from the veterinarian's half-crazed with pain, and
mamma held him in her lap in my little sitting room for the rest of
the afternoon. Whenever I think of my mother I see her with Pierrot
tucked under her arm, or on the foot of her bed, or with his little
paws on the door of the carriage, looking out for big dogs that we
might pass and at whom he could bark in his own ferocious way. He
feared nothing, and had a gallantry of spirit that belied his small body.

We were all, of course, in mourning because of Uncle Arthur's
death, but one afternoon we drove to Frederic's new house to see
the beautiful decorations for the tea that Dora was giving for his
sister, Florence. His great studio was hung with tapestry, and made
a most perfect and effective setting. Although I could not be
Adelaide's maid of honor, I was, none the less, in the midst of all
the preparations for her wedding—the opening of wedding presents,
arranging the decorations for the church, and all the excitement
that she shared with me as much as possible. Her wedding was on
December 6, and I helped her dress, and from the back of the
church had a glimpse of the really beautiful ceremony. After the
wedding she and Ned came to Aunt Dell's house. A little table for
two was laid before the fire in the upstairs sitting room, where they
had dinner before taking the train to Hot Springs. Helen was still
abroad, and that evening, feeling a little sad, I sat down and wrote
her all about the wedding.

The next day I went to Ottawa, where Aunt Dell, my mother and Mrs. Eames had gone the previous day. While I was there something very sad was to happen.

The previous summer before we sailed, my mare, Duchess, had been put on a farm seven miles from the house at Ottawa. The arrangements had all been made by my father, and I supposed, of course, that she was being given simple care and shelter at night. I started out the next day to see her, with the happiest anticipation. I wrote in my diary, "Find my poor Duchess with a great fistula on her neck. She had not been under a roof for six months—nothing to eat but corn husks. She came running to the fence at the sound of my voice to greet me. I led her back as best I could by holding her halter over the back of the buggy. We put her in the box stall

Catherine on Duchess

of the old stable, and blanketed and fed her, and I telephoned to the veterinarian in Chicago." The next day he came, and said the best thing to do was to have her killed. In the early afternoon I said goodbye to her, and they led her out to the second Deer Park and shot her. A little later I drove to the spot where three men were digging her grave. It was almost dark when they finished. It was a sad end for so beautiful and distinguished a mare. She had carried the Master at Meadowbrook, and her wisdom and sagacity had insured my safety through the years I had owned her. I felt very bitter and rebellious.

On December 16 I went with my mother to the first Thomas concert in the new Orchestra Hall. My mother had the third box from the stage on the left side as you face the orchestra. I can see her today, seated in the front of the box in her beautiful sable cape, wearing a little toque made of iridescent feathers, her sable muff in her lap. It was afterwards said that Mr. Thomas was disappointed in the acoustics of the hall. However that may be, he was only to live a short time longer. His funeral was to take place just three weeks from that afternoon.

On Christmas night we all went to dinner at Mrs. MacVeagh's, and on December 30 I left for Washington with Jenny. My father and Adelaide, who had returned from her wedding trip, and Pierrot went to the station to see us off. It was New Year's Eve when I reached Washington, and that night, dressed in my beautiful pink satin ball gown, I dined at Mrs. John R. McLean's, and sat next to the Prince de Bearn and Robert Goelet. There was afterwards a dance and cotillion. I did not know very many men, but the few old friends I had looked after me, and I had a pleasant evening.

Thus began the New Year.

THE CHRONICLE OF CATHERINE EDDY BEVERIDGE

1905

Opposite: Abby, Spencer and Catherine

INTRODUCTION

~ 1905 ~

ALTHOUGH IN 1905 Catherine again wintered in Washington and traveled for large parts of the year in Europe, a note of strain begins to creep into her account of this time. Part of the strain was undoubtedly owing to her father's troubled financial situation, which in April 1907 would culminate in his bankruptcy. Augustus's stewardship of Abby's fortune, part of which he had invested in a business venture that later failed, jeopardized the social standing of the Eddys. Delia stepped in to shore up their finances, and Abby and she embarked on a course of action that, while responding to painful realities, cleverly concealed the Eddys' growing difficulties. Augustus Eddy's glaring neglect of Catherine's beloved horse, Duchess, which she dramatically related in her 1904 narrative, signaled his distracted mind and strained pocketbook, for he was generally a responsible executor of others' affairs. Likewise, the steps that Mrs. Eddy took in 1905 to secure and furnish an apartment in Washington, which to outsiders might signify an expansion of the family's resources, actually anticipated the day when the Eddys would be forced to sell their Chicago home and move into the one that Delia owned. Undoubtedly, these changes, occurring at the periphery of Catherine's consciousness, made more urgent the question of her marrying.

As if on cue, an eligible European suitor materialized. Alfred zu Dohna, scion of an ancient German landed family, appeared one day on the Eddys' doorstep, bearing a letter of introduction from an eminent clergyman of their acquaintance. Dohna began courting Catherine at once. The unrelenting attentions he paid her, as he trailed the Eddys on their customary transatlantic hegira, suggest the intensity of his attraction to a young woman as at home in German culture as she was well connected in American society.

Despite Dohna's illustrious pedigree, both Abby and Catherine regarded him, and what he represented, with misgiving. Though Catherine found it flattering to be pursued by such a distinguished suitor, she could not coax herself to love so colorless a figure. And though Abby's efforts had long been directed toward uniting her daughter with a man of Dohna's type, she loved Catherine too much to marry her off opportunistically. The appeal of Dohna's noble title and vast lands may have waned when Abby confronted the fact that, were Catherine to marry a European aristocrat, she would be fated to leave her mother and country behind. Both women struggled with their feelings about Dohna for weeks, as he dogged them from Chicago to the East Coast and, finally, to his native Germany. September brought a happy distraction, for, in England, a little less than ten months after Arthur Caton's death, Delia and Marshall Field were married. Their careful efforts to marry surreptitiously were faithfully reported in American newspapers, and, with American society watching at a respectful distance, the couple were at last united in matrimony. A sensational event soon eclipsed the Fields' happiness, however, for in late November, less than three months after their marriage, Marshall Field Jr. shot himself and died, leaving a beautiful wife and three children behind.

The circumstances of Marshall's death, at just thirty-seven years of age, aroused widespread speculation that he had committed suicide. Marshall, who was an experienced hunter, shot himself in his dressing room with an automatic revolver. The shot entered his abdomen just below the ribs and by some "wonderful chance" missed his stomach and intestines before perforating his liver. He was too severely wounded to offer any account of what had happened, but friends claimed that he had injured himself while "testing" a new weapon. Alternatively, it was claimed that Marshall was contemplating a hunting trip and had the gun with him in his room for that reason. It slipped from his hand and hit the floor, or perhaps he had touched the trigger as the gun was falling. In any event, the firearm was turned toward him and discharged frontally in such a way that he wounded himself fatally. At the inquest into his death, a parade of witnesses labored to dispel the idea that he had committed suicide, and a coroner's jury ruled the death accidental.

Mr. Field was not present on the occasion, but filed an affidavit asserting of his son that "[h]is family relations were happy." Catherine suggests otherwise, observing matter-of-factly that Marshall "had been the cause of bitter disappointment" and "had given his father endless anxiety." Given the senior Field's lack of confidence in his son, it is difficult to see how the younger man could have been happy. In contrast to his hard-driving father, referred to as "Chicago's merchant prince," Marshall was hesitant and retiring. After leaving Harvard without graduating, he never applied himself to anything. Newspapers friendly to the family claimed that ill health accounted for Marshall's lack of achievement. Whatever the truth, his frailties had disqualified him from any role in his father's vast business empire. Without him, his wife and children faced a more uncertain future.

Albert J. Beveridge

ON NEW YEAR'S DAY I lunched at the Boardmans', and dined at the Austrian Embassy, where I sat next to Faramond and Count Hoyos. I wore my beautiful blue taffeta dress. After dinner we walked across the street through the chancellery to Mrs. Slater's house.

The next day I went with Mrs. Slater to the Diplomatic breakfast at the Hays', where I was very glad to see Alice and Helen again. The news had come of the fall of Port Arthur, and caused great excitement. That afternoon I went to the Secretary of the Navy's[50] to "receive" as was the custom. There were a great many naval officers, and I had a good time. Tuesday I lunched with the Myers, our friends of Borca, in their house on Farragut Square. Walden Myer was in clerical clothes, and looked very much more dignified and important than he had in the Dolomites. I sat between him and Count de Chambrun. The house, to my amazement, was indescribably beautiful. It was pure American Gothic, built by Upjohn, the architect of Trinity Church in New York. Inside, the rooms opened on a rectangular hall two stories high, with a gallery around it on the second floor. Everything in the house was American Gothic or Victorian, even to the private chapel. The house has long since been torn down to make way for the Army & Navy Club. It was a superb example of the house of that period, and should have been preserved. That same afternoon I went with Mrs. Slater to a musicale at Mrs. McLean's, where Schumann-Heink sang. I dined that night at Margaretta MacVeagh's, and wore Aunt Dell's pink dress and braided my hair on top of my head.

The following days were full of engagements. On January 6 Mrs. Slater gave a dinner. I wrote in my diary, "Sat next Gilmore and de Chambrun, who was very fresh, but amusing. Afterwards talked to John Lodge. Some of the people—Alice Roosevelt, Boardman, Wetmore, Lodges, de Tuyles, Polly Morton, Katherine Elkins, Matilde Townsend, Mitchell, McCawley, Sala, Gurney, Ewart, Longworth, Bonaparte, etc."

On Sunday Beveridge came to tea, but seemed to make no impression on the pages of my diary. One day we lunched at the de Tuyles. He was the first Secretary of the Netherlands Legation, and she was very beautiful—tall and blonde. They had a wonderful chef, and the day is memorable, as we had a dish that afterwards became one of my mother's favorite lunches. It consisted of a huge capon that

[50] Paul Morton.

had been very carefully steamed, and was served whole on an enormous platter. Around it were little even mounds of vegetables, all cut with the same fine cutter—not balls, but a little elongated—carrots, turnips, potatoes, beans. A marvelous sauce was served, made from the bouillon in which the capon had cooked, and to which cream and very finely chopped parsley and celery had been added. I think my mother, with her usual genius, improved upon it, for under her guiding hand it became a most magnificent dish for a Sunday luncheon party.

I now went to Mrs. Munn's to spend a few days. I was glad to be with them again. Charlie was still there on his vacation, and we all had a good time together. I continued to dine out every night, and on the 12th went to the White House Diplomatic reception. I had supper at Alice Roosevelt's table, with Polly Morton and three or four men.

The next day I went to New York with Mrs. Slater, where my mother and father and Aunt Dell had already arrived. They told me that my beloved Trilby[51] had been lost for several days. I went to stay with Mrs. Vanderbilt for a night, and she took me to call on old Mrs. Astor. I was always glad that I had seen the interior of that very ugly house. I saw Emily Rogers, and went to the theatre with her and her brother. They wanted me to stay on with them, but it was not possible, as I had planned to go to Philadelphia to spend a night with Alice Littleton, and to go to the opera, to hear *Tristan and Isolde*. I met my mother on the train as it passed through Philadelphia, and we went together to Washington. We were looking for a house, and the next day we went about with Mrs. Munn and an agent. There was one on Rhode Island Avenue that we particularly liked, but nothing came of it.

When we reached Chicago two days later there was still no Trilby. I was really heartbroken. The news from Russia was very disturbing, and we were in some anxiety about Spencer, but a cable came from him saying, "No danger—things calmer."[52] It was really the beginning of the great revolution.

Three days later, after dinner, MacGregor heard a meow outside the door. He rushed to open it, and in flew Trilby, who tore upstairs, never stopping until she reached the third floor. How glad we were!

[51] Catherine's cat, named after the heroine of the popular George de Maurier novel.

[52] On January 22, the czar's chief of security, Grand Duke Vladimir, whose wife had so impressed Catherine during her Petersburg stay, decided to use force to dispel a large but peaceful crowd of labor demonstrators who had converged on the Winter Palace to offer petitions to the czar. Police fired on the crowd, killing several hundred workers and wounding many others, turning a peaceful Sabbath into "Bloody Sunday." The massacre set off a year of labor strikes and peasant uprisings, collectively known as the Revolution of 1905.

In the middle of February I began to read Houston Stewart Chamberlain's *Life of Wagner*. A few years later appeared his *Foundations of the 19th Century*, which had a greater influence on my life than any other book I ever read.

My mother's Sunday lunches began, and our usual busy days followed. We gave a dinner for Adelaide and Ned—the Stones, the Joe Coleman, Jr.'s, Farquhars, Bartletts, Spragues, George Porter, Keiths, etc.—a lovely table, and they stayed late. We were all beginning to play bridge.

My mother seemed quite re-established in health, and every day my diary gave the details of her life, her dinners, and the friends that came to her house. On Tuesday—her day at home—there were sometimes twenty or twenty-five persons for tea. Aunt Dell was, of course, in mourning. Mrs. Eames and Mrs. Bellas spent a great deal of time with her, and she went often to Ottawa, where she busied herself with putting the old house to rights.

On March 4, Elsie Porter was married in Paris to Edwin Mende, a young doctor. His father was a famous diagnostician in Zurich, to whom Mr. Field often went for a general examination. Elsie's mother had been under his care, and in this way Elsie had known the son, who was studying to be an oculist. I was sorry not to be in Paris for the wedding. Elsie was to live in Bern, and in the years to come I often visited her. Our friendship was to grow stronger in spite of long separations.

One evening my mother and father and I went to dine at Mrs. MacVeagh's. The guest of honor was Mr. Henry James. Robert Herrick, the novelist, was also there, and after dinner he came to talk to me. Eight years before I had studied with him, going every morning to his apartment near the University of Chicago. I met Mr. James, and he remembered me in London, and asked about Spencer and the Hays. He talked to my mother after dinner.

Late one afternoon I came home with mamma after a busy day and found that two young Germans had left a letter of introduction from Dr. Hall, and their very foreign-looking visiting cards. One was a Dr. Wahlen, and the other the Burggraf Alfred zu Dohna-Mallmitz. Their visit was to have some repercussions in my life for the next few months.

A few days later I met Count Dohna at a dinner given by Mrs. Lathrop. He was about thirty years old, with very blond hair, a somewhat aquiline nose, and a chin that seemed to recede into his collar. All in all, it was a face not devoid of distinction. His English was far from fluent, and he had a quiet and unresponsive manner. Mrs. Hall had known his sister, Daisy von Dohna, and Dohna, himself, had been a student at the University of Gottingen. He was the eldest son of the Burggraf, and belonged to one of the oldest families in Europe. One branch of the family—the Dohna Schlodiens—was mediatized. The family estate was in Silesia. He had been sent with the young man who accompanied him to study agricultural methods in America, but, as things turned out, his studies did not prove to be very burdensome. He came to tea on Sunday, and thereafter we saw him almost every day.

Mrs. Vanderbilt arrived in Chicago on her way from California in a private car. She spent the day with us, first going to see Aunt Dell, and then to 1601. I wrote in my diary how proud I was of the house, the beautiful table and the delicious lunch, all of which Mrs. Vanderbilt appreciated and admired. She wanted my mother and me to go to New York in her car, but, of course, we refused, and left ourselves on the late afternoon train. We were on our way to Atlantic City, where we had never been before. We arrived in a heavy rainstorm, and found splendid rooms awaiting us in the Marlborough Hotel. We were about to unpack when we discovered that dogs were not allowed! They refused to make an exception, even for one as small as little Pierrot, and we telephoned wildly to different hotels and finally found something at the Chelsea. The rooms were not as good, but the view was splendid, and we were finally settled.

Who should arrive the next morning but Dohna! We were completely surprised, and not altogether pleased, but we ended by having a pleasant time with him. He made excursions with my mother and me, and one day Dr. and Mrs. Hall came to lunch with us. A few days later when we went to New York we all five went to the play. By this time his intentions were very serious, and I had some difficulty in treating the matter lightly. Mamma and I went back to Chicago, and the persistent letters followed—written in German, but in English script, so that it was easy for me to

Dr. Thomas C. Hall and Mrs. Hall

read them. But I was busy and not too preoccupied with the new situation. We now spent much of our time in Ottawa, where the snowballs and lilacs were coming into bloom.

On May 5 Herbert and Mary Stone, the Bartletts and the undaunted Dohna, who had arrived from the East, came to Ottawa for the week-end. Herbert and Frederic were very amusing, and we all had a gay time.

On Sunday Frederic, Herbert, Dohna, Mary, Dora and I went out in some local motor that had been hired for the day to Starved Rock.[53] Coming back the brakes refused to work, and the hill being steep and rough, they turned the car into a bank against a fallen tree, where it balanced for a moment, and finally settled on the road. It was a very close call, and we all crawled out as best we could and walked to the foot of the hill. We decided not to tell Aunt Dell, but when we arrived at the house where she sat in the great bay window behind the ample and delicious Ottawa tea table, she saw at once that something had happened; but it was all forgotten in a moment, as we were young and hungry.

Mamma and I left again for New York the 12th of May. Dohna remained in Chicago, and went to Monticello to visit Robert Allerton. We were home again in a few days. At this time there came to Chicago another young foreign visitor, Benno de Siebert, a Secretary of the Russian Embassy. He was far more intelligent than Dohna—tall and slender. He belonged to one of the great German families in Baltic Russia, and was at heart very German, both in his culture and taste. Siebert was a most kind and charming friend, and afterwards very devoted to Helen.

At last Dohna left for New York, and the next days we were very busy preparing for our departure. We sailed on June 6, and, undismayed, Dohna was on the boat. We left him finally to pursue his voyage to Bremen, and we landed as usual at Cherbourg. Helen was in Paris, and I remember to this day our long conversations on the balcony of the hotel—and how much I had to tell her! Dohna, and de Siebert—all the events of the spring at home. It was the same busy Paris—fittings and drives in the Bois. We were only there ten days, and started on our way to visit Spencer in St. Petersburg.

We arrived in Berlin early in the morning, where Dohna met us, and we walked across to the old Hotel Continental, where nice

[53] Starved Rock is a needle-like rock formation jutting up from the plain outside Ottawa. According to legend, a band of Illiniwek Indians resorted to the butte in the fighting that broke out after they killed Pontiac, the famed chief of the Ottawa tribe. Potawatomies who were allied with the Ottawas besieged the rock, and the Illiniwek starved.

rooms were awaiting us, and a huge German bouquet. Dohna's
father was in town, and asked my mother and me to lunch with
him. He did not look at all like his son, and was much more
homme du monde. That evening Dohna took us to the Zoological
Gardens to dine. In his own setting he appeared, of course, to
advantage, and I remember the first little feeling of uncertainty
creeping into my mind.

We left the next day for St. Petersburg. Spencer met us, and we
found a pleasant apartment awaiting us at the same Hotel d'Europe
where I had stayed with Elsie. Spencer had rented what they called
a "cabin" on one of the islands of the Neva, with Baron Foster of
the Austrian Embassy, and another young man whose name I have
forgotten. We went to see his quarters after lunch, and then to watch
the polo. The Princesses Belloselsky and Cantacuzéne were there,
Mrs. Meyer, our Ambassadress, and Lady Hardinge, the wife of the
new British Ambassador. No one watched the polo, and everyone
talked. That night Spencer came to dine with us, and stayed until
11. The night was a bright as day.

The next morning it was warm, with the sun shining. I went out
with mamma and the courier for very serious sight-seeing. Spencer

*From left to right:
Robert Sanderson
McCormick
(Ambassador
to France) and
Mrs. McCormick,
Spencer Eddy, and
Robert Wood Bliss.*

lunched with us and we all went to the Hermitage. That evening we dined in Spencer's cabin. It was not really a cabin, but a charming little bungalow. We had an excellent dinner, very well served. The polo ponies were sent for, and came up to the door, where we gave them sugar. Spencer drove back with us and spent the night in town at his apartment.

The following day we went to the Hermitage again, to Fabergé's, and various shops, and Thursday we lunched at the American Embassy. Prince and Princess Cantacuzéne were there, Robert Bliss, our second Secretary, the Bavarian Minister, and Foster. There was no polo, as it was raining hard. That evening we went to dine with Spencer on the island—Foster, Lord Cranley and Beaumont, of the British Embassy.

The next day was my birthday, and Spencer gave me the beautiful little jade Fabergé frame. I went with my mother to his apartment in town, where we met him and the paper hanger whom my mother had sent for to refreshen his rooms. In the afternoon we went to a portrait exhibition, and then to the Alexander Nevsky monastery to hear the monks sing. I wrote in my diary, "Very bad news from Odessa, and even as near as Riga, where some troops had bolted and gone no one knows where."

Mamma was early out the next day to see about furniture covering for Spencer's apartment. At lunch time, although we did not expect him, he came in to tell us the sad news of Mr. Hay's death. It was a great blow to Spencer. He had, indeed, lost his most important, wisest and kindest friend. That evening I wrote in my diary, "the news of the rioting all over Russia is no better."

One day we lunched at the British Embassy. The Ambassador was charming.[54] I can remember him even after all these years, although I have forgotten the pleasant young men whose names I noted in my diary. It was the same beautiful embassy that I had known with the Scotts, only now it was summer, and after lunch we went out on the balcony. That same evening we dined at the American Embassy.

The 4th of July was a wonderful day. My mother, Spencer and I went with the Princess Orloff on her yacht to Peterhof. We started about noon, in a driving rain. Princess Cantacuzéne, Prince Belloselsky and Foster made up the party. We had lunch on board, and soon afterwards the sun came out. Carriages met us at Peterhof and we drove through the park, where the fountains were playing. We were shown through part of the palace, and as we were continuing our drive through the gardens a huge Cossack stepped out to speak to us, and the carriages stopped. He said to the Princess Orloff that we could not go further as the Empress and the Imperial children were having tea in the pavilion we were approaching. There in the distance we saw three little tethered ponies. I often remembered that scene when I read of the horrors of the final revolution in Russia. We had tea on the yacht going back, and a quiet evening with Spencer at the hotel.

The next day we lunched at the Spanish Embassy with the Duke and Duchess d'Arcos. The Duchess d'Arcos, an American, was an old friend of my mother's, and we had a very pleasant time. We left that afternoon for Berlin. The Ambassador, himself, came to the station to say goodbye. We were very sorry to leave Spencer. He looked miserable and forlorn. Mr. Hay's death had been his first great sorrow.

We spent two days in Berlin, where Dohna met us. We saw the Pergamon marbles for the first time, and the new museum.[55] We went to the play—*Jugend* and *Fritzchen*—with Keinz acting. Dohna's brother was there—very amusing and bright, and like the Burggraf. He was engaged to be married. On the 9th we left for Frankfort, and spent the night in the beautiful old Frankforterhof I knew so well.

[55] The Kaiser Friedrich Museum, designed by Ernst von Ihne, housed a collection of engravings and Renaissance works from the Old and New Museums.

We were soon settled in the villa at Schwalbach. Dohna came the 18th. My mother, who I think was beginning to be a little worried by the turn things had taken, met him at the station, and had a talk with him before he saw me. The weather was gray and cold, but we went for long walks though the wood road to the Platte, and down by Unter dem Buchen to Hubertsquellen and Fishbach, and Hettenheim. One evening we went to the Riesemuhle and had trout, and with my mother we went on several picnics.

Spencer arrived on the 25th. His coming only added to the confusion in my mind. I hoped that he would, in a few words, settle it all for me and probably send Dohna packing, but nothing of the kind happened. Even in my childhood, with Mlle. Cognier, I had never taken so many or such varied walks. Sometimes Spencer would go with us. There was hardly a little village in all that lovely section of the Taunus mountains that we did not know. Mrs. Williams and Laura were at the Allee Saal, Mrs. Gordon Dexter, and Baroness von Hutten, whose husband, the German Minister to China, had been murdered in the Boxer rebellion; and we sometimes lunched or dined together.

One day Spencer, Dohna and I went by motor to Heidelberg. We had two pannes on the way, and arrived about 2:30. Dohna's sister, Daisy, was there, very ill under the care of a famous specialist. While he visited her, Spencer and I went to the Schloss, and I saw for the first time that great ruin and the even more beautiful view. We had another tire coming back to Wiesbaden, where we arrived at 10 o'clock and took a late train back to Schwalbach.

It came time for Dohna to join his regiment for the summer maneuvers. This he was loathe to do, and saw Dr. Franz, who wrote out an excuse for him, to the effect that he was *"blutarmig."*[56] The old Hofrath said, with a twinkle in his eye, *"Die alte familien sind immer blutarmig."*

[56] Anemic. The doctor continues, "The old families always have anemia."

Our conversations grew more and more serious, and we talked to each other with great frankness. He told me about the estate of Mallmitz, and the great forests that were cut in rotation. He explained

Alfred Dohna and Spencer

that the Emperor would doubtless make me "*edel*" [noble] as the eldest son, by a clause in his grandfather's will, was obliged to marry in the nobility. He told me about his sisters and his brother in the navy who was next in line. This brother was destined to become one of the great heroes of the World War, and did finally inherit Mallmitz after Alfred Dohna's death.

On August 2 my mother and I went to Munich, where we met Aunt Dell. We were on our way again to Borca. At Innsbruck Cousin Mollie and Helen joined us, and we all went on together. I can remember through all these years my happiness at having Helen with me, and the walks and talks we had together. There were rainy days and sunny days, with the tops of the Dolomites clear and pink. One day we motored to Cadore for lunch, where we saw Titian's house, and on to the Bosca di San Marco. We drove to Cortina in the afternoons for coffee at the incomparable Konditorei.

Mr. Field joined us on the 9th, so that we were a large party. Spencer and I began to take some very long walks; sometimes Helen went with us, and a little boy to carry the tea basket. One day I got up at 5:30 and, with Helen and Spencer, went to Cortina by motor, where we had a delicious breakfast. Spencer left us there and went on to Toblach to meet my father, who had come from America. Helen and I spent a pleasant morning in shops and walking about until the motor came through on its way back with my father and Spencer. My companionship with Helen, the happy days in the Dolomites, and perhaps the right atmosphere to think things out clearly in my own mind, had made me decide that I could not marry Dohna. I wrote him a very definite and final letter that he could not possibly misunderstand.

Helen Birch

Helen and Cousin Mollie left for Venice, and Spencer and I continued our walks together. We were never to have such close companionship again. One day I wrote, "Such a day! Start at 9:30, cross the river at Borca and climb higher than every before. Have lunch on a sheltered meadow, where we build a fire of pine brushwood and cook ham and eggs. We left my father there and Spencer and I go still higher to a great projecting rock. The ground was covered with Edelweiss and rare Alpine flowers. I smelled for the first time the delicious perfume of the little picoli neri;[57] and the view!—mountain after mountain, crag after crag, and two great purple valleys stretching to the Adriatic. Never had I seen so wonderful and awe-inspiring a sight. Get back about 7, having walked twenty miles—four and a half hours of it steady climbing."

A few days later a telegram came from Dohna saying, among other things, that he would be in Toblach on Tuesday. We all decide that I had best go to Venice, so Spencer and I hastily plan to leave the next day. It was great fun! We were off in the morning at 7 o'clock, over the beautiful road to Belluno. We arrived in Venice about 2. Helen met us, and at 4 she and I started to Torcello in a motor boat. We dined at the Lido at 9:30, and came back to Venice just as the moon, very red, came up over the sea.

Dohna arrived at Borca and saw my mother, and was finally made to understand that I would not marry him. I had one more 39-page letter from him, and that ended it. Alas! I was not in love with him, but I was a little in love, and have remained so to this day, with the Schloss at Mallmitz and the orangerie that I was never to see!

Spencer and I left shortly for Paris, where my mother and father and Aunt Dell soon joined us. We were at the Hotel du Rhin. Preparations were now being made for Aunt Dell's marriage to Mr. Field. Every effort was made to keep it secret, and my father left to make the final plans in England. Spencer and Mr. Field left for London two days later, and Aunt Dell, my mother and I followed them on September 3. Helen was to go with us, but her train from Venice was late, and she missed every connection, and only reached London the following night. We were all at Claridge's.

On Tuesday, September 5, Aunt Dell and Mr. Field were married. I wrote in my diary, "At first a dull day, but the sun comes out a little later. Aunt Dell never looked better—wears gray chiffon with lace tunic, and gray and silver hat with long gray plumes." They were married by the Canon in St. Margaret's, Westminster, a very beautiful and impressive church. At Claridge's afterwards there was a wedding breakfast. The Ambassador and Mrs. Reid, Jack Carter, Albertine and Marshall, Ethel Beatty, Spencer, the Crossleys, Helen, the Canon, Mrs. Dexter, Mrs. John Clark, Mr. Joseph Field, Mr. William Monroe, Mrs. Dibblee, and my father and mother.

Menu.

——▸◂——

Melon de Cantaloup

———

Œufs Pochés Mornay

———

Whitebait

———

Côtelettes d'Agneau Grillées
Petits Pois au Beurre
Pommes Parisienne

———

Perdreaux à la Broche
Salade Niçoise

———

Soufflé Palmyre
Friandises

———

Corbeilles de Fruits

*The menu served
at the wedding of
Marshall and Delia Field*

The next day we went by train to Wrest Hall, a country place that
the Ambassador had rented—Mrs. Dexter, my mother and father,
Helen and I. It was an interesting house, with a beautiful garden laid
out by Le Nôtre. Every night we went to the play, and Friday we left
for Paris. The next morning, September 9, Spencer started for his
post in St. Petersburg. He was really engaged to be married to Lurline
Spreckels, although there followed a period of doubt and uncertainty.

That same afternoon Helen and I, with her faithful Agnes,[58] went by
train to Chartres. It was a dark and dismal day. It rained from time

58 Agnes Meehan (b. ca. 1870),
Helen's maid.

to time. We drove at once to the Cathedral, and stayed there all afternoon. I thought it more beautiful than anything else in the world. We had been reading Huysmans' *Cathedral* again, and we were determined to see the Cathedral at all times and hours as he had described it. As it grew dark we had tea at a patisserie. A fair was going on outside our rooms in the hotel, and there was a great racket all night, but we managed to sleep for a few hours. We arose before five o'clock to go to early mass in the crypt. I wrote, "There were too many lamps—more than in the time of Durtal, I am sure." We saw the little, black, shadowy figures of old French women, and some aged men, and we smelled that crypty, misty, foggy Huysman air. Then we hurried back to Paris. It was only September 11, and Helen went back to join her mother in Venice. We were not to sail until October 18, and there were five long weeks ahead of us in Paris.

Mr. Field and Aunt Dell arrived from London, and stayed at the Hotel Bristol across the street. It was very strange to be separated from Aunt Dell, and she came often to see us, and for long talks with my mother. On September 14, with Marie, a maid we had taken to London, I left for Bern and a visit to Elsie.

She lived in a cozy villa in a suburb. Edwin, her husband, came home every day to lunch. He was not tall, had curly hair, but was distinctly intelligent and a very strong character. The first day after lunch we went to the old town, and had tea in a little Konditorei under an arcade. In the evening there was a concert. We went for walks in the beautiful wood, and for excursions in the lovely country around Bern—to Freiburg, to Thun, to Sollerthun. I was back in Paris by the 25th.

My father left for America with the Dibblees a few days later, and our usual busy life in Paris continued. One memorable day my mother and I went with Mr. Field and Aunt Dell to see the chateau of Vaux le Vicomte. It had belonged once to Fouquet, and it was there that the great fete was given in honor of Louis XIV. The chateau was opened for us, and we walked through those beautiful rooms that I have never forgotten. The family was not at home, but comfortable chairs were in the great salon, and bowls of flowers on the tables—all the evidence of life that great historic monuments usually lack. Next to Versailles and Fontainebleau, it is probably the greatest of the houses of France.

Elsie Porter Mende
as a young matron

One day I bought a little lady dog—a maltese like Pierrot, but not nearly as fine—in fact, she was rather big and clumsy as time wore on. My mother was very distressed, but it could not be helped—I had bought her, and she was mine. She was very gentle, and promptly went to sleep on my bed, where she slept quietly all night.

One day Hazel Trudeau, whose husband had died, brought her little baby to see us. Hazel was indescribably beautiful in her long widow's veil, and a little Mary Stuart cap coming down in a point over her forehead. A few years later she was to marry Lavery, the portrait painter, and to become one of the great figures in London. I went to see Lurline, my future sister-in-law, and thought her quite nice, but I could not be enthusiastic. Spencer was lost to us, and entering an alien world. Just before we left Helen and Cousin Mollie came from Vienna and I had two or three days with them. The last thing we did before I sailed was to go to hear the Vie de Bohème at the Opera Comique.

My mother and I, Jenny and the two little dogs sailed on the 18th. It was windy and rainy on the tender. The Myers were on the boat, and Mr. and Mrs. Frederick Keep, who had arranged to have us sit at their table with Mr. Boardman, Mr. Hall McCormick, and Russell Tyson.

We arrived in Chicago on October 28, where Aunt Dell met us. She and Mr. Field had sailed a week earlier. I found my dear Trilby well. That evening we went to the horse show.

Our life in Chicago began again, only now there was a great change. Aunt Dell had left her own beautiful house on Calumet Avenue. She could not bear, at first, to dismantle or touch it. It was open, and in perfect order. Sometimes the lights would be lit and she and Mr. Field would go over there to spend the evening. It was really not until after Mr. Field's death that she actually brought her things to his house. Mr. Field's house on Prairie Avenue had been built by Hunt, and was a superb example of his architecture. It had a high stoop that nevertheless had great dignity, reaching from the street to the drawing room floor, and a mansarde roof. The ceilings were very high, and the house, as an actual shell, was infinitely better than Aunt Dell's, but it lacked her great dining room, and, of course, contained nothing of interest.

Albertine Field

I saw a great deal of Ruth Hanna, and began to see more of Albertine Field. Albertine was ten years older than I, but I never felt the slightest difference in age—she was so beautiful, so young in mind and temperament.

My mother's Sunday lunches began again. On the 19th we had Ruth Hanna, Ellen Waller, Louise Gaylord, Pauline Kohlsaat, Mary and Herbert, Eames, James Deering, George Porter, Ben Cable, Howard Gillette, Min Palmer, Marshall and Albertine.

Three days later we heard a dreadful piece of news: Marshall had shot himself in his sitting room on Prairie Avenue. Aunt Dell and Mr. Field were in New York at the Holland House, and they started home on a special train. The newspapers were full of the accident, and all the horrible publicity that Aunt Dell and poor Mr. Field abhorred. Marshall was taken to the hospital, where his condition proved to be very serious. My mother went to see what she could do for Albertine. Marshall lived until the 27th. He had given his father endless anxiety and had been the cause of bitter disappointment, but he was a lovable, pleasant fellow with charming manners, and Albertine adored him. Albertine and her boys moved to Aunt Dell's. She was really heartbroken.

Von Siebert came to Chicago, and brought word from the State Department that Spencer had sent in a dispatch from a town near St. Petersburg. The news in Russia had been very disquieting, and we were anxious.[59] I was glad to see Siebert, and we had some pleasant days together. Helen was home, and Adelaide, and we seemed from the pages of my diary to have been very gay. One evening my mother had another pergola dinner—just as it had been three years before for Mrs. Slater. Helen and I sat on the back stairs and ate the dinner on our laps that MacGregor handed us, but came down later. Joe Smith, the Herbert Stones, Lathrops, Blairs, Beales, Meekers were there. While he was in Chicago Joe Smith did a little drawing of me.

On December 19 I say in my diary, "Cable from Spencer, saying he was really engaged." Evidently after our departure from Paris there had been some doubt about it. It would have been better for him had he decided the other way.

Stanley and Katharine McCormick came back to Chicago, and Mrs. McCormick gave them a large reception, at which I poured tea. In the midst of all this jumble of engagements, one morning, December 21, Beveridge telephoned me, and asked if he might come to see me. I had an engagement to go with mamma to the Fortnightly[60] to hear Mrs. Craigie, but I slipped away early and came back to the house. It was the first and only time that Albert was ever in 1601. When I started to pour his tea, I said, "How do you take your tea?" and he said, "How do you take yours?" I laughed—"With cream and no sugar." He answered, "That's the way I'll always take mine."

New Year's Eve we dined quietly at Aunt Dell's. Cousin Mollie was ill and could not come, but Helen, my mother and father and I were there. I came home and went into my little back room and read Matthew Arnold until after 12. It was the first quiet New Year that I had had in many years.

[59] Unrest had increased in Russia in September and October, as the first soviets, or workers' councils, were formed and a general strike took hold. In various parts of the empire, especially in Petersburg, the soviets were assuming the character of revolutionary governments. Under pressure, Nicholas had issued a proclamation, his "October Manifesto," establishing a legislature (the Duma), but many activists were not satisfied. Though unrest eventually dissipated without further violence in St. Petersburg, fighting broke out elsewhere and blood was shed as the army moved to quell the people.

[60] The Fortnightly was a leading Chicago women's club, which the Eddys' friend, Emily MacVeagh, had helped found.

THE CHRONICLE OF CATHERINE EDDY BEVERIDGE

1906

INTRODUCTION

~ 1906 ~

THE NEW YEAR IN CHICAGO BEGAN with an elaborate charitable bazaar modeled on the Kirmess, a traditional fair held in the Netherlands. Chicago's Kirmess lasted over a number of days and included an auction, a costume-dress dance assembly, and other activities at Orchestra Hall. Barely discernible over the din of this gayety, a faint note of trouble sounded: Marshall Field, who had gone to New York to change his will, had caught cold. His condition rapidly worsened, and within a few days he had died. He was third largest taxpayer in the United States. He left an estate worth roughly $120 million and a family grappling with the sudden loss of its patriarch. For with two sudden deaths and a marriage, the configuration of the Field family was strangely changed. The deaths of the family's principal males left only Delia, Albertine and her children, and Mr. Field's sole surviving child, Ethel, behind. What was to happen to them, and to the vast estate of Marshall Field?

Of the three women, Albertine's future was most uncertain. Though Delia, like Albertine, had just been widowed, Delia had a substantial fortune of her own, a secure social identity, and no children to take care of. Ethel, who was closer to Albertine in age, was married to the dashing and popular British naval officer David Beatty. Though she counted on money from her father's estate to help her maintain a high profile in English society, her husband's brilliant reputation and the couple's status as

favorites of the British royal family gave them some security. Albertine's situation was far more marginal. The daughter of a prosperous Chicago brewer, recently deceased, she faced a severe loss of fortune and status now that her living connection with the Fields was gone. Catherine tells us that Marshall Field Jr. had died intestate, which is not quite true. Marshall Field Jr.'s will was impounded, making it impossible to learn what it contained. Given the informal character of many wills of that time, one wonders whether the document offered insights into Marshall's temperament or his state of mind just prior to his death, prompting the family to suppress it. In any event, Marshall Jr.'s estate was not large, and his untimely death prior to his father's increased the chance that Albertine would enjoy a smaller portion of the senior Field's estate than she might have otherwise.

Field's will showed that he cared much less for the charming women who surrounded him than for the perpetuation of his name and large fortune. Unlike the recently deceased Russell Sage, whose affection and respect for his wife had impelled him to make her the sole executrix of his $100 million estate, Field had made relatively small bequests to his female relatives. He had also taken care to keep his fortune from falling into the hands of his now-deceased son. Instead, Field placed the vast bulk of his estate in trust for his grandchildren — especially his male grandchildren,

Marshall III and Henry. Even they were to be kept at arm's length from their inheritance for decades. Though they soon began receiving large sums of interest from their shares of their grandfather's estate, they were not to come into control of the principal until they reached thirty-five years of age. In the meantime, the estate was to be administered by a board of trustees. "Public opinion was shocked," and with good reason. Even the $8 million that Field left for a new Museum of Natural History in Chicago seemed niggardly.

Still, outraged expectation rather than the threat of real hardship assailed Ethel and Albertine. Each had been provided for adequately. Albertine inherited at least $1 million from Field. She also received a very ample allowance ensuring that she could care for her children comfortably. Ethel received several millions. Thinking, though, of the great riches that might have been theirs, Albertine and Ethel entreated Delia to join them in contesting the will. She refused because, in 1905, Field and she had signed a prenuptial agreement. Under its terms, Delia was to receive $2 million and to inherit the Field mansion and all its contents. Being wealthy in her own right and not wanting her husband's money, she had relinquished any further claim to his estate. The excessively restrictive character of Marshall Field's ironclad will irked even its principal beneficiaries, however, who continued to challenge its provisions into the 1920s.

Field's death, though traumatic, had only an indirect effect on Catherine's family. Far more consequential was Spencer's 1906 marriage to Lurline Spreckels. Abby and Catherine both disapproved of Spencer's decision to marry Lurline, a California heiress whose grandfather, Claus Spreckels, had made an immense fortune from Hawaiian sugar. In fact, the match dissatisfied both families. The Spreckelses regarded the cosmopolitan Spencer as an opportunistic "upstart," while the Eddys disdained the Spreckelses' new wealth, dubious social credentials, and vulgar public squabbles over money. Abby worried that Lurline's extravagant and careless ways would be Spencer's undoing. She worried that Lurline would undermine Spencer's fragile work ethic, encourage his tendency to be profligate, and destroy his career in diplomacy. Whether or not Abby was correct, Spencer did quit the diplomatic corps a few years later. His marriage to Lurline ended in divorce in 1923, and he never found a meaningful occupation subsequently.

Spencer's choice only intensified Abby's determination that Catherine's marriage conform to the wishes of her family. This determination set mother and daughter on a collision course, however, for as memories of Alfred zu Dohna faded from Catherine's consciousness, she discovered that she was in love with the fiery Indiana senator, Albert Beveridge.

New Year's Day I lunched at Helen's. I had asked Margaretta MacVeagh to come to Chicago for Mrs. Palmer's ball on the 5th. Margaretta had a devoted admirer, Howard Gillette, who was also a great friend of Adelaide's and of mine. He and I plunged at once into busy list-making in preparation for her visit. We also planned to give a dance in Aunt Dell's old house after the Kirmess the following week.

Margaretta arrived the day of the ball. It was bitterly cold. There was a dinner at our house before the dance. Helen and I wore identical dresses that Aunt Dell had had made for us at Worth's the previous autumn. They were green taffeta, covered with pailletted tulle. We carried enormous bouquets of lily-of-the-valley. I danced the cotillion with Eames MacVeagh, who was an old friend, but a new admirer. I have never forgotten that evening. The cotillion was very gay, with all sorts of elaborate figures that took us dancing through those beautiful rooms. On Sunday we had a lunch as usual—Howard Gillette, Clive Runnells, Mrs. Armour, the Stanley Fields, the Keiths, the Honore Palmers, and Herbert Stone, and that night a big dinner at the Stanley McCormick's.

The next morning I went to see Aunt Dell, who was leaving for New York with Mr. Field. He had an appointment there with Mr. Milburn, the lawyer, who was preparing a new will. Alas! We were, all unknowing, on the very brink of tragedy. The following day word came from New York that Mr. Field had been taken seriously ill on the train; but the first report proved to be exaggerated, and we went on with our gayety.

The next day we had at first good news about Mr. Field, and we decided to go on with the dance, but later came the word that his illness had been diagnosed as pneumonia, and in spite of a telegram from Aunt Dell, we gave it up. That night we dined at the Stanley Field's before going again to the Kirmess. On Friday Margaretta left for Washington, and Jenny and I took the 20th Century for New York. Mr. Field and Aunt Dell were at the Holland House; Albertine was also there. Mr. Field was decidedly better. Dr. Billings had come on from Chicago, and was working with the New York doctors. That evening there was a consultation, and Mr. Field not so well. All four doctors spent the night with him. The next day (Sunday) he was not expected to live from hour to hour. My father came that afternoon. We all sat up until 3:30 in the morning. But the next day he was

better, and everyone was hopeful and happy. We all had tea in Aunt
Dell's room, and Mr. Field continued to hold his own, but the next
day he sank gradually, and died at 4 o'clock in the afternoon. I wrote
in my diary, "I am so sorry for Aunt Dell. There is nothing I can do
or say. I cared so much for him, too. It is all very strange and sad."
And so it was.

We left for Chicago. Albertine and I went to stay with Aunt Dell at
her house, where my mother met us. The weather was cold and
gray. Frederic and Dora came the next day to arrange the fabulous
flowers that kept coming until the last moment. There was a service
at the house, and then we went to the old First Presbyterian Church. After
Graceland, there was a memorial service at the Auditorium. All the
employees of Marshall Field & Company were there, and the great
hall was crowded. When Aunt Dell came in the orchestra played
the Luther Hymn and a Bach choral. There was a short address. I
remember that it ended "Marshall Field—hail and farewell." It was
a very stirring tribute.

The next days snow fell, the wind howled, and it was bitterly cold.
Helen and I sat in the back sitting room at 1905, writing hundreds

of envelopes for the cards of acknowledgment that had to be sent. The will was read and published, and public opinion was shocked. Chicago was only given $8,000,000 for a possible Museum, and the rest of the will was concerned with a heavy trust for the benefit of the two young boys, Marshall and Henry.

I continued to stay at Aunt Dell's house. Albertine and I occupied the north bedroom, the room with the lovely Venetian glass chandelier. One of my early memories had been of that room. When my grandfather lay very ill just before his death, my mother sent me with Jenny to carry a note to Mrs. Field.[61] She was in bed, and we went up to her room. When she had read the note and asked Jenny about my grandfather, she said to me, "Catherine, would you like to see Albertine's wedding dress?" Jenny and I went into the north bedroom, and there, stretched out on the bed, was a shimmering white satin bridal dress and a long tulle veil. And here I was now, in that same room with Albertine, in the midst of such heavy tragedy.

It was all very depressing. I remember the countless and endless discussions about the will. I can see Albertine in a beautiful white cloth wrapper, perched at the foot of Aunt Dell's bed, her dark eyes looking even larger than their wont in her pale face. Albertine found herself in a very serious situation by the terms of Mr. Field's will. Her husband, Marshall, had died intestate, and she had only one-third of his very small estate. She received not a penny from Mr. Field's will. In fairness to Mr. Field, it must always be remembered that this and many other things would have been righted and changed in the will Mr. Milburn was preparing for him in New York.

On February 7 Ethel and David Beatty arrived from England. Ethel felt, too, that she had been unjustly treated by her father, and she and Albertine went down on their knees to Aunt Dell, begging her to break the will, but this Aunt Dell refused to do.

A few days later I started on my way to Washington, where I was to visit Mrs. Slater, and also Margaretta and Mrs. Munn. It was, for me, the most momentous visit of my life.

Mrs. Slater's house was on 18th Street. It was a perfect town house of the period, filled with French furniture, but austere in its lines. The great drawing room on the second floor stretched across the front of the house, with a marble mantel at either end. The room

[61] The first Mrs. Marshall Field, Nannie Scott Field (d. 1896), whom Marshall Field had married in 1863.

was ever afterward enshrined in my heart, because it was there that I first met my Albert; but this February day when I entered it again there was nothing farther from my thoughts. That evening I went alone to a musicale at the White House. It took some courage to go alone, but I met Mrs. Lodge and went upstairs with her, where Marjorie Nott was waiting for me. I saw de Siebert and many others, and Alice Roosevelt was very nice and friendly. It was just a few days before her wedding to Nick Longworth.

The next night there was a dance at Mrs. Townsend's. Butler Ames, Chambrun, Count Bernstorff and Billy Hitt all asked me for the cotillion. I danced with Butler Ames, and drove home with Mrs. Davis (who was afterwards Mrs. McCawley) at 4 A.M.

Olivia Thorndike was in Washington, and the next day we went for a walk together, and lunched at Mrs. Munn's. That afternoon she and I went with Alice Roosevelt, Chandler Hale, Billy Hitt and others for tea at the Mayflower. Spencer arrived in Washington that day, and dined with us at Mrs. Slater's.

The next day was Thursday, February 15. Butler Ames called for me in his motor, and took me to the House, where we sat in the gallery and listened for half an hour. We were to meet Mrs. Slater, and lunch with Beveridge in the Senate dining room. Mrs. Slater met us, as had been arranged, but there was no Albert. We walked through the long corridor to the door of his committee room. I felt that this was an undignified thing for us to do, and I remember standing back as far as possible from the door. A moment later Albert rushed out. He was intently preoccupied by a bill that he was introducing that day. We went to the dining room, but in a few moments he hurried off. Later he came up to the gallery and sat with us. I drove back with Mrs. Slater in her brougham. I hardly heard was she said to me. I was in love!

The next day we lunched with Spencer at the New Willard—Mrs. Slater, Margaretta, Count Zichy, Count Wenkheim and Butler Ames. I dined alone with Spencer that evening. The next night we dined at the Larz Andersons' in their new house.

On Sunday there was a big luncheon of thirty or forty at the Country Club, where I sat next to Fred Hale, who was always very nice and friendly to me.

Albert J. Beveridge

Mrs. Slater's tea that afternoon was crowded. Albert was there, but my diary only mentions his name. The next day, Monday, I moved to Margaretta's. That night she gave a dinner. Spencer came, and stayed on afterward and talked to us.

The following day I lunched at the Warders', where "Chambrun was very amusing;" then to Mr. George Smalley's, the famous correspondent of the London Times, for tea; and then back to Margaretta's as fast as I could fly, to meet Albert. While I was giving him his tea Mr. MacVeagh came in, and they had an interesting talk together.

The next afternoon Butler Ames came to tea "in spite of all we could do, and Mr. Smalley, too." I dined at Katherine Elkins' and went on with Edith Root to the Bachelors'. De Siebert had sent me a large bouquet of lilies-of-the-valley and orchids, and Butler Ames gardenias. I danced the cotillion with Siebert. I had a wonderful time. I sent Jenny away and stayed to the very end, and drove home with Edith Root.

Mr. Wayne MacVeagh, Margaretta's father, was a great wit and a very charming man. He had been Attorney General under Cleveland. At luncheon the next day he began to tease me about Albert, and this teasing continued throughout my visit, much to my deep, and I suppose very visible confusion. All in all I had never been as gay or had a better time.

On the 23rd Albert telephoned me to say goodbye. I felt very awkward and stupid at the telephone. Jenny moved my things to Mrs. Munn's, and that night I went to a theatre party and then to the Italian Embassy to supper. Ronald Lindsey, Ulysses Grant, Seeds, Lord Eustace Percy, Margaretta, Martha Cameron, Edith Root and de Chambrun were at our table. Dinner followed dinner, and two cotillions, and at last I went to New York with Mrs. Munn. From New York I went to Lakewood to spend ten days with Albertine, who had rented a house there for the Spring. Spencer sailed to return to his post on the 14th. I was not to see him again until just before his marriage in May. With Mrs. Munn and Carrie Louise I went to Farmington for a few days. Mrs. Munn had taken a little house there in order to be near the boys, who were at school in Simsbury. We went to the school play, which was very amusing, and came back to Farmington in a sleigh by starlight. Then I joined my mother at the Shoreham in Washington.

Carrie Louise and Charlie Munn

Soon we were back in Chicago. It was now the end of March. Early
in April something very sad happened. My darling Trilby had not
been well, and it was finally decided to chloroform her. It seemed to
me a final break with my little girlhood. Trilby must have been ten
or twelve years old. She was a daughter of Charlotte, a beautiful little New England cat that we had brought home one summer from
Manchester. Her father belonged to Mrs. Barker, our neighbor, so
although she was a short-haired cat, she was, in a sense, pedigreed,
and had all the manners of a lady of high degree. She had been my
constant companion, sleeping at the foot of my bed, and following
us about with almost dog-like tenacity. Her birth had been very

Trilby

eventful. Her mother, like all cats, loved perfume, and always chose to lie on something silky and scented. One evening before her accouchement she could not be found. We looked for her high and low and called, but all in vain. It was not until late that evening when my mother opened one of the long drawers of her bureau (that now stands in my room in Beverly Farms) that Charlotte was found, with her three newly-born little kittens, in the very midst of my mother's lovely lingerie. From that moment Trilby became our special and beloved pet. Those rare summers that we stayed in America and went to the North Shore, she went with us. As I think of the animals I have loved, Trilby assumes a very important place in my affections—a place that was never to be filled until my beautiful Goldie and her orange progeny came into our lives.

Butler Ames came out to Chicago and stayed some time. I would always try to make him talk about Albert, whom he greatly admired. We sailed for Europe on April 17. We were a large party—my mother and father, Aunt Dell, Albertine and her boys, Helen and Looly Hooper, Mr. Adams' niece, who had been put in my mother's care. Mr. Spreckels, Spencer's future father-in-law, was also on the boat, and a Mrs. Robinson, a friend of Mrs. Spreckels, from California. While we were on the ocean came the news of the San Francisco earthquake. With the limited wireless facilities of those days we heard very few details, but the definite word that San Francisco had been

Lurline Spreckels

demolished. Albertine landed at Plymouth. She was very happy to be approaching England again, where she was to live for the rest of her short life.

We arrived at Cherbourg after dark. "It began to rain, and was very uncomfortable on the tender. Greatest confusion, and we had no end of bother about compartments. Aunt Dell went in the wagon-lits and we in other section of train. Helen and I sat up all night, quite cold." Such was the journey from Cherbourg to Paris in 1906.

April 26 was a dark and rainy day. We went to the Mairie of the 16th Arrondissemont at 10:30 for Spencer's civil marriage—my mother and father, Aunt Dell, Mr. and Mrs. Spreckels, and one or two others. Spencer's witnesses were Blanchard, of the Embassy, and Paxton Hibben, and Lurline's witnesses Elisha Dyer and Mr. Irwin. The wedding took place two days later in what is now the American Cathedral, in Paris. We stood in the choir as if it were a chapel. Jim Whigham was Spencer's best man. There was a breakfast at the Spreckels' apartment, where Mr. McCormick, the Ambassador, made a speech and Spencer answered very nicely. They went off in the rain to Fontainebleau.

My father left for America with Mr. Spreckels on May 11, and I left the following day for London, where I was to spend a short time with Albertine. I have always remembered that visit with pleasure. We were at Claridge's, where Albertine's sitting room was always heavy with the fragrance of flowers, and especially the lovely Madonna lilies that were in bloom at that season. She had her car and an excellent chauffeur, and we made many long excursions and drives. I wrote in my diary on the 13th: "After lunch we go from Henley to Oxford. See it first from the top of a hill, lying in a hollow of blossoming trees. Think all the time of the Scholar Gypsy and wish I had it with me."[62] I saw something of Lady Elcho, who was in London. Albertine and I went often to the opera, where Caruso and Melba were singing. We saw Ethel and David often, and I went with Ethel to many interesting shops and sales. It was at this time that I bought the lovely linen curtains that were first in the Washington apartment, and now hang every Spring in the drawing room at 4164.[63] Helen was in London at Cousin Ella's. One day we went together to see Mrs. Robinson, a famous fortune teller of the period. She was a little, stuffy woman in a sunny apartment,

Cousin Ella

[62] Matthew Arnold's 1858 poem "The Scholar-Gipsy," an elegy on his Oxford years, descants on the beauty of the countryside around Oxford.

[63] The Beveridges' Indianapolis house, at 4164 Washington Boulevard.

where you smelled the dinner cooking, and there was nothing mysterious or any of the trappings of clairvoyance about her, but she was indeed an extraordinary person. She said to me, "You will marry a man in public life. If you were an English girl I would say that your husband would be a member of the Government." Needless to say, I never forgot what she told me, and as my mind was entirely preoccupied by thoughts of Albert, it made me very happy.

I remember a day when we motored to Leamington, where I had been once with my mother as a little girl. I remember the hills covered with primrose and wild hyacinths, and that inexpressibly beautiful and sweet-smelling English countryside of May. We went to Kenilworth and climbed over the ruins, and from there to Warwick Castle,[64] where Lord Warwick's launch took us down the river to lunch at the shooting lodge. From there we motored on to Stratford and back to Leamington, where we spent the night.

I went back to Paris on May 27. Lurline had been ill, and there was a question as to what Spencer should do, as his time was up and he was expected at his post.

My mother and I had some very pleasant shopping to do. Before leaving America she had taken an apartment in Washington for three years. We had only seen the plans on paper, as the building was not yet completed. It was built by Bruce Price and de Sibour for the Warder estate, and was supposed to be a replica of a Paris apartment. It was on the corner of 16th Street and M—a block from Scott Circle. There was only one apartment on each floor. We had brought from America the measurements of the windows so that the curtains could be ordered in Paris, and my mother had evidently made careful plans about what should be taken to Washington from Chicago, and what should be bought abroad expressly for the apartment.

On May 30 Aunt Dell, mamma and I went to Tesniers, and Aunt Dell bought the gray bedroom furniture for me that is now in what we call her room in Beverly Farms. In the meantime we were making our plans to go with Mrs. Slater and Miss Gwynn to Sweden and Norway, two countries I had never seen. Albertine and her boys came to Paris, and almost every day was spent with them. Finally we left for Berlin, where Jenny and Aunt Dell's Michael left us to go to Carlsbad, where they were to await our return from Scandinavia. That night we left for Copenhagen.

[64] The castle at Kenilworth was a gift of Queen Elizabeth to the Earl of Leicester, where he entertained Her Majesty in 1575. Warwick Castle was the seat of the Grevilles at this time. Lord Warwick and his beautiful wife, Frances Maynard, Countess of Warwick (known as "Daisy"), occupied the place.

We arrived there early in the morning. The little dogs, Aunt Dell's Flossie and my mother's Pierrot, had to be smuggled because of the quarantine. We went to the Thorwaldsen Museum, where I saw the originals of the beautiful Day and Night that were on the walls in the little dining room of the Allee-Saal in Schwalbach. We saw a beautiful Baroque Palace, and went to some celebrated shops, and took the evening train to Stockholm. From there we made an excursion to Saltsjobaden, a "charming place on an inlet of the sea. Sailboats and yachts, and lilacs blooming everywhere." We chartered a boat and went though the lovely waterways, and around countless islands that dotted the coast.

It was now bright daylight all night long, and difficult to adjust one's mind to sleep. On June 19 we started on our way to Trondhjem. The train stopped at little stations for our meals—such wonderful meals!—with tall, thin glasses of delicious Swedish coffee, topped with whipped cream. We were on our way to witness an historic occasion—the coronation of the first King of Norway.[65] When we arrived in Trondhjem flags were waving, there were warships in the harbor—a gay and festive scene. Mrs. Slater's sister was Lady Herbert, the wife of the British Minister. In the afternoon we walked about in the little town, and stopped in front of the palace, where a crowd had assembled. While we stood there the Queen and the Prince of Wales[66] came to the window.

The coronation took place on June 22. The King, who had been called to the throne by the Norwegians, was a Danish prince, and the Queen had been, before her marriage, Princess Maude of England, the daughter of Edward VII. I wrote in my diary: "We left for the cathedral at 9:30. We wore light, high-necked gowns, as we had been instructed on our invitations. We had excellent seats in the transept, where the two thrones were placed. It was a very picturesque and beautiful sight. The Prince and Princess of Wales, Prince Henry of Prussia, the Crown Prince of Denmark, the Grand Duke Michael of Russia, and many others were there.[67] After the ceremony of the coronation the King and Queen walked down the aisle with their long velvet robes, crowns on their heads, and sceptres in their hands, and all the men-of-war in the harbor fired salutes until the cathedral resounded. It was a very inspiring moment."

[65] Actually, the first modern king, Haakon VII, who reigned from 1905 to 1957.

[66] Queen Alexandra and her son, the future King George V.

[67] Prince George (1865–1936) and his wife, Mary, Princess of Wales (1867–1953), later Queen Mary; Prince Henry of Prussia, Kaiser Wilhelm's brother; the Crown Prince of Denmark, later King Christian X (1870–1947), Haakon's brother; and the Grand Duke Michael, Spencer's friend.

Adgangstegn

til

Kroningen i Trondhjems Domkirke

den 22de Juni 1906

for Mrs. Eddy

Indgang 13 *Plads i Kolonne* VII *No* 577

Kirken aabnes Kl: 9 Fm.

De anmodes om at indtage Deres Plads inden Kl. 10½ Fm.

I Tilfælde af Forfald maa Kortet uopholdelig sendes tilbage til Statens Kroningskomité, Adresse Stiftsgaarden, eller Underretning meddeles Komitéen.

Invitation to the coronation.

*Left to right: Abby Eddy,
Miss Gwynn, and
Delia Caton Field on
an excursion in the fjords.*

The next day the sun was shining. We went to the palace to be presented—all of us except Aunt Dell, who, because of her mourning, did not go. There was a long defillée. The King and Queen were seated, and we made a reverence as we passed. The very simple palace was charming. In the afternoon we went to a concert, where all the royalties were present. We sat not very far behind the Princess of Wales (afterwards Queen Mary), and I have often thought of how straight she sat, without touching the back of her chair, through all the long program that followed. From there we went to see the national dances and gymnastics that took place in a stadium in the open air. The King and Queen were in a pavilion at one end, which was decorated with garlands of hemlock and countless bright flags.

The next day we left in a boat for Molde. After breakfast the next morning we went up on deck. The landscape looked like the far North—a long coastline of snow-capped mountains, and the sea gray and cold. From here we made excursions and tours of the surrounding fjords. It rained day after day, but from time to time the clouds parted and we had views of the gloomy rocks and sheer, cold mountains. The waterfalls were beautiful, and came down seemingly out of the clouds, like long, white veils. Every day we ate incomparable salmon, cooked to the Queen's taste,[68] and generally served with flawless Hollandaise sauce. We drove often in little, one-horse cabriolets that were quite comfortable. Finally we reached Christiania (now Oslo), and then returned by way of Copenhagen to Berlin.

While we were in Berlin we did some shopping for the apartment, and the four little Italian arm chairs that are now in the marquetry room were bought at that time. Aunt Dell's motor, a Mercedes, met us in Berlin,[69] and she and I drove in it to Dresden, my mother going by train. From Dresden I motored with Aunt Dell to Carlsbad, where Cousin Mollie and Helen were already installed at the Königsvilla. Never had I been so glad to see Helen! I went to Munich for a day with Spencer and Lurline. Lurline was still ailing, and Spencer was very discouraged and blue. It was warm and sultry in Carlsbad, and not at all like our beautiful and rural Schwalbach, but it was, of course, pleasant to be with Helen, and the life I led in her company was very agreeable. We would get up in the morning by six o'clock and go for a long walk to the Kaiser Park for

[68] Probably Queen Maude, who was apparently aboard.

[69] On her trips to Europe, Delia traveled with a car, a retinue of servants, and a great volume of her own household belongings, which she shipped over to use.

breakfast outdoors under the lime trees. On the way we would stop at a bakery and buy our bread. Everyone had their own waitress at the little restaurants. They wore tags on the front of their dresses bearing their names—Katie, Annie, Lottie, etc. The tables were covered with bright red and white tablecloths, and we drank the delicious Austrian coffee of that day and ate the good German bread and fresh butter. Sometimes we would walk to the Posthof for breakfast. There were concerts in the afternoon, and in the evening Cousin Mollie often took us to an operetta or a play. We took long walks through the beautiful woods. Aunt Dell often laughed about her Carlsbad days, remembering these long tramps when she carried her white serge train over her arm! Such was the fashion of the time.

One day I drove with my mother to Perkenhammer, where she ordered the white service with her monogram in blue that we use to this day. The shops in Carlsbad were famous. An excellent tailor from Vienna made us suits in loden cloth, and the celebrated Braun, who had also a shop in Berlin, was a constant and never-ending source of entertainment on rainy days. We drove often to Giesshubler, where we drank the incomparable water from the spring, and had wonderful suppers of trout.

Ethel   Albertine David. Lady Mary Foley

Luncheon on the moors – Invercauld – 1906

In the meantime I had been asked to go with Albertine on a visit to the Beattys in Scotland. I was sorry to leave Helen and Carlsbad, and my thoughts were so constantly in America that I looked forward with almost no interest at all to the unique and delightful visit that was ahead of me.

I left with the maid, Marie, spent a day in Paris, and then went to London, where Albertine met me at the station. We left London on August 7 in Albertine's car, and spent the night at York. We had time before dusk to see the cathedral.

We spent a night at Edinburgh, and went on the next day to Invercauld. That same afternoon I went out for a long walk with David across the moors. Invercauld is one of the great estates of Scotland, with excellent shooting. The Beattys had leased it from the Farquarson family. The large house had been built in the 19th Century, in the architectural style of a baronial castle. It was surrounded by the most beautiful of Scotch landscapes. It was only a short distance from Balmoral, in the heart of the Highlands. When we arrived there were only two other guests there—Mr. Lowther and Lady Mary Foley. Mr. Lowther was the brother of the Earl of Lonsdale. After dinner, to my delight, a piper wearing the Farquarson plaid marched three times around the table and piped us out to the drawing room.

A house party arrived on the 11th—Lord and Lady Hyde, and three men. I wrote: "No one very interesting, though the Hydes are nice—she very young looking, and dreadfully shy." In the evening Albertine always played bridge. She was the only woman who did so, and I can see her now, so beautiful, with her charming smile, going off with three men to the little room where the card table was set up.[70] Left to our devices, the remaining ladies would sit around the lamp snipping chintz. Yards of bright-colored, flowered cretonnes had been sent up from London, and from these we would cut flowers and bouquets and paste them on paper lamp shades and boxes, to be sold at a bazaar.

Monday, August 13, the shooting began. I quote from my diary: "The men start out about 8:30. We leave at 11 and drive to a certain point, where we find hill ponies. I only ride a little way, and go on foot for two or three miles more through the heather. Have lunch in

[70] The morality of bridge playing was a subject Edith Wharton plumbed in masterful descriptions of Lily Bart at the bridge table in *The House of Mirth* (1905). Catherine, though envious of the bold Albertine, politely endured a dull evening with the ladies, making goods for a charity bazaar.

the pouring rain and then follow two of the guns and see them shoot eight or nine brace; then back to Invercauld, drenched."

And a few days later: "David goes deer stalking and kills a stag Royal. We see it after tea—rather an unpleasant sight. Work on boxes, and after I am in bed Albertine comes up and we talk until nearly 2."

What we were talking about was Albert, for I had unburdened my heart to Albertine, and she, like the darling she was, listened to me by the hour. Day after day we went in the rain to meet the guns for lunch in the moors. Sometimes there was a little low table or an inverted box that we could sit on. It rained constantly, but no one even spoke of the weather or seemed to notice it. For the most part it was a fine, soft rain, with low mists on the mountains. The luncheons that were served to us were perfection—hot bouillon and chaudfroids of chicken, and all sorts of delicious dishes. There was a private golf course on the estate, and a professional, and every day Albertine and I and sometimes Ethel would take a lesson. The bazaar at Braemar took place, and presumably all our boxes and lamp shades were sold. On Sundays everyone was supposed to come down to breakfast in order that the servants would have an opportunity to go to church. It was my first experience of a great English breakfast. The table was set, and not a manservant appeared except to bring in occasionally a tea pot. The breakfast dishes were spread on the sideboard—a great array of magnificent silver covered dishes, many of them with hot lamps under them. There would be eggs, and toast, and fish, and bacon, and sometimes a tiny broiled baby grouse whose mother had been shot, and who had been finished by a gamekeeper. The English, who are such proverbially poor cooks, have, after all, furnished the world with the two best meals of the day—breakfast and tea.

From week to week the house party changed, and different young men made their appearance. Aunt Dell arrived on August 30, and I was very glad indeed to see her. The Prince and Princess of Wales were at Abergeldie, and David was often asked to shoot with the Prince. One evening when we had started dinner a telephone call came from Balmoral. The King asked Mrs. Beatty to come to Balmoral to dinner. For some reason they were short a lady, and Ethel was to act as hostess. There was great flurry and excitement, and a car was ordered, and she hurried off. Albertine's two boys were there with us, and little Gwennie. Ethel's baby, David, was only a year or two old. I spent many hours playing cricket with Marshall and Henry, and we were all often with the children in the pleasant, comfortable English way. Lord Warwick arrived early in September. He was an old and devoted friend of Albertine's, and loved his bridge with her after dinner. The shooting changed—the guns now stood in the butts, and the beaters, thirty or forty strong, walked through the heather driving the grouse. One day I sat in a butt with a young naval officer whom David had asked, perhaps on my account. He was a very nice, shy young man, and quite inarticulate. When we had been there some time he said to me, "You know, I have a confession to make, if you won't give me away to Captain Beatty. I really don't know anything about shooting at all, and I feel quite embarrassed about what I am going to do this afternoon." I told him he needn't bother about me, as I thoroughly disliked seeing anyone shoot grouse, and it ended in our having a very pleasant conversation.

One day we went to see the games at Braemar. Ethel and David, Albertine and the boys were presented to the Prince and Princess of Wales. The games were very dull, but the kilts were beautiful.

Aunt Dell and I left on September 7. I wrote in my diary: "Ethel has been very good to have me so long—a month and a day since I arrived." We spent a day or two in Edinburgh, saw Holyrood and St. Giles, but I thought it a dull town. We drove in a carriage to Rosslyn Abbey. We walked through the ruins, and up and down a little garden path in the sunshine. The chapel itself very charming "a jewel in the midst of this grim Scotland."

We were a few days in London at Claridge's, where Albertine joined us. Then we all went to Paris.

It was now the middle of September, and I left with Aunt Dell, Mrs. Slater and Miss Gwynn to go to Biarritz, where we stayed at a very beautiful hotel hanging over the sea. Aunt Dell and Mrs. Slater both had their cars, so we were all ready for our excursions and our trip back to Paris. A telegram came just at this point that Spencer had been appointed First Secretary of the Embassy in Berlin.

We went one day to San Sebastian and saw a Concour Hippique. The King and Queen were in a box,[71] and we saw many pretty women. That was my only glimpse of Spain!

[71] Alfonso XII (1886–1941), king of Spain, was just beginning his long, ineffectual reign. In 1906, he married Princess Victoria Eugenia of Battenburg (1887–1969). They narrowly escaped assassination on their wedding day; thirty-seven others were killed.

From Biarritz in the two motors we went to Pau, Lourdes, Toulouse, Carcassonne, and Nimes, where we saw the beautiful amphitheatre in the moonlight. From Nimes we went to Grenoble and Aix, where we took the train for Paris. I was very glad to see my mother, who looked well, and welcomed me by making some American coffee for breakfast. I had only a chance to see Helen for a moment, as she sailed that same day for home.

We ourselves sailed on the Kaiser Wilhelm der Grosse a little earlier than usual, on October 24. Albertine, Mrs. Slater and Miss Gwynn were with us. The evening of our arrival in New York I stood with Albertine on the upper deck. It was a very warm night for October. The lights from the tall buildings seemed piled up into the sky. My father met us, and I stayed late on the dock sending the trunks to the right places. Then we went to the Waldorf, where "I had some oysters"—always our first treat on reaching America.

Two days later we went to Washington to see the apartment. Some busy days followed. We stayed at the Willard Hotel, but spent every day unpacking the furniture that had come from Paris. Mrs. Munn expected to be away for the greater part of the winter, and my mother took over her stable with Rosamond, the coachman. It was almost the last of fine carriages and horses. The era of the motor had begun.

On November 6 we left for Chicago. Aunt Dell and Albertine arrived the same day, coming from New York.

We had come to a very important decision, and that was to give up 1601 Michigan Avenue—the house where I was born—and to move into Aunt Dell's house on Calumet Avenue. The corner on 16th Street had become noisier, and the neighborhood increasingly bad, so that it seemed from every point of view the only thing to do. I wrote in my diary: "After dinner go through the rooms and then sit in my little back room till very late. All my memories come crowding in—the Christmas trees, Monday, Choo Choo, Trilby—Jake and Edward—my grandfather and grandmother—all my little girlhood—all my life."[72]

The next day we left for Washington and the new apartment where we found flowers awaiting us from Mrs. Slater. My new bedroom furniture from Paris was all installed, and I slept in my beautiful

[72] Jake was presumably a servant, like Edward Pender, the Eddys' coachman. This was the home in which Abby and Delia as well as Catherine and Spencer had grown up. While it is true that the neighborhood was changing, Mr. Eddy's financial troubles most likely prompted the Eddys to sell the house.

gray bed for the first time. Albertine was our first visitor. She only stayed for a few days. Mamma and I were busy from morning till night, moving furniture and hanging pictures. As the apartment took shape it grew prettier and prettier. There were three rooms facing on 16th Street. To the right was a large, square drawing room, with a French marble mantel. We had in it my mother's Lenbach portrait, tapestry from 1601, the four little Italian chairs that are now in the marquetry room in Beverly Farms, and two French commodes my mother had bought in Paris. There was a smaller sitting room—long and narrow—with another marble mantel, and three French windows opening on a balcony. In this room we put the lovely Adam furniture that my mother had given me for my sitting room at home. At the windows hung the linen curtains that are the summer curtains now in the drawing room in Indianapolis. The dining room corresponded to the large drawing room, and was the prettiest room of all. The table and chairs came from Krieger in Paris. The curtains, now in the marquetry room, were of heavy blue satin, with pale yellow stripe. There was a marble buffet table that is now in the hall at Beverly Farms, and the beautiful Italian commode and very high mirror that is now in the Italian room. The room was very finished and correct. It is a pity that we never had photographs taken of the apartment.

Edward Pender,
coachman to F.F. Spencer
for over 30 years, and
the Eddys' coachman.

Sunday evening, December 2, I was in my room when the telephone rang. I knew instantly who was on the other end of the wire. I heard MacGregor speaking. Of course, it was Albert, who asked if he could come to see me that evening. I was so excited that I began to shiver, and I remember, before he came, sitting on the radiator in front of my window in an effort to get warm! Albert looked worn and tired, but we had a pleasant talk together.

A few days later I went out to Chicago to take part in a bazaar that was afterwards to become famous. It was held in the old Coliseum on Wabash Avenue.[73] The scenery had been designed by Frederic Bartlett, who transformed that great, barren convention hall into Paris of the 18th Century. There was a Place Vendome, and streets of little French shops that had been taken by various ladies. Helen and I were in Mrs. Watson Blair's booth. We wore black and white striped dresses and bright pink aprons. It was a very de luxe boutique, and we sold novelties from Cartier and from Paris that had been brought over for the occasion. We had to work very hard, as the crowd was enormous. It lasted two or three nights, and thousands of dollars were made for the Passavant Hospital.

Tuesday I was in Washington again, and Albert telephoned and asked if he could come to see me the following evening. He left that night on the midnight train for Cincinnati, where he was to make a speech on Child Labor.

Our busy days continued—dinners and Sunday luncheons, and the many calls that filled the Washington afternoons of that period. On Christmas day I received one very large red rose from Albert. On the 31st I wrote in my diary: "Raining all day. Go to the Pages without my hat for a tea. When I get back the telephone rings and the operator said 'New York wants to speak to you.' I had dull visions of Butler Ames, and was rather cross when they couldn't get the connection. But who was it but someone very nice, who said— 'I am telephoning to wish you a Happy New Year!'"

[73] The Coliseum, which stood on Wabash between Fourteenth and Sixteenth streets, accommodated fifteen thousand people; it was second in capacity only to Madison Square Garden.

Dec. 26"

Dear Senator Beveridge

Just a word
to tell you how much I
appreciate your charming
thought of me — I hope

that you have enjoyed
your holiday & that you
have had the rest you needed

With every wish for a
Happy New Year believe
me Always sincerely

Catharine Spencer Eddy

Miss Spencer Eddy is Bride of Mr. Albert J. Beverid

MR. & MRS. ALBERT J. BEVERIDGE

Religious Ceremony Performed at American Embassy in Berlin by the Rev. Dr. Hall.

[SPECIAL TO THE HERALD.]

BERLIN, Wednesday.—In sunny summer weather the marriage of Miss Catherine Spencer Eddy and Mr. Albert J. Beveridge, United States Senator for Indiana, was solemnized here to-day. Owing to the wishes of the families, the ceremony was conducted with a simpli-

States Senator from Vermont, w pressly remained in Berlin for th ding, although pressing business c ed with the Immigration Com called him to Paris, acted as bes the only bridesmaid being Miss Birch, who wore a mauve-colored hat.

After the Ceremony.

After the register had been sig all present the whole party left t Spencer Eddy's residence in the zollernstrasse, the former mans Prince Hohenlohe - Langenburg, was beautifully decorated with li

THE CHRONICLE OF CATHERINE EDDY BEVERIDGE

1907

Opposite: New York Herald, *Paris Edition, August 8, 1907.*

INTRODUCTION

❧ 1907 ❧

AGAINST THE KALEIDOSCOPIC BACKDROP of Washington's winter season, Catherine's romance with Albert deepened. She went often to see him in the Senate, and they contrived to meet socially. Their courtship attracted notice. Many friends offered the couple encouragement, but Catherine's growing attachment to Albert dismayed her mother. Abby worried that marriage to Albert would represent too much of a change for Catherine, exposing her to unaccustomed hardships and burdening her with unwanted cares and responsibilities. How could a public man care for Catherine adequately? If Albert were to fail in politics, where would that leave Catherine socially? And how could she bear to give up a glamorous life in order to live in Indiana? Delia's and Abby's influential friend Mrs. Slater shared her misgivings. As Catherine grew more and more certain that her happiness depended on Albert, she found herself at odds with her mother, who had been dearer to her than any other person. Catherine and Albert struggled toward the altar despite Abby's opposition. By the summer, news of their impending marriage had reached the papers.

Journalists offered some amusing estimates of the match. Some newspapers depicted Catherine as an "ambitious Cupid" who had snared one of Washington's most eligible men. Others opined that Albert had made a prudent match, one that would enable him to draw on the Spreckels and Field fortunes were he to run for the presidency. Still others pointed to the illustrious marriages that Delia and Spencer had made as proofs that the Spencers were a ruthlessly opportunistic family. These stories were strangely at odds with the family's own conviction that Catherine was marrying for love alone. Though sustained by her love for Albert, Catherine, her physicians warned, was in danger of being made ill by the controversy. There was only one thing to be done. In Berlin in August she and Albert were married. After an elegant ceremony and feast, they were off on an idyllic honeymoon in the Dolomites and Italy.

Returning to the States in the autumn, Catherine struggled to establish her married life on a sound footing. Her mother's warnings now assumed some pertinence, but Catherine was very determined to make a success of things. After a show of independence, Albert and she accepted the use of Abby's beautiful flat on Washington's Sixteenth Street, where Catherine became the mistress of her own domain and began to get the hang of official entertaining. Her first visit to Indianapolis was less satisfying. Dutifully trying to adjust to an unfamiliar place in the early stages of pregnancy, and worried once again about her mother's health, she found her confidence in her marriage wavering. By Christmas, however, she had mastered her doubts and anxieties. Jubilantly happy with the events of the year, she looks forward to 1908 and to the birth of her first child.

Menu cover design and luncheon served at the
wedding of Catherine and Albert, August 7, 1907.

DÉJEUNER 7 AOÛT 1907

CONSOMMÉ FROID EN TASSES

OEUFS À L'AMÉRICAINE

SAUMON DU RHIN MONTPELLIER
SAUCE VERTE

POULARDE À LA DEMIDOFF
SAUCE SUPRÊME

JAMBONS À LA STRASBOURGEOISE

SALADE JAVANAISE

MELONS À LA PARISIENNE

GATEAU DE MARIAGE

THERE WAS A LITTLE GROUP that I saw very often that winter in Washington, not only at dinners and dances, but often at lunch. There was Cecil Higgins, of the British Embassy, who was clever and keen, and very attractive; there was Fred Hale, who was always friendly, and came to see me often; Benno de Siebert was a devoted friend, and Butler Ames was always at my beck and call. There was de Thal, a Russian, who was very musical, and Count Hatzfeldt, of the German Embassy. The German Ambassador was Speck von Sternburg. His wife was an American, and I liked her, perhaps because she was a friend of Albert's. I saw something of Edith Root, and I became a great friend of Lucretia Le Bourgeois, a niece of Mrs. Herbert Wadsworth. Lucretia had an interesting mind, and drew and painted with unusual talent and originality. I went to many parties with Martha Cameron. She was to marry Ronald Lindsey, but her life was to be very short.[74] My mother, who seemed to be well, dined out almost as often as I did. My father came on occasionally from Chicago.

[74] She married Lindsay in 1909 and died in 1918.

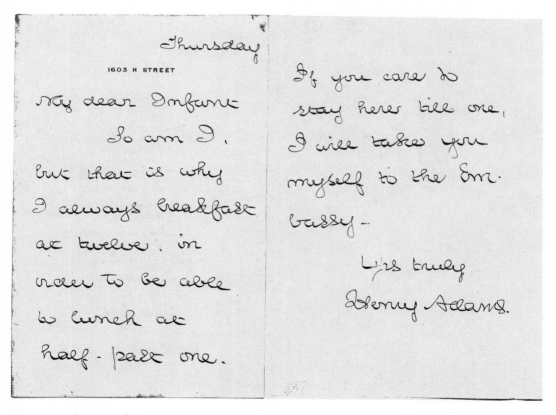

Thursday

1603 H STREET

My dear Infant

So am I, but that is why I always breakfast at twelve, in order to be able to lunch at half-past one.

If you care to stay here till one, I will take you myself to the Embassy—

Yrs truly
Henry Adams.

From Henry Adams to Catherine

On January 2, I wrote: "Breakfast at Mr. Adams' (that meant the 12
o'clock lunch) and afterward Mr. Adams, who for once breaks his
rule of never lunching out, went with me to the German Embassy
for a half past one lunch"—two lunches in one day! At that time the
walls of the Embassy were literally covered with fabulous Chinese
porcelains that belonged to Sternburg. That evening I went with my
mother to a musicale at the White House.

Eames MacVeagh came from Chicago to see me. On the Sunday
after his arrival we had our first luncheon in the apartment, the
Sternburgs, Mrs. Slater, Edith Root, Count Hatzfeldt, Ronald Lindsey,
the Thorons and Albert. The apartment was greatly admired, much
to my mother's pleasure.

I saw Albert every day. As often as I could I would go to the Senate,
where his secretary, Tom Shipp, would take me into the Senate
gallery. Sometimes I would walk to the Capitol with him, and I
would see him occasionally at parties. One evening I went to dine
with Edith Root. She and I were afterwards going to a theatre party
that Albert was giving. Only her father and mother were there.
The conversation turned to Albert, and, much to my surprise, the
Secretary of State, who was not at all friendly to him, said that there
was no man in Washington with his brilliance of mind and indefatigable industry. After dinner Baroness Sternburg came by for us, and
we went on to the theatre. The play was *The Musicmaster*,[75] and
our little party sat in two boxes. Louise Foraker, Katherine Elkins,
Senator Brandegee, Frank McCoy, who was afterwards to become
a Brigadier General, Butler Ames, and a few others. Afterwards we
went to the New Willard for supper.

[75] A 1904 play by Charles Klein.

Every Saturday night there was a dinner and dance at the John R.
McLeans'. The McLeans lived in an enormous house on McPherson
Square. Mrs. McLean was delicate and never dined out, but all
Washington came to her. I remember the library, where the bookcases that lined the wall were only four or five feet high, in the
fashion of the nineties. On the top of these bookcases were literally
hundreds of signed and framed photographs. At the beginning of
the winter certain young girls were invited to all these dances, and
occasionally we would receive an invitation to the dinner that always
preceded them. The dances were over very early, and supper was

served at 12 o'clock. I would often see Albert there, and once or twice I danced with him. Much as I was in love with him, I preferred to dance with Higgins! Both Mr. and Mrs. McLean were very fond of Albert. Their son, Ned, had developed poorly, and was without ambition and very backward in his studies. Some years before Mr. McLean had asked Albert if Ned could go to his office and spend his mornings there. They hoped in that way to inspire him with some desire to work and improve his mind, but it failed to influence him.

Mr. Walter Berry was very kind to me that winter. He was an older man with a fine literary taste. He was a devoted and life-long friend of Mrs. Wharton, the novelist. I was very much flattered to have him come to see me. He was interested in my collection of 18th Century French books, and one day he sent me a present to be added to my little library. It was a 15th Century illuminated book of hours, which I have always treasured.

On January 26 Helen came to visit me. She found me in the depth of despair. My love affair was growing daily more difficult. But her coming steadied me, and I dried my tears and went with her to countless parties. De Siebert was devoted to Helen, and she had a very good time. Washington was gay, and as much as two young girls could be, we were in the midst of it all.

[76] Albert had prepared four days' material on the subject of child labor, which he was presenting on the floor of the Senate to shame his colleagues and to focus the nation's attention on the problem. State legislatures had been slow to regulate child labor, prompting Beveridge to seek federal legislation.

On January 29 we heard Albert continue his great speech on Child Labor which he had begun some days before.[76] He stood at his seat completely surrounded by law and reference books, from which he frequently quoted without hesitation or delay. It was a thrilling moment for me. At this point he began to give me his articles for the *Saturday Evening Post* to read in manuscript, and I made my first hesitant little suggestions on the margin of the pages.

Mrs. Vanderbilt came to Washington, and we gave a luncheon for her, and that same evening Helen and I dined at Mrs. Munn's. Albert was to have been there, but was asked to the White House, and, by a strange coincidence, sat next to my mother. The next day being Sunday, we had another lunch, and in the afternoon de Siebert and I went to the station with Helen. I could not bear to let her go, and came back to the apartment very low in my mind. Just as I entered the door the telephone rang. It was Gifford Pinchot, asking when he might come to see me.

Albert had talked about him so much, and with such admiration, that I naturally shared his opinion. It is hard for me to realize this, and to remember it now. He was also in my eyes a somewhat romantic person. He had been engaged many years before to Miss Laura Houghteling, of Chicago. She was one of two sisters, both beautiful, witty and amusing. She had been engaged to some young man whose name I do not remember. One morning she walked into her mother's room and said, "I know you are my mother, but beyond that I have no memory of who I am." It was some form of rare aphasia, but there were many persons who said it was only a means to rid herself of her suitor, of whom she had grown tired. In all events, this lack of memory persisted. The poor, distraught fiancé arrived and had to be introduced to her, as were all her old friends. Finally, in the course of time, she became engaged to Gifford Pinchot. Then she developed tuberculosis, and was taken to Aiken, where she died. Gifford was unconsolable. He put on a black tie, and a very large black border on his visiting cards, and devoted himself to his work, and also to spiritualism. He hoped in this way to get into communication with his betrothed. At this period I think he was actually and whole-heartedly friendly to Albert.[77] In all events, he came to see me in Albert's interest. He advised delay and caution, and discussed the matter with me from all angles. It was a subject interesting enough to bring him to see me several times.

My dear Albertine was our next guest. Apparently all the men I had danced with turned up to play bridge with her. "They play bridge, and no one will go home," I wrote in my diary. She was there only a few days.

My love affair continued its stormy course, but I was saved from too much misery and self pity by innumerable parties. As I look in retrospect on those busy days, I cannot but marvel at the complete social preoccupation of that epoch. In spite of all the gaiety it was a hard period for me—I have no desire to recreate it in my mind. I adored my mother, and could not entirely blame her for the senseless opposition to my marriage. She had been interested and pleased by Albert's attention to me in Washington in the Spring of 1904. All the nonsense was the result of Mrs. Slater's influence upon Aunt Dell, and, indirectly, upon my mother. Their perspective and reasoning was distorted. Albert and I often said in after years that had Mr. Field

[77] Pinchot and Beveridge eventually came to a parting of ways over the role of George Perkins in the Progressive Party but were reconciled towards the end of Beveridge's life.

been alive their attitude would have been very different. Mr. Field knew Albert slightly, and liked him. Touched with prophecy, he had teased me about him — I, who had never even see him at that time, but who had read his *Russian Advance*! Alas — Mr. Field was not there, and Albert and I had to fight our battle alone.

In April we went back to Chicago, and to 1910 Calumet Avenue. Delia McGarry and MacGregor had dismantled 1601 and placed everything in Aunt Dell's house. The house itself was as familiar to me as our own, and my mother's furniture and pictures fitted into their new setting. But neither she nor I took much interest in it. I think she was beginning to feel none too well, and I, with the complete selfishness of youth, could think of nothing but my own problems.

On April 7 Albert came from Indianapolis to Chicago. He saw my mother, and from that moment he said we were engaged. The date and moment meant nothing to me — I had considered myself engaged to him for many long months! That evening McCutcheon and Helen came to dine, and Albert left again on the midnight train.

Albert came often to Chicago. On April 27 (Grant's birthday) he made a speech at Galena that created a great sensation at the time. I was being drawn into the vortex of his busy life. Articles were constantly sent to me to read in manuscript, sometimes speeches were submitted to me — all very flattering. Long distance telephone calls, telegrams, letters — it was a new world, and a vastly more interesting one than anything I had ever known. Adelaide and Ned were thrilled by my engagement. Ned had always admired Albert, had read his articles in the Saturday Evening Post, and their love and encouragement at this moment in my life meant a great deal to me.

[78] In 1908, the Imperial Expanded Metal Co., which Catherine's father owned, filed for bankruptcy. Abby's letters to Catherine suggest that Abby had furnished her husband with the initial capital. Augustus's troubles forced the disposition of some of the family's assets, including property in Indiana and, perhaps, their Chicago home. The experience accounts for the fierce tone of Abby's advice to Catherine about managing her money.

To make matters harder for my mother, my father's business affairs came to a crisis, and she had to live through days of seeing lawyers and bankers, and ended by assuming, with Aunt Dell's help, much of the indebtedness.[78] As I look back through thirty-five years, my heart is heavy for them both. I was then a violent partisan of my mother's — I still am, and always shall be — but I see my father with more understanding eyes, and with greater sympathy. My father would have had a happier and more successful life had he been able to be an architect or a painter, for he was undoubtedly gifted with artistic talent. He had little aptitude for business, although he insisted always upon working. I still think that in her married life my mother was severely tried, and bitterly disappointed. But my father had qualities that drew people to him, and had his life been directed in a different channel, he might have achieved success.

Albert went with us to New York on May 12. The next day I lunched with him at Sherry's. He had asked the George Perkinses and Mr. and Mrs. Joseph Hamblen Sears, the publisher. I liked them all, and was very happy. The next day we sailed—my father and mother, Jenny and little Pierrot. In the very early morning I drove to Hoboken with Albert. The Kaiser Wilhelm sailed at 7:30.

All that first day at sea I received Marconigrams[79] at regular intervals. My cabin was full of flowers from George Perkins and Albert's cousin, Edward McClain. Every day, all the way over, I received a box of flowers from Albert, with a letter, and the day before we landed, another wireless.

On the boat were the Charlemagne Towers. They had been very kind to me in Russia. Now he was our Ambassador in Berlin, and Spencer's chief. Mrs. Tower said to me that she had heard of my engagement to Albert. It came to me as a little shock, for no one except my intimate friends had talked of it. She spoke of him with such enthusiasm it put me in a little glow of happiness.[80]

We stayed at the Continentale in Paris for a few busy days, and on the 24th took the Nord Express to Berlin.

Mr. Spreckels met us with the news that Lurline was already in labor. The baby, Spencer, Jr., was born the next morning, Sunday the 26th. The famous Hofrat, who delivered him, said: "*Nun, nun, Genadige Frau, warum beklagen sie sich, Sie bekommen doch ein Sontags kind!*"[81]

I remember him in his beautiful cradle that same day, his little head so like Spencer's, and the sweet-faced Schwester Emilie Kassner, who was to care for him so many years, and to love him always. The next evening we dined at the Embassy, and the Ambassador made a little speech and drank the health of the baby.

I stayed in Berlin until June 4. It was very pleasant. We saw new pictures, and went to the opera to hear what was almost the first performance of Richard Strauss's *Salomé*.[82] As we took our places my

[79] Named for their inventor, Nobel Prize–winning Italian physicist Guglielmo Marconi (1874–1937), who in 1896 devised the first successful radio telegraph. In 1901, he sent the first radio signals across the Atlantic, defying skeptics who believed that, because of the Earth's curvature, radio waves could travel no more than a few hundred miles. Even so, Catherine received marconigrams only on the first and last day of her voyage, indicating the practical problems that remained.

[80] Albert met Ambassador and Mrs. Tower while traveling in Russia; Tower supplied Beveridge with introductions to leading Russian figures.

[81] "Now, now, dear lady, why are you complaining, after all, you are going to have a Sunday child!" Folklore extols Sunday's child as full of grace.

[82] *Salomé* had had its first performance in Dresden on December 9, 1905. The work tested the sensibilities of some operagoers, who found its profoundly erotic story, sensuous music, and libretto by Oscar Wilde perverse and repulsive. The kaiser initially opposed its performance in Berlin.

mother whispered to me, "Look who is sitting next to you." It was Muck, the conductor of the Boston Symphony, whom I had always greatly admired. I spent a few days in Spencer's apartment, and went with him once or twice for drives in his long Mercedes car, stopping at Wannsee for tea on our return.

One day, never to be forgotten, we went to see the emperor review the troops. Thanks to Spencer and Prince Thurn and Taxis, we had a wonderful position just behind the Imperial Family. The Empress was there, and the Crown Princess.[83] The garde du corps passed, and the cream of the army. It was a magnificent spectacle. Miss Janet Perkins, who had given me lessons as a little girl, came to lunch, and we went to see her in the Botanical Museum, where she had an honored place, with many young men as her assistants. She was one of the most distinguished of living botanists.

On June 3 came a cable from Albert, saying "If I can sail 11th why not event 29th?"—but nothing came of that. However, I was now seriously thinking about the date of the marriage. Mr. and Mrs. Tower, who were very interested, offered the Embassy, but, of course, nothing could be decided until the time of Albert's arrival.

On June 4 James Deering came to Berlin. We all had tea and then dined together, and he and Spencer went with me to the station to see me off. I was on my way to visit Albertine in London.

Albertine had a nice flat at 11 Mount Street. Her boys were in school in England, and she was beginning to go out in the world again.[84] That beautiful Albertine! I can see her before her dressing table being coiffed for the evening—her dark eyes, her long lashes, and her lovely mouth with its entrancing smile. I stayed with her in London for ten days. We went several times to the opera. One night there was a gala performance for the King and Queen of Denmark.[85] Albertine had a dinner that evening—"Ethel and David,[86] Lord R. Innes-Kerr, Craig Wadsworth, and some others. There were marvelous jewels to be seen at the opera, and many picturesque Indians in their beautiful costumes. Cecil Higgins and Lord R. came back to supper."

We saw Ethel and David often, lunching and dining together. One lovely Sunday morning we drove out to see Albertine's new place in the country—Danesbury.[87] Lord Warwick and Cecil Higgins went

[83] The German empress Auguste Viktoria (1858–1921) and her daughter Viktoria Louise (1892–1980).

[84] Characteristically, Albertine was defying the wishes of her late father-in-law, whose will dictated that his grandsons be educated in America and groomed to take part in American business. The boys were raised in England and educated at Eton and Oxford.

[85] King Frederick VIII (1843–1912) and Queen Louise (1851–1926). Frederick, who was the father of Haakon VII of Norway, had assumed the throne in 1906.

[86] The Beattys.

[87] Albertine subsequently set herself up in London at 2 Carleton Terrace, where her lavish entertainments made her popular with Americans abroad. Her quest to remarry ended on September 3, 1908, when she married Maldwin Drummond, a man of good birth but scant fortune, who was a cousin of the Earl of Perth. Rumor had it that King Edward had hoped Albertine would marry the Prince of Teck, brother of the Princess of Wales. After her marriage, Albertine resided at her husband's Southampton estate, eventually selling her London home to Otto Kahn. She died in 1915, at just forty-two years of age.

with us. The house was still full of workmen, and we sat out under the great trees and had our lunch.

One evening Albertine and I dined alone, and went to see Ethel dressed for the Court ball. Ethel, too, was very beautiful; her features were not perfect like Albertine's, but she had beautiful eyes, and a lovely, slender figure. She was always dressed by Callot[88]—simple, straight lines, and superb embroideries on tulle and chiffon. On June 13 I wrote: "A cable from Albert, who is in Minneapolis making a speech. In the afternoon go with Albertine to a bazaar that the Queen opens. Dinner here. Lord Warwick, Mr. and Lady Eva Dugdale, Lord R. Innes-Kerr and Grant Smith."

On June 15 I left for Paris. The crossing was unpleasant, and the train late. I found mamma and my father at the station, where they had been waiting for hours. Butler Ames was in Paris, and lunched with us the next day at the Ritz. On the 18th my engagement was published in the *New York Herald*.

That same day came a cable from Aunt Dell, telling us of Hugo Birch's sudden death in Mexico. He was Helen's brother. Cousin Molly and Helen were on the ocean coming to Europe. On the 20th my father went to Cherbourg to meet them, and the next day they arrived in Paris. Helen and I were constantly together for the days that followed.

On the 24th the valet de chambre of our floor at the Continental came in great excitement to say that Mademoiselle was desired at the telephone. In those days the French telephones were notoriously primitive, and no one thought of telephoning when it could be avoided. What was my surprise to hear Albert's voice! He was in Cherbourg. The next day he came at 10:30 to see me. We lunched at Laurents—my mother and father, Albert and John McCutcheon,[89] who had come with him from America.

Before we left Paris I tried on the lining of my wedding dress at Worth's.

On July 1 my mother and father and I went to Contrexéville, where mamma was to take the cure. Albert left for Caux. While we were in Contrexéville it was decided that my marriage should take place in Berlin on August 7. Dr. Hall was in Göttingen, and would marry us.

Albertine Field

[88] Callot Soeurs was a Paris design firm founded by three sisters, the most active of whom was Marie Callot Berger. The firm, known for its use of gossamer fabrics and elaborate beaded and embroidered designs, reached its prime in the 1910s; in frequenting it, Ethel was somewhat ahead of her time.

[89] McCutcheon recollects the trip in his autobiography, *Drawn from Memory*. It appears that even on the boat Albert did not view his marriage as entirely likely. McCutcheon recalls him as "a fine companion, always interesting, always amusing." Only on reaching Paris did Albert's hope of marrying Catherine acquire some certainty.

I remember one day going with my father in a small motor bus with six other passengers to Domremy. There was "one nice French girl with her father. I talk to her and find her very interesting. Domrémy is a quaint village." We saw Jeanne D'Arc's house, the church where she was christened, and the ugly modern basilica built on the spot where she tended her sheep and saw her visions. Across the Meuse was the hill where Julien, the Apostate, had his camp. Another day we drove to see the famous oak dating from the 11th Century, called "Chéne des Partisans."

Albert arrived the 11th. He and I drove to the famous old tree and made tea under its shade. Another day he procured a motor, and he and I, with my mother, drove to Domrémy. The country of the Vosges is not beautiful as are the surroundings of Schwalbach, but it is none the less a pleasant countryside. Before we left I drove with my mother to Vittel, and we selected the lovely Epinal service that I have used so much—plates of all sizes, candlesticks, urns and serving dishes.

On July 18 we were back in Paris, and I tried on my wedding dress. Another fitting July 20. Mademoiselle Cognier went with me to shops and errands, and I poured out my heart to her. On the 21st I left for Berne to visit Elsie.

Dr. Thomas Cumming Hall

She met me the next morning in her new motor, and we drove to her pretty house in the Thunstrasse, where I saw Molly for the first time—a baby of eight or nine months, and my godchild. I had so much to tell Edwin and Elsie, so much to ask them! They seemed so secure in their young married life—so wise, as indeed they were. Two days later Albert arrived. We motored all together to an inn on the banks of a mountain stream, where we dined on fresh boiled trout au bleu, and returned in the moonlight.

My mother sent Spencer from Berlin to Berne to urge a postponement of the marriage. Elsie and Edwin opposed this scheme, and sent for Dr. Mende to come from Zurich. I had grown very thin, and must have appeared delicate and anything but well. Dr. Mende was very firm. He wrote to my mother, and gave me every encouragement.

I took the night train to Paris on July 20, and after a "horrible day" there, left that same evening for Berlin. Albert going from Berne, arrived at Spencer's apartment at 11:30. On the 4th my mother and father arrived from Paris, and the next day came Edwin and Elsie from Berne. Helen and Cousin Molly, Mrs. Munn with Carrie Louise and Charlie, and a little later Dr. and Mrs. Hall, from Göttingen.

August 7 was an overcast, cool day. I dressed fairly early in my wedding dress, and drove with my father to the civil marriage. From there to the Embassy. We were in a carriage, my father and I, the coachman and footmen with white boutoniéres, and a white bow on the whip. I can remember my father speaking to me very kindly and gently, and telling me what responsibilities I would carry as the wife of a public man. I remember my startled feeling when we really arrived at the door of thEmbassy. We went upstairs and into the great marble room where the ceremony was to take place. I can remember Dr. Hall—how tall he seemed, and magnificent in his black robe!

My wedding bouquet!

HERMANN RIEMANN
BLUMEN-AUSSTELLUNG
HOFLIEFERANT SR. MAJESTÄT DES KAISERS U. KÖNIGS
BERLIN W., TIERGARTEN-STRASSE 8.
FERNSPRECHER: AMT 6, No. 5197.

We were married! "Helen threw back my veil, Dr. Hall shook hands with us. Behind me stood my mother, and I stopped to embrace her. Down the great staircase into the carriage, and to Spencer's."

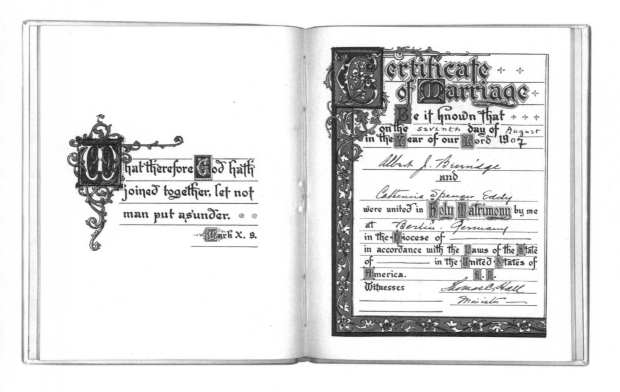

On the honeymoon

Spencer's apartment belonged to the Prince Hohenlohe-Langenburg. It was really a beautiful house, occupying two floors, joined by a large English staircase. The rooms that day were full of flowers, and great tubs of blue hydrangeas. The wedding breakfast was served on an E-shaped table. At one end of the room stood a tall wedding cake, made by Spencer's chef. The Ambassador proposed my health, and Albert responded. Then Dr. Hall made a most perfect little speech, speaking of Albert's wonderful career, and what his life meant to America, and how happy all who loved me should be to give me into his strong hands and keeping. His words seemed to still all trouble and uncertainty in my heart, and to bring the peace and joy that never left me again until the end of Albert's life.

From the stairs I threw my bouquet, and Helen caught it. I can remember the room as I dressed, stepping out of my wonderful wedding lingerie, and slipping into another chemise almost as fabulously beautiful! I wore a gray Creed suit, and a large blue hat, and a blue veil.

We were off! I can see Carrie Louise and Charlie and Helen pelting us with rice and slippers, and last of all, Spencer's face at the carriage window. It was a gay wedding—not sad.

Now we were on the train on our way to Dresden. We dined that night on the terrace of the Bellevue. Before us flowed the beautiful Elbe, where my heart and thoughts return to this day.

From Dresden we went to Munich, where we spent a few days at the Russischerhof, and to Hohenschwangau, where we spent a night. There we found a luxurious motor to take us to Borca, in the Dolomites. We spent the first night at Brennerbad, in the cold, bracing mountain air. We had a jolly little dinner, and sat afterward on our balcony. A very nice hotel, that I had often passed on the train. Breakfast on the same balcony that enchanted us, and down the Brenner pass to Toblach, and on to Cortina—then in Austria— where we gave up the motor.

Albert was overwhelmed by the beauty of the Dolomites, which he had never seen before. We went by carriage to Borca, and decided to stay there. We had a sitting room and bedroom at the end of the hotel, just over Mr. Field's old rooms. One wonderful day followed another. With a small boy to carry our basket, we would climb the side of Mount Pelmo and sit on an Alpine meadow under the larches, and eat our lunch of chicken and chianti. Sometimes we drove to Cortina in the afternoon. All the Munn family arrived, not knowing we were there, but they only stayed a day. Elsie and Edwin arrived in their car and persuaded us to go with them to Venice for a few days. Edwin was a brilliant driver, and traveled at great speed. Down that heavenly valley we flew to Vittorio, bathed in warm sunlight, where we lunched amidst the oleanders. How often in after years did Elsie speak of that drive. It was one of the happiest days of our lives. At Mestre Charlie met us with a launch, and took us to the Grand Hotel, where Mrs. Munn had engaged rooms for us—a sitting room on the Grand Canal, Elsie and Edwin on one side, and Albert and I on the other. We lunched and dined at the Castello Nero, went to the Lido for tea, and sat on the piazza for coffee. One night Albert and I took a boat to the Rialto, and walked into the slums, where the houses almost met overhead, and where, in the setting of a Shakespearean play, men were brawling and quarreling.

We motored back to Borca with Edwin and Elsie, and they went on to Switzerland. The beautiful days continued. We always lunched on the mountainside. On August 17 we went "up on the hill over San Vito, and had lunch where we had lunched once before. Finish *Sir Nigel*,[90] and I read *The Tempest* while Albert sleeps with his head in my lap." Sometimes we climbed the sides of Antelao—more rugged and steep than Pelmo, and built a fragrant fire and had tea from our tea basket. Helen and Cousin Molly arrived in Cortina. Helen would come to us for our picnic lunch, and the next day we would dine with Cousin Molly in Cortina. On September 3 they passed through Borca at 9:30 on their way to Venice.

On September 7 we "take our last luncheon up near the old and best place, make a fire and fry polenta. We are very sad at the thought of leaving, and in the afternoon take the tea basket to the little woods. After dinner go out for a walk in the starlight."

The next morning we left for Toblach in a landau. It was a beautiful, cloudless day. I looked back at Pelmo. Perhaps I would never see it again, and I wanted to remember it vividly, and carry its inspiration always through my life.

[90] A new novel by Arthur Conan Doyle.

We spent a day and night at Zurich on our return. "Arrive very early
and go to the Baur au Lac, where we have a most delicious breakfast. We lunch at the Mende's, long-distance Elsie, and decide to go
to Berne. Go up to the Dolders' for tea. Have a perfect little dinner
on the terrace by the river.["] There are very few hotels in the world
comparable to the Baur au Lac, —on one side, the river flowing
through paved banks in crystal clearness; in front, the garden that
stretches to the lake. Wagner lived there for a time, and I think
began to write *Tristan and Isolde* in the corner suite. The food was
delicious. What perfect dinners and lunches we have had there on

Elsie Porter Mende with Catherine in Berne

the terrace by the river! I can see my mother and father and Mr. Field—Aunt Dell in a beautiful white serge suit and a lace veil thrown back from her pointed hat—my dear Helen and Frederic, and memories of Elsie and her children. There is something about Zurich that makes me feel that I have lived there in the past, and as if it were beckoning me to return. How I loved to walk on the Bahnhofstrasse, with its beautiful shops! In the morning, the street full of stands loaded with flowers and vegetables, and at twelve, in the twinkling of an eye, all signs of the market vanished as if by magic. The hazy, opalescent lake, and the steamers plying to the bordering villages—sometimes boys swimming near the shore would scatter to left and right of the little steamer's bow as she nosed in to the dock; and by every landing a terrace with an arbor overhead— tables, with bright tablecloths, and, should you desire to land, a delicious lunch or a glass of beer and cheese to welcome you.

From Zurich we went to Berne for a day with Elsie and Edwin. The next morning Albert and I "went to walk in the woods, where we so often before discussed our troubles." Now the wind had blown them all away. After lunch we left for Paris, and arrived very late that night. In our sitting room was a little supper put there by Jenny, and a note from my mother.

We had only a week in Paris before sailing. There were busy days for me. Albert and I lunched at the Café De Paris every day, or at Henry's. I had many fittings, and much to see—my beautiful Boin Tabouret silver service from Spencer, and other presents I was to select. My mother had given me my earrings, and the pearl ring that Evelyn wears now.

On the 18th we left for Cherbourg. My mother and father were sailing with us. Charlie Munn was on board, bound for his last year at Harvard. Aunt Dell met us when we landed on the 24th. Albert wished very much to take me to Washington, Connecticut to see Mrs. Platt, the wife of the Senator he had so greatly revered, so we spent a night with her in her pretty house, sleeping in a great four-poster bed. Her maid was Charlotte Anderson, who later was to live with us for so many years.

On the 28th we were in Washington seeing houses. I was determined not to live in our apartment. We stayed in Albert's old rooms at the

91 A hotel on Fourteenth Street just off Thomas Circle. Albert's quarters consisted of two rooms, furnished with dark Japanese furniture.

92 Albert had acquired the house at 4166, and some adjacent land, before his marriage. Catherine and he built a new house on the open land the following year.

93 Not in reality; Catherine moved from Indianapolis in the late 1940s. For the rest of her life she divided her time between Beverly Farms, Massachusetts; Switzerland; and Fort Lauderdale, Florida.

Portland.91 On October 1 Aunt Dell telephoned from New York to say that mamma would be genuinely distressed if we did not take the apartment, and Aunt Dell begged me to reconsider. They made such an issue of it that we agreed to go to 1155, and the house hunting was over.

On our way to Indianapolis we stopped at Greenfield, Ohio, to see Albert's cousins, the McClains. Edward L. McClain had built up a great business from small beginnings, and continued to live in the little town that owed its prosperity to his factories. As a French industrial family would live, the house, with its lawns and flowers, was next to the factory itself. While we were there we drove over Highland County, and saw the scenes of Albert's childhood, and where his mother's pioneer family had lived.

The day we were in Greenfield a telegram came from New York that struck terror to my heart. Dr. Tuttle had found a recurrence of my mother's trouble. It was undecided what would be done, and I was told to go on to Indiana, but my heart was heavy.

We arrived in Indianapolis. It was a long drive in those days from the station to 4166 Washington Boulevard92—from 38th Street, a dirt road, bumpy and rough. It was dark when we reached the house, and the lights shone through the windows and the open door. The next morning I looked out on the great forest trees I was to know so well, now in their beautiful autumn coloring. To the south stretched the grove where our own house was to be built, and where I was to live for the rest of my life.93 We were only in Indianapolis for a few days. On October 9 we decided to go to New York. Mamma did not know we were coming, and I first saw Dr. Tuttle in our room at the Waldorf. He said that the operation would be a desperate one, and held out little hope for her final recovery. Then I decided to let her know that we were there, and went straight to her room. The operation turned out more favorably than Dr. Tuttle had expected, and it did prolong her life for over a year. Fortunately, I could not look into the future, and, being young and happy, my hopes soared. I stayed in New York until she seemed on the road to recovery, and on October 29 started for Indianapolis again. At every stop a Western Union boy walked through the train calling my name, with a telegram from Albert, and in the morning—I suppose at Richmond—a

messenger brought a bunch of violets. Albert wanted to cheer me
after my hard experience in New York. Two days later we went to
Chicago. Mr. Birch met us at the station. We slept in my old beds
in the middle bedroom, and I was very glad to be there. I had a
great deal to do for my mother and Aunt Dell, in the house and at
the bank.[94] Adelaide and McCutcheon came to lunch, and we took
the afternoon train to Indianapolis.

The next day was Sunday. Twenty persons came in the afternoon.
How I managed to give them tea I do not know, but I was young
and resourceful. Encouraging news came from mamma, but a week
later I had to leave hurriedly again—she had had a turn for the
worse. However, it only retarded her recovery, and she really began
to improve. But I stayed in New York, and Albert joined me. We
were at the Plaza. Our rooms were very high up, overlooking the
park. Helen landed, and we were together for a few days. I met
Albert's friends, David Graham Phillips and Frank Munsey. We
dined with the George Perkins'—a large dinner in our honor.
Finally mamma left the hospital and came to the Plaza, and I then
went to Washington, where MacGregor had the apartment in perfect order to welcome us.[95]

I was happy to unpack in my lovely surroundings. I had a new
cook and maid, and a young butler named Walter Fluke—
I plunged into the busy housekeeping I have always loved. Our
engagements began. On Sunday, the first, we lunched at the
Herbert Parsons. The Jusserands, Miss Emmet, the painter, Mrs.
Keep, Mr. Gillett, who was afterwards to be Speaker of the House,
and Burton, just defeated for mayor of Cleveland. The next day
Aunt Dell, Mrs. Slater and Miss Gwynn came to lunch. All was
forgiven! Mrs. Slater was a good loser, and became a zealous advocate of Albert's. Alas! she had caused us a great deal of trouble,
but I never would have had him had it not been for her, so I
treasured no rancor, and forgave her, too. Senators began to dine
with us, one or two at a time—Frye, Hansborough, Gallinger,
Dillingham. Albert went to the first Gridiron dinner[96] since our
marriage, and "I have a poached egg in bed." I had begun to think
that perhaps I was enciente. That very night I wrote to my mother
to tell her of my surmise.

[94] With her mother ill and her aunt away, Catherine assumed responsibility for the large house at 1601 Calumet, which was now her Chicago residence. From a succession of sickbeds out east, Abby sent forth a long stream of letters advising Catherine on how to manage. Catherine also looked after Abby's financial affairs.

[95] The newlyweds attracted attention on their return to the capital. The *New York Times* reported that, Beveridge having appeared in the Senate three times that week, each time in a new suit, "his colleagues are having a great deal of fun about his trousseau."

[96] A Washington press club, founded in 1885.

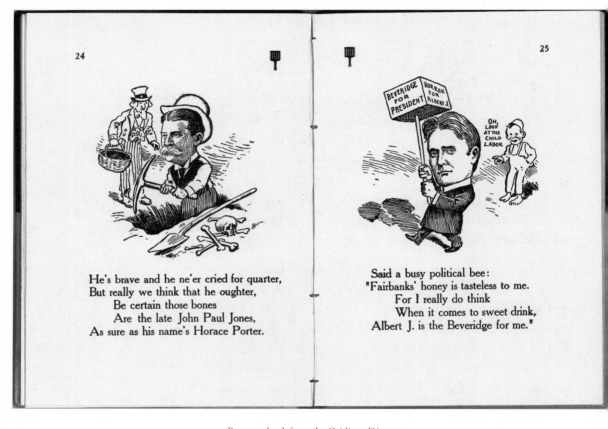

He's brave and he ne'er cried for quarter,
But really we think that he oughter,
    Be certain those bones
    Are the late John Paul Jones,
As sure as his name's Horace Porter.

Said a busy political bee:
"Fairbanks' honey is tasteless to me.
    For I really do think
    When it comes to sweet drink,
Albert J. is the Beveridge for me."

Program book from the Gridiron Dinner

On December 15 I left for Chicago, where I found my mother looking well. I spent two days with her, and then returned to the Claypool in Indianapolis.[97] Albert was very busy. He had enormous patronage to dispense. The line of men waiting outside his office door in the Claypool Building stretched from the door to the elevator. It was almost impossible for him to see every one. I was alone all day in what was, for me, a dreary place, knowing no one, hungry, and supplementing the poor hotel fare by crackers and fruit bought at the Columbia Grocery across the street. I telephoned Mamma, who reproved me severely, and for the one and only time in my married life, my heart wavered. I could not contemplate life in Indianapolis. But the days passed. On the 21st I went to a little tea at Mrs. Jameson's, and met Booth Tarkington. I tried to return the calls that I had received, driving about in a large Horace Wood landau. The streets were slippery with ice and sleet—the distances obscure. I did not know where anyone lived. On December 23rd I took an early morning train to Chicago. Albert was to come the next day. That was Christmas eve, and momma sent for Dr. Cary, who said that I was undoubtedly enceinte—my baby would be born in August.

On Christmas day I wrote in my diary: "Albert sleeps a little later, and I have breakfast with mamma. Never had nicer presents. We all go to Aunt Dell's for luncheon, and in the afternoon to the Bartletts', where I am godmother to their baby, Frederic Clay, Jr." Robert Allerton and Will Hibbard were the godfathers. The christening was in the studio, before a beautiful triptych that Frederic had painted for the occasion. I held Clay. He was sniffling a little, and I was fearful that he would choke and cry, but he was good. Dr. Cary was there, and gave me a knowing twinkle. We had dinner at my mother's—"quite a jolly dinner—the Birches and Mr. Montgomery, and the Milburns. Afterward a man who tells stories, and a wonderful trained dog came in as a surprise. Albert takes the midnight train to Indianapolis."

There is no entry in my diary for the remaining days of 1907, but I know we were in Indianapolis on New Year's Eve, and went to a supper party at the German House,[98] where we heard the bells ring the New Year in.

[97] The Claypool, a big working hotel at the corner of Illinois and Washington. English novelist John Cowper Powys once visited the place. "I can see now the leather chairs of the old writing room there," he wrote, "and the deep capacious inkpots on the tables at which the unwearied drummers wrote their buyers, their employers, and their girls."

[98] Das Deutsche Haus, a popular social and cultural club at the corner of Michigan and New Jersey, founded in 1894 by several German organizations.

On the rocks at the Rockmere Cottage
Manchester — Taken a few days before
Albert Jr was born (Aug 21) 1908

1908

Opposite: Catherine and Albert on the rocks at the Rockwell Cottage, Manchester

INTRODUCTION

~ 1908 ~

CATHERINE'S ACCOUNT OF 1908 looks out onto a purely domestic landscape. It was the first time in years that she did not go abroad. Marriage had focused her attention on things closer at hand. Catherine's deep love for Albert infused her life with new meaning, and she found herself fully occupied with the excitement of the Washington social season, her husband's hectic political career, and the impending birth of her first baby. The year rushed by breathlessly, jammed with White House dinners, romantic rambles with Albert in Rock Creek Park, contentious Senate debates, and election-year intrigues.

The year was a momentous one for Albert and the Republican Party. The party's progressive and conservative wings were joined in a struggle for supremacy, while individuals of both persuasions sought to claim the mantle of party leader. As Roosevelt's highly popular presidency drew to an end, the party struggled to remain united behind his designated successor. Bland and judicious, William Howard Taft was a difficult man to rally around. Progressive Republicans, though eager to retain power and uphold the dominant position of their party, doubted that their reform-minded agenda would receive much support from their new leader. They forged ahead uncertainly. Albert found himself in a particularly awkward position. He declined to become Taft's running mate (a move that, we can see now, would have placed Beveridge within nearer reach of the presidency) but labored to support Taft's candidacy. Albert campaigned nationally for Taft, hoping especially to deliver Indiana to him. Embroiled in political affairs for much of the year, and often away from home, Albert remained in Catherine's eyes a deeply interesting and romantic figure. Despite Albert's heroic exertions, the Democrats triumphed at election time in his home state, signaling the growth of an opposition that imperiled his own political future.

As Albert tirelessly crisscrossed the country, passionately exhorting Americans to do the right thing, Catherine remained at home, her thoughts centered on a marvelous new being. For, on August 21, after a morning spent proofing one of her husband's speeches, Catherine had given birth to a son, Albert Jr. The gratifications of motherhood, coupled with her husband's evident devotion, were to buoy Catherine through one of life's greatest difficulties. Her mother's health, never fully recovered, had once again begun to fail, and on January 2, 1909, Abby died, leaving Catherine to face the future with a hard-won maturity compounded of grief and joy.

Catherine Edd
1888

This little sketch made when I was just seven
yrs old must have been largely drawn by my father.
It is of the Rockwell cottage where in 1908, just 20 yrs
later, my son was born. The windows either side of the
chimney my room —

ALBERT AND I LEFT FOR WASHINGTON on New Year's day. The weeks that followed were happy ones, gay for me, and busy and interesting for Albert, who was working for his Tariff Commission.[99] On the 3rd we dined at the White House. The President[100] took me out to dinner, and I wrote in my diary, "He is the most brilliant and versatile person with whom I ever talked." I wore a pale blue satin dress, made by Worth, that is still in a trunk in Beverly Farms. It was a beautiful dress of the period, made with a train. Around my throat was a new dog collar given me by Aunt Dell and my mother. There was a large diamond placque in front, and the pearls were quite large. Some years later Cartier took it back, and gave me what had been paid for it. The money went to help pay for Beverly Farms.[101] It was a strange fashion that would bind a pretty young throat with a stiff collar, no matter how magnificent.

The Munns were in Washington, and I saw them often. Mrs. Munn was very kind, and took me to see Dr. Hardin, who was to look after me during the months ahead. On January 7 we dined at the Vice-President's.[102] The dinner was for the President and Mrs. Roosevelt. Mr. Justice Day took me out, and on his other side was Mrs. Roosevelt, who, of course, sat at the Vice-President's right. During dinner the President leaned across the table and drank my health in the light Moselle wine that was always served to him at dinners. After dinner, when the gentlemen came in from the smoking room, the President walked through the long drawing room and sat down by me. Needless to say, I was very complimented and pleased. This evening I had worn my black velvet. It was also made by Worth. The President said, "May I say to you that you are wearing a very beautiful and becoming gown?" By this time I fear my head was completely turned.

The next night we went to Senator Depew's. The dinner was for the Vice-President, and as Mrs. Fairbanks was not there, I sat on the Senator's right. Among the guests was Elinor Glyn, the novelist, who had at the moment a very ill-deserved vogue. I talked afterward to Mr. Vogel, the Swiss Minister. On the 9th we went to the diplomatic reception at the White House, and I saw many persons I knew. We took the German Ambassador, who was already stricken by the terrible illness that caused his death, and Baroness Sternburg home in our carriage, as their motor had not come in time. It was bitterly cold now. On the 10th Mrs. Slater had a dinner, and I sat next to

[99] Albert was pushing for the creation of a tariff commission, an independent panel of experts that would advise both houses of Congress on tariff issues and proposed changes. The idea threatened legislators who had shaped the tariff over the years to suit the interests of their constituencies. Nonetheless, the proposal had attracted the support of some manufacturers, heightening dissension within the dominant Republican Party.

[100] Theodore Roosevelt.

[101] A large beaux arts house in Beverly Farms, Masachusetts, purchased in 1912 from the Birches. It remained the family's summer home until the 1970s.

[102] Charles W. Fairbanks.

Baron Hengelmüller. It was dull for me, but after dinner I had "a pleasant time talking to Mr. Howard." The next day Albert lunched with me, and we dined at the Keans'. After dinner I talked to Mr. Justice Holmes. As we left Mrs. Holmes said: "Whenever it is time to go home and I want to find the Justice I always try to think, who is the youngest and prettiest woman here, and there I always find him." The next day was Sunday, and "the Justice came to tea, and was utterly charming and delightful." That same evening we dined at the McLeans', and I sat next to Mr. McLean—very different from the Saturday parties and the good times of last winter.

Secretary Wilson came occasionally to dine. He was a great Secretary of Agriculture, and a very interesting man. On the 15th we dined with the Garfields. Mr. Garfield was the Secretary of the Interior. That evening I sat on his right, and on his other side was Alice Longworth. Afterward we all went to a reception at the Vice-President's for the President and Mrs. Roosevelt. The following day was a Thursday, and I was at home. I wrote in my diary, "Fifty-eight come to call in the afternoon, and I have my hands full." On Sunday we had a luncheon—Mrs. Hobson, the Chandler Hales, Miss Gwynn, Alice Griswold, Helen Ernst, the Russian Ambassador,[103] the Swiss Minister, Craig Wadsworth and Mr. Howard. On the 21st we dined at the Robert Bacons'. The next Thursday there was a heavy snowstorm, and "I am spared many callers. Mrs. Slater, Mrs. Ellis, Mrs. Vanderbilt, Vogel, and two funny women."

The next Sunday we had another luncheon of twelve. That evening when Albert and I were about to sup on cold chicken and a baked potato, in walked Senator Frye! I had said to him (he was a very lonely old man) that he must come any Sunday he felt so disposed and we were at home, and he had taken me at my word. "I rushed to the kitchen and Kewley, the cook, in twenty minutes had soup, beefsteak and vegetables; then the cold ham, and I made a fondu in the chafing dish, and it really was not bad at all." It was not the last time that such emergencies arose.

Occasionally Albert went to a men's dinner—on the 28th to the Secretary of State,[104] and again to Mr. Justice Harlan's. The next Thursday I had "sixty-six here in the afternoon. Fortunately the nice ones come more or less together. The men all at the end, when

[103] Baron Roman Romanovich Rosen.

[104] Elihu Root.

105 Albert gave a speech in the Senate on February 5 recommending the creation of a tariff commission.

106 Portuguese anarchists assassinated King Carlos I (1863–1908) and his eldest son, Prince Luís Filipe (1887–1908), as they rode through Lisbon in an open carriage.

Albert comes in, and it is really very pleasant." Sometimes, of course, we dined alone, and those were happy evenings. Albert would give me a speech or article to read. At this period it was always his Tariff speech.[105] On February 1 we dined at the British Embassy. I sat between Brun, the Danish Minister, and Nick Longworth. The Bryces were in the Embassy at that time. The dinner was not exactly gay—on the contrary, very quiet—and in the midst of it, suddenly Senator Frye, who sat next to Lady Bryce across the table, peered around the flowers at me and said in quite a loud voice, "Peek-a-boo." It doesn't sound very funny as I write it, but it made us all laugh, and I have remembered it to this day. As we left the Embassy we were told the news that the King of Portugal had been assasinated.[106]

Albert's cousins, the McClains, came for a six-day visit. Apparently I was equal to the emergency, but it must have been hard. The first evening we went to a reception of the Indiana Society, and I shook hands with five hundred persons; the next night we had a dinner— Monsignor O'Connell, Senator and Mrs. La Follette, Senator Bryan (a very young Senator from Florida, whose untimely death occurred a few weeks later), Lucretia, Helen Ernst, Mr. and Mrs. Harlan, Admiral and Mrs. Barker, Mr. Royaards and Miss Upham. I wrote in my diary, "La Follette and O'Connell were very brilliant and amusing. They certainly represented the old and the new."

The next day a blizzard was raging. I went with the McClains to the Senate to hear Albert make his Tariff speech. I thought it one of the best things he had ever done, and was very proud of him. That evening Albert and I dined at Senator Cullom's, and I sat next to Sternburg. The next night we took the McClains to a reception at the White House, and they seemed to enjoy it immensely. The following day we gave another dinner—the Vice-President and Mrs. Fairbanks, Justice and Mrs. Harlan, Senator and Mrs. Flint, Mrs. Hanna, Senator Hemenway, Senator Frye, Mrs. Somers, my great aunt, General and Mrs. Bell, and the Secretary and Mrs. Garfield. That was the occasion that Albert loved to describe. I had sent to New York for some fresh caviar, and it was served in two large blocks of ice. When it was offered to Justice Harlan he was intent upon what he was saying, and put in his spoon

Senator & Mrs. Beveridge will please present this card at the door of The White House Tuesday evening, January the tenth

once, and then again, and then once more. The precious delicacy
was rapidly disappearing. I was horror-struck. At last he saw what he
had done, and said, "Bless my soul, I have taken all the caviar."

A little later we went to Chicago—Butler Ames with us. There was
a banquet at the Hamilton Club[107] that evening, and my mother
and I sat hidden in the balcony to hear Albert's speech. Aunt Dell
and Mrs. MacVeagh were also there. He was given a great ovation.
The next day after lunch Albert and I left for Wabash. They held
the train for us at Ft. Wayne, and we arrived at our destination
about 6:30. We stayed at Mr. and Mrs. Pettits'. After dinner, while
I was changing my dress, I heard a band that had come to serenade
Albert in front of the Pettit's house, and when we went out on the
porch, there was a procession of men carrying lanterns, stretching
as far as we could see. Flags were flying, fireworks were going off,
and crowds lined the street all the way to the Opera House. It was
a very enthusiastic crowd, and Albert was cheered repeatedly, and
many men took off their hats to me so that I had to bow and wave
to them. Albert made an excellent speech, constantly interrupted by
applause, and after it was over we went to the back of the Opera
House and shook hands with 2500 persons.

I will always remember the Pettits—he was Albert's United States
Marshal—a very nice man, with a gentle, pleasant manner. I wanted
very much to reach Chicago again in time for the concert Friday
afternoon. There was a train that left Wabash at 4:30 a.m. We went
to bed for a nap, and were called by those kind people, who had hot
coffee waiting for us, and we caught the train to Ft. Wayne. It was,
of course, still dark, and we walked up and down on the platform
waiting for the 20th Century that took us to Chicago, where we
arrived at 9 o'clock. I wrote in my diary: "We go to the concert—
all Wagner. I hear *Tristan* for the first time with Albert. Everyone
crowds into the box to meet him. Miss Keep fairly hugs him, and
Mrs. Watson Blair said to Mrs. MacVeagh, "I see it all! I see it all!
He is the most attractive man I ever met." There was a little tea at
my mother's after the concert, and in the evening we all go to see
The Man From Home.[108]

I stayed at my mother's a week longer. I was very happy. I saw
Adelaide and the Bartletts constantly, and Albertine, who happened
to be in Chicago. Helen must have been in Florida. My mother

[107] A men's club in Chicago that Albert
had addressed as early as 1896.

[108] A comedy by Booth Tarkington and
Harry Leon Wilson that went on from
its midwestern success to become a
New York hit. In it, a straight-talking
Indiana lawyer travels to Europe to prevent his young ward from marrying an
undeserving English aristocrat.

took me to Miss Dodd at Field's to plan for my clothes in the months to come. A great blizzard struck Chicago on the 18th, but I went cheerfully to the north side. One evening Mamma "suddenly decided to go to the Deering ball." It must have been Barbara Deering's coming-out party. I was so glad to have her go. She wore her beautiful gray satin (in a trunk at Beverly Farms) and her pearls. How beautiful she was! I was happy that I can remember her dressing that evening, Jenny lacing her bodice, and I, curled in the chair by her bureau, watching her as I had done as a little girl.

My mother and I, with Jenny and Pierrot, left for Washington. Albert met us, looking very pale. He had had a severe attack of ptomaine poisoning, with two doctors and a nurse, and had not wanted to frighten me by letting me know. He felt better the next day, and we went to Secretary Wilson's dinner for the President. I sat between Senator Dolliver and Speaker Cannon. Cannon kept chewing a huge cigar all through dinner. When the waiter started to pour his glass of champagne he said, in quite a loud voice, "My God, can't you bring me some whiskey?" It was a new experience for me. My mother was awake when we came in, and I sat on her bed and told her all about it. The next day, the 26th, was her birthday. In the evening we all three dined at Mrs. Slater's. "A beautiful dinner. Mamma looks very pretty and so young." I had a really good time. It was a happy moment for me. I was still hopeful for my mother's continued health, I loved my Albert, who was at the height of his political life. Before we left Mrs. Slater's that evening, mamma told her about the baby.

Dinner followed dinner. Miss Mabel Boardman, Mrs. Leiter, the Frederick Keeps. Often I sat on the host's right, and had to leave first. With all my lovely jewels I had no wrist watch that I could wear in the evening. I was too short-sighted to see a clock on the mantel. I sometimes secreted a little watch in my glove. I never carried an evening bag then. Instead of an evening bag I held an ostrich feather fan, with my monogram in diamonds on the shell stick.

On March 1 we had a Sunday lunch. "Thanks to Mamma, the table is really beautiful." The guests were Mrs. Slater, Senator and Mrs. Depew, Senator Dillingham, Mr. and Mrs. Crowninshield (Louise Crowninshield, whom I was to know so well in the years to come on the North Shore), Mrs. Williams, Justice Moody and

General Ernst. My mother rented a motor while she was in Washington, and it made calls much easier for me. In it I would often take Albert a hot lunch to the Capitol, for he still showed the effects of his illness. The Duchess of Sutherland came to Washington, and there were many dinners in her honor. While I hardly knew her, I had a very vivid memory of her at the Russian Court balls. She was very tall, and quite beautiful, and became an intimate friend of Ethel Beatty's. One evening she was at the Bourke Cockrans where we dined. I sat next to the Italian Ambassador, and Esme Howard, and talked to the Vice-President after dinner. The next Sunday we were at home, and in the afternoon my mother, Albert and I went in the motor to the Cabin John road with a tea basket, and made tea in the woods. My father came from Chicago, and he and my mother, Jenny and Pierrot left for Aiken. Evidently my mother had given us the motor for a few days longer, for one Saturday afternoon Albert and I drove out again about eight miles on the same Cabin John road, then so beautiful, and went into the woods with the basket and book and rug, made a fire, and had our tea by a little brook. It was as warm as a May day, and the ground green with rock ferns, laurel, and moss.

Whenever George Perkins and Dr. Shaw came to Washington, they dined with us. George Perkins was a friend of Albert's early manhood, and his success in life aroused in Albert an admiration that he felt for few men. He was dynamic, full of energy, fond of bantering, a good friend to Albert in those years when I first knew him. His wife

George Perkins

[109] Albert being among those who left the Republican Party for the Progressive Party in 1912.

[110] *Un mariage de la main gauche* is one lacking official recognition. The Italian royal family apparently frowned on the idea of the duke's marrying a woman who was neither noble nor Catholic; for its part Katherine's family was opposed to a union that might paradoxically diminish her social status.

was dull, and life in his house on the Hudson could not have been very satisfying—all his great energy was spent in his business, and in his taste for politics.

Dr. Albert Shaw was a true and devoted friend to the very last. He did a great deal for Albert, and his advice was usually good. He was inclined to be prolix, and did not mind being chaffed about it—but his letters were clear and to the point. They are today the most interesting letters in the files. Both George Perkins and Dr. Shaw were great admirers of the President. In that respect they perhaps hurt Albert and drove him too violently and without reserve into the Roosevelt camp.[109]

On the 16th Albert had a triumphant debate with Tillman, much to everyone's pleasure, and that same evening almost the whole Indiana delegation dined with us—twenty-four in all.

Katherine Elkins had been a friend of Albert's, and I, too, was very fond of her. Just at this time she was involved in a love affair with the Duke of the Abruzzi. On the 19th I lunched at the George Meyers' and Abruzzi and Katherine were there. I sat next to him, and found him "very pleasant and good-looking." Senator Elkins finally refused to let her marry him, as it would have been a marriage a main gauche—there were other rumors at the time, but it was her father's opposition that ended it.[110] Nevertheless, had she married him, her life would have been, to my way of thinking, far more interesting than life in Warrenton, VA, with Billy Hitt. That same evening we dined at the Elkins', and, of course, he was there, too. After dinner Katherine told me to leave first, so evidently he stayed on. He was really in love with her, poor fellow.

The next night we dined at Senator DuPont's. Louise Crowninshield presided at her father's dinners. The Senator took me out. He had been a general in the civil war, and Albert admired him, as well he might. He had a white mustache, and a very military bearing.

The next day word came from Aiken that Jenny was ill with pneumonia. She was very ill indeed, and my mother had finally to leave her in Aiken to finish her convalescence, but she made a perfect recovery, and lived to see Albert, Jr. grow to manhood. I loved her dearly from the first day she came to me when I was barely four years old, until her death at Beverly Farms in 1934.

In 1884 Mr. and Mrs. Walters, who were friends of my mother's
in Buffalo, wrote to ask her if she could place an excellent child's
nurse who had been with their little girl, Lucy,
and who was desirous of going to Chicago. My
mother answered that she would, herself, be glad
to engage her to be my nurse, and the matter was
thus arranged. I had had a French nurse, Lena,
and in what few words I had to say, I was bilin-
gual. She departed, and I was told that Jenny was
coming. When she arrived at the house my
mother was not at home, and my grandmother
welcomed her, and took her into my nursery.
There stood the little chest of drawers that now is
in the middle bedroom at 4164, and my grandmother said, "You may keep your things in that."
This, Jenny told me many years later, but
although I was only three and a half, I think I

Jenny Byrne

can remember her coming and taking her hand and going
downstairs with her, probably to my supper.

She was very pretty. Her hair grew low on her forehead, thick and
wavy. It was prematurely white hair, lovely in quality. She had fine
features—a beautiful, delicate nose, and a sweet smile. She was very
neat in her person, and always dressed soberly, as was proper and
expected in those days.

She was born in Watertown, New York, April 29, 1842. Her parents
had come from Ireland, and she was a Catholic. There was no
fanaticism in her religion, and she was not very strict in its obser-
vances, but she liked to go to church, and enjoyed the music of the
mass. She had been engaged to a young man who was killed in the
civil war, and later had another suitor who afterwards made his way
in the world and became a leading citizen of Cattaraugus County,
New York. She would not marry him. All this my mother told me.
I never spoke to Jenny about it, or asked her questions, as I might
well have done the latter years of her life.

She had almost no life apart from my mother and me. She rarely
went out by herself. Her dresses were made by Miss Dargan, a dressmaker who lived in a little wooden house with a high stoop, on
Elm Street. It was a great event when Jenny and I would drive with

Edward and the roans to the North Side for a fitting. I would look on, and Miss Dargan would give me cookies. The house stood until a few years ago, just opposite Wienhoeber, the florist.

From the very first she was devoted to my mother. Gradually, as I grew older, she became my mother's personal maid, and served her with single-hearted devotion. Our journeys to Europe opened a new world to her. Paris she soon knew as well or better than Chicago. Schwalbach, the Engadine, everywhere she was respected and known. When Therese came to Aunt Dell, she and Jenny became great friends. Therese was very much younger, but loved Jenny dearly, and as their summers were spent together in Europe, this was a happy time for her.

But she worked very hard. It was no sinecure to be a personal maid in the beginning of the century. There were no wardrobe trunks, but long trunks, with three trays, very difficult to lift alone, and so many trunks! Women of fashion often returned from abroad with twenty or more of these huge boxes. Elsewhere I have described Charles, of Goyard's. It was he who taught Jenny to pack so well that a dress was bound to be unpacked as fresh as when it was first folded. It required a good mind to keep the keys accessible and divided, the trunks counted and numbered. Jenny at a douane or zollampt was efficient and expert. She understood a little French, but never spoke a word of it, and made herself clear without any effort. When we traveled she wore my mother's jewels suspended in a chamois bag from her trim little waist. I can see her today, one of the most vivid memories of those I loved.

She had beautiful, unerring taste. Whether her contact with my mother helped this or not, I do not know. She showered me all my life with presents that I needed and enjoyed. It was the greatest pleasure of her life to give to me, and later to my children.

To the very end her mind was clear, her memory accurate and her eyesight perfect, a very slight deafness after her 90th year her only concession to time.

The last years of her life she lived in the large end room at Beverly Farms, sewing and busy by day, and playing solitaire in the evenings. Sometimes Catherine,[111] when the children were young,

[111] Catherine MacGregor, who worked for the Beveridges, was the daughter of Alexander MacGregor, one of Delia's most trusted menservants.

would sit with her, and later Miss Murphy played "Miss Millikin" with her. In July, 1934, I was obliged to go to Indianapolis, and Jenny packed my bags—she was then 92 years old. I was leaving little Fex in Beverly Farms, and did not wish to say goodbye, as he would sense a separation. Jenny was seated by the fireplace in my room with Fex in her lap. Catherine MacGregor happened to be with her. I said in my usual voice, "I'll slip quietly out and won't say goodbye," and Jenny said, "That's right." I looked back at the door and waved my hand. The next day I was out on the lawn at 4164, and Esther called me. It was long distance, and Dr. Parkhurst, who said Jenny was very ill. I hurried back to Beverly Farms, but she died a few hours before I arrived. She is buried, as my mother had arranged, in my grandfather Spencer's lot at Graceland. I made that last journey with her quite alone. It seemed right and fitting for me to do so—we had traveled so much together, and so far.

Katharine McCormick came to Washington to spend a week with me. Stanley had had a complete mental breakdown, and was never to recover, but then she was still full of hope and plans for the future. On March 28 Albert left to go to Indianapolis for the State Convention.

Count and Countess de Buisseret, who had been very kind to me when I was a young girl in Vienna, were now in Washington, where he was the Belgian Minister. He was as popular in Washington as he had been in Vienna, where they called him affectionately *"the Halbe Porzion."*[112] They were young and friendly, and I was glad to see them. Alas, they were both to die tragically during the first World War. My mother and father returned from Aiken, and my mother was not at all well. Her happy respite was over. Albert had had one of his great successes at the Convention, but his candidate for the nomination for Governor was defeated, and Watson[113] was nominated. On the 3rd he arrived, very late. I had fallen asleep over Boswell's *Johnson* while I waited for him, but how glad I was to see him!

My mother left for New York, and on April 10 Albert and I followed her there, where we stayed a day or two at the Plaza, and then left for Boston. We were looking for a house on the North Shore for the summer. We stayed two days with Mrs. Dexter and Katharine, and went by train to Manchester, where we saw some dreary cottages,

[112] "The Half Portion."

[113] Albert had backed Charles Wesley Miller (1863–1923). The nomination went to James E. Watson (1864–1948), a U.S. congressman.

and I asked to see the Rockwell house, where I had spent two summers of my childhood, and was told that it possibly was for rent. We came to no conclusion. That evening Albert dined in Cambridge, and Mrs. Dexter, Katharine and I went later to hear him speak at the Harvard Union Hall before a great crowd of students.

The next day, April 14, Dr. Newell came to see me at Mrs. Dexter's—very different from modern procedure, where I would certainly be expected to go to his office. We made plans for my confinement in August, and for a nurse. I liked him very much.

We returned to New York, where my mother was still at the Plaza, and left the next day with George Perkins for Washington. Dr. Shaw was also in Washington when we arrived, and every day one or the other, or both, breakfasted or dined with us. Great consultations were going on at the White House. I wrote on April 16: "Dr. Shaw comes to dinner. He says the President talked to him for two hours, and used Albert's words as though they were his own (Albert having seen him in the morning). Mr. Perkins goes off to the White House, and we go to the opera—*La Boheme*."

Easter Sunday we went to St. Patrick's. Someone recognized Albert, and gave us splendid seats, and that afternoon we went to our favorite picnic spot on the Cabin John Road, and made tea on a carpet of wild flowers. Our life was now comparatively quiet, and with the exception of my growing anxiety about my mother, very happy. I wrote on April 21: "Wonderful, wonderful day! Am out almost all the time. Go to the Senate, but come away before A speaks. Get him at 5:30, and we drive down the Mall, and walk home from the White Lot. Have a nice little dinner by ourselves, and I read till late in A's study." The fight for the four Battleships was on,[114] and there was great activity, Albert speaking in the Senate, consultation at the White House, and conferences at our apartment—on April 26 eight or ten Senators early Sunday morning. But the bill was defeated. The next day I wrote: "Albert starts away early. Very hot, sultry day. Go up to Senate about three. The most dramatic scene imaginable—A speaks well for ten minutes. Then Aldrich attacks him in the most ugly manner—and Senator Smith springs to his feet and defends A, saying "The whole country listens to the Senator from Indiana, and it comes with poor grace from the Senator from Rhode Island ." The wildest applause, both

[114] Catherine refers to a Senate debate over a bill authorizing four new battleships, a measure in keeping with Roosevelt's belief in a strong navy. Old Guard Republicans closed ranks against it, while the weaker, and typically younger, insurgents urged its consideration. Catherine was particularly proud of this episode in her husband's career, which is treated at some length in Claude Bowers's *Beveridge and the Progressive Era*.

after A's short speech and after Mr. Smith's. Am so proud of him. It is a real triumph, in spite of their being defeated. We go to see Keller after dinner."—Keller being a magician, and Albert enjoying it hugely. Part of what Senator Smith actually said was—

> The American people are accustomed to listen to the Senator from Indiana and to recognize his brilliant attainments. There is not a Senator upon this side of the Chamber who does not recognize his ability when help is needed in elections and campaigns. He is able to state his views then to your satisfaction and sometimes to your advantage. It is his ability and his character and courage that have again and again come to the rescue of Senators in doubtful states when their elections were pending.

On April 28 Katherine Elkins and I lunched together, and she poured out her heart to me about Abruzzi. She stayed all afternoon, and that same evening Jenny arrived from Aiken with a trained nurse, looking wonderfully well considering how ill she had been.

There was an old mill in Rock Creek Park that had been turned into a tea house, with little tables out on the bank of the stream. It was a quiet and pleasant spot, and Albert and I went there day after day for our tea. The park was beautiful then, and unspoiled by motors. There were paths bordering Rock Creek where we would walk—sometimes Albert on one side and I on the other, for the fun of meeting on a rustic bridge farther on. We had a carriage by the month—mostly a Victoria—and the era of the afternoon drive had not quite drawn to a close.

Albert's mother came for a visit. She was a very old lady, frail looking, with a sweet and winning smile. Albert was the one bright spot in her long life. She was very proud of him, but I never felt, in listening to Albert's occasional accounts of his childhood, that she had spared him much of the unnecessary toil of those early heartbreaking days. She had, however, in her simple way, the faculty of winning the affection of all who knew her well. I wish, in thinking of this visit, that I had asked her more questions about Albert's boyhood.

One Sunday we went to Baltimore to see Albert's friend, Monsignor O'Connell,[115] consecrated Bishop. It was a very long ceremony—two and a half hours before the sermon—and when that began we left, and had lunch at the hotel. I saw Lucretia le Bourgeois and

[115] On May 3, Monsignor Dennis J. O'Connell was consecrated Titular Bishop of Sabate. The grand high mass was preceded by an elaborate procession of seminarians, acolytes, Catholic University faculty members, abbots, and archbishops, adding to the length of the ceremony.

Margaretta MacVeagh very often. In and out they go on the pages of my little book. Baroness von Sternburg, Comtesse de Buisseret, Mrs. Slater, Katherine Elkins.

One day the Indianapolis architect, Clarence Martindale, came to see us about our new house. I wanted him to see the apartment, for we had decided to make the downstairs rooms as nearly like the apartment as possible. He measured the French windows and the cove of the ceiling and the detail of the rooms. Unfortunately, he was neither a very good nor a practical architect, and we were, for our part, building a house at too long a range, so that we were both to blame. Nevertheless, the house has stood the brunt of time very well. For the outside he copied to some extent a picture of a house on Long Island, torn out of a *Country Life* by my mother. The architect's name meant nothing to me then—it was Mr. Charles Platt.

On May 14 Albert gave a very notable man's dinner. I went early to the market to buy flowers, and was busy all day with the table. It was a dinner of eighteen—the French Ambassador, Mr. Jusserand; Justice Holmes; Secretary Garfield; the Assistant Secretary of State, Robert Bacon; Senator Hemenway; Governor Hanly of Indiana; Dr. Albert Shaw; Mr. Sears and Mr. Munsey (all three from New York for the dinner); Robert Underwood Johnson, the editor of *The Century*; Dr. Remsen, the president of Johns Hopkins University; Dr. Angell, the president of the University of Michigan; Dr. Northrup, the president of the University of Minnesota; Mr. Chase Osborn; Judge Hannis Taylor; Scott Bone, the editor of the *Washington Herald*; and Gifford Pinchot. I remember Albert telling me how completely out of place Hemenway and Hanly had appeared in that brilliant gathering, sitting for the most part silent.

Albert had expected to be chosen as temporary Chairman of the Convention.[116] To everyone's surprise, Burrows of Michigan, was selected—a dull, old, dry-as-dust man. There were many signs of coming political storms, but I was too happy living to spend much time scanning the sky.

Spencer came to Washington for a few days. One of the most serious mistakes I ever made was to ask Albert to use his influence to advance him. With Albert's enthusiasm, and thinking to please me,

[116] The Republican national convention was coming up. The temporary chairman was expected to give the keynote address. Albert wished to be chosen, both to burnish his reputation and to promote the Progressive cause. Accounts of the politics of the selection conflict. One historian asserts that Beveridge already knew from conversations with Roosevelt that he was not to be the convention's chairman. Another claims, to the contrary, that Roosevelt wrote the convention's organizers asking that Beveridge be selected, but that, as a slap at the president, the request was denied. The chairmanship went instead to Senator Julius C. Burrows.

and above all, my mother, he went to unnecessary lengths. It did Albert harm in his relationship with the President, and was a grave error in judgment, but of that I was blissfully unaware. While Spencer was with us Albert gave a dinner to the Senators who had stood by him in the Battleship fight—twenty-one Senators, and Spencer, who made twenty-two. It was gay and animated, as only a man's dinner could be. Even Spencer was called on to speak, and Albert said he did very well. The next morning we all three break-fasted in the sitting room, and Albert left for New York for a day, and Spencer for Chicago.

On May 29 occurred La Follette's filibuster against the Currency Bill.[117] I wrote in my diary: "Albert comes away from Senate, where La Follette has been speaking since 11 o'clock, and we go for a drive. When we get back they have sent the Sergeant-at-Arms for him, so he has to hurry off again. Comes back about midnight, but they telephone for him and he goes up in taxicab—gets back at 3 something, and has to go again!! At last comes home, and goes to bed about 5—La Follette still talking.["] And the next day—"In the afternoon go up to Senate and get A. The filibuster is broken—feel very sorry for poor La Follette. A furious thunder storm on our way back. Albert returns for night session, and Congress adjourns for good this year."

On June 4 Albert gave another dinner—this time to a little group of newspaper men who called themselves The Rockyboy Band of Wandering Indians. Albert was the Chief, and their reunions were very hilarious. Berryman, the cartoonist, drew for it. There were poems by Ira Bennett. John Cal O'Laughlin was a member, Tom Shipp and John McCutcheon, and many others. Everyone had an Indian name. The night of the 4th they elected new members, and stayed till twelve—it was a gay dinner.

Spencer and Lurline came from Chicago, where they had been with my mother, and Albert left the next day for Indianapolis, stopping on his way in Philadelphia, to see George Lorimer. I can remember to this day how sorry I was to have him go! Count Hatzfeldt came to lunch, and we went to the Mill for tea, where we met the George Youngs.[118] George Young, who had been Spencer's friend in Constantinople, was now in the British Embassy in Washington.

[117] La Follette spoke for eighteen hours against the Aldrich-Vreeland currency bill, railing against the concentration of power in the nation's financial and industrial systems and establishing a Senate record for filibustering that stood until 1953.

[118] In 1906, George Young was posted to Washington as attaché at the British embassy. Since Catherine had met him in Constantinople, he had married Jessie Helen Ilbert (d. 1946), whose father, Sir Courtenay Peregrine Ilbert (1841–1924), was a gifted parliamentary draftsman and clerk of the House of Commons.

Berryman on Beveridge

He had married Helen Courtney, the daughter of Sir William Courtney, who had been for many years the Speaker of the House of Commons. She was lovely looking, very animated and charming. In their families she and George united all that was best in the intellectual life of England. She was expecting a baby in September, so with that bond we at once became great friends, a friendship that has lasted through the years. The Embassy was to be in Manchester that summer on Smith's Point, so that we were to see something of each other in the months ahead. The next evening they came to dinner with John Barret, and the following day Spencer and Lurline lunched with them.

When Spencer and Lurline left on June 11, we started at once to close the apartment for the summer. My mother had sent MacGregor to help me, and we all worked hard.

On the 15th I left for New York, where I stayed for a day at the Plaza with Spencer and Lurline, and then to Boston, where Aunt Dell met me.

During these days the Convention was in full swing in Chicago. My mother and father were there, and Albert stayed with them at the Calumet Avenue house. On Friday, the 19th, early in the morning he was offered the nomination for the Vice-Presidency. I think it was Hitchcock who urged it on the telephone. Albert turned to my mother, and asked her if he should take it. My mother advised him to do so, but he positively refused. Although he asked her advice, I know he did not consider it for a moment. Had he taken it, his life would have followed another course. My mother gave him good political advice, but the brave years of insurgency and political defeat that were to come led to his greater fame, and his decision cannot be regretted now.

On the 20th I was in the Rockwell cottage in Manchester. The place was full of happy memories for me. My grandfather had rented it for two summers after my grandmother's death, and Helen and I, as little girls, had had months of the Singing Beach, the rocks and the Essex Woods—memories that could never be forgotten. It was not just a rented cottage, but a place that my family had loved, and where now my son would be born.

Albert, summer 1908 in Manchester

On the sea side of the Rockwell cottage a lawn stretches to the rocky shore. The rocks rise high above the water and are somewhat precipitous. It is the open sea that breaks on them—nothing between our coast and Spain. At the time of the full moon there is a silver patch across the water, and the scene at all times had grandeur and great beauty. To the right is the end of Smith's Point, and on the other side of the Point is the little Bay of Manchester and the Back Beach.

The house itself must have been built in the early 80's. There was a fairly large and very comfortable sitting room, a little panelled German room with a cozy fire, and a dining room that faced the sea. The hall was as high as the house, with a skylight and gallery leading to the bedrooms above.

The noble rocks took Albert's fancy. Some rough wooden steps led to a ledge not too high above the water, and there he had a seat built to surprise me. We had our tea there every fair day, and some-times MacGregor would bring down our picnic supper and we would make a fire and stay there far into the night. Albert hired a rowboat and kept it pulled up on the Back Beach. Often in the late afternoon we would row out onto the bay to one of the three little islands within easy reach. One evening "we donned our pirate clothes, took our supper in a basket, and rowed first to an island where we hoped to land, but found no beach; then to another island where we could land, and where we discovered a fisherman making lobster pots. We built a fire out on the rocks (the fisherman's dog sitting beside us) and ate our supper with the sunset on one side and the sea on the other."

Albert had a horse, and rode in the morning. Occasionally I would meet him on the Singing Beach, where he had a swim, and we would drive back together. Sometimes the wind would blow and the rain beat against the windows, and those were happy days. We would light a fire in the little German room and read and work and have our tea there.

Aunt Dell had rented a house in Dublin, and my mother and father were there. My mother came to Manchester for ten days the end of June, and returned to Dublin and came again the 30th of July to stay until after my confinement.

A few men were coming and going constantly, seeing Albert on political matters. His young secretary, Metcalf, sat on the front porch typing, typing. Katharine Dexter often spent a night; the Munn family came and went—Charlie, Carrie Louise, Mrs. Munn, who loved Aunt Dell and my mother so dearly.

In Berlin Lurline had engaged a German Schwester to care for my baby. She was a friend of little Spencer's Schwester Emilie Kassner, and her name was Schwester Anna Marie. She was one of the best nurses in all Germany. She arrived on the 4th of August in her lovely uniform. If I could only have kept her! It proved impractical. She did not know a word of English. Dr. Newell's German was limited, and Miss Haggerty, Dr. Newell's nurse, was jealous and not accommodating. The Schwester did remain for a few weeks after the baby's birth, and then returned to Germany. Had I been wiser and braver, I would have kept her—to everyone's benefit and well being.[119]

The layette was unpacked and ready—all from Paris. My mother had sent my own lovely French baby dresses abroad to be washed and renovated. All the little shirts and woolens came from Madame Frank on the Rue de la Paix—the beautiful christening coat, the old lace and embroidered cape with its down-like undercoat covered with finest handkerchief linen or mull. No little royal prince could have had more beautiful things. My own cradle with the ormolu cupids had been newly re-upholstered, and stood ready with its lovely curtain sweeping the floor, and my own Moise had been sent back from Paris where it had been refreshened with a new garniture.

On August 18 I put my desk in order, and on the 19th I went to drive and spent the evening with Albert, reading poetry aloud. On the 20th my confinement seemed imminent, but nothing happened, and I slept all night as usual. The morning of the 21st I went into my mother's room, where they brought my tray and coffee, but I knew then the time had come. During these days Albert had been busy dictating, and Metcalf typing, in preparation for the Presidential campaign ahead. The 20th I had been given a speech to read. Again, the morning of the 21st, when I had begun to be in labor, Albert brought me some corrected pages—perhaps to divert me. I read them till I could read no more. Dr. Newell had been summoned

[119] In a few months, Catherine would be back in Chicago, no longer under the care of Dr. Newell or Miss Haggerty. Since she herself spoke German, she and the nurse would have had no trouble communicating. On the long train ride to the Midwest, Albert Jr. was to fall dangerously ill—presumably from bad milk—and had a worrying and uneven convalescence.

by telephone, and came in his motor from Boston, but before he arrived Dr. Washburn, in Manchester, had to be sent for. As such things go, it was a hard but brief struggle. At five minutes past three in the afternoon Albert, Jr. was born. My mother, standing by the door, went to tell Albert in the next room—he put his head on his arms and burst into tears.

I was very ill after the comparatively normal birth—a dilatation pressing against my heart. I lay unconscious for several hours, but Dr. Newell was clever and resourceful, and undoubtedly saved my life. Night had fallen before I saw the baby.

He was a very fine little fellow—so blonde that even the day after his birth his color was only pink. His hair was very smooth and the most brilliant gold that can possibly be imagined. Almost all babies are born with a darkish fuzz that wears away, but not Albert—his little head was neat like a boy's, and the wonderful color of his hair and skin made him a really beautiful baby. The Schwester was happily at home with the French layette. She dressed him at first not in a dress, but in a long, fine, flannel petticoat. Around his waist she bound a broad blue taffeta ribbon that served really as a binder. It was brought around and tied in a large flat bow in front. Then the little French shirts, one inside the other like jackets—linen and thin, thin flannel. Some of them are still in the baby clothes as they came from Paris—in three sizes. On September 12 I was up for the first time, and watched the baby having his bath by the fire in my room. At that time three weeks in bed was not unusual.

Albert had left the 3rd or 4th of September to speak with Hughes[120] at Youngstown, Ohio. He was soon to begin a campaign trip to the coast. But he returned to Manchester, and on the 18th the Munns came in the evening, and for a surprise there were fireworks, and at the end "C A T H E R I N E" in large illuminated letters, with a gold waterfall all around it![121] On September 25 Albert left for New York, where he spoke at Carnegie Hall before a great crowd, and at Terre Haute on September 29 he replied to Bryan on Labor. . . .[122] "The address was the second of a series of three replies, the first of which he made at Carnegie Hall, New York, on Trusts." These speeches had all been dictated on the rocks and in the garden of the Rockwell cottage.

[120] This was the first of many stump speeches Albert made during the 1908 presidential election on behalf of his party. Throughout the fall he campaigned hard, though he himself was not up for reelection. He had hoped to postpone going on the stump until late September, but Taft persuaded him to appear at Youngstown with New York governor Charles Evans Hughes to open Taft's campaign in Ohio. Hughes (1862–1948), later a U.S. Supreme Court justice and secretary of state, had established his reform credentials by exposing irregularities in New York's utilities and life insurance industries. Like Albert, he was a keenly sought-after Republican speaker.

[121] From afar, Abby wrote wistfully, "wish I could have seen your name—only Queens have that done."

[122] Albert had been tapped to follow the route of William Jennings Bryan's speaking tour, answering the Great Commoner's speeches with those of a Republican cast. Speaking on trusts, labor, and the tariff, Albert dogged Bryan from New York City to Terre Haute, Indiana, to North Dakota. Bryan's popularity and forensic skills made him difficult to beat, but Albert, who had debated Bryan before, understood his opponent's vulnerabilities.

In the meantime the baby, Miss Haggerty and I left for Chicago. We stopped for a few hours at the Touraine,[123] where my mother and father and Aunt Dell had been staying for a few days, and then to the South Station. It was September 30 when we arrived in Chicago. Albert met us, coming from Terre Haute, and we drove in Aunt Dell's motor to the Calumet Avenue house. The baby was not well. On the train something had gone wrong with his formula, and he was to have a long illness from some kind of milk poisoning.

Albert was about to leave on his campaign trip. I was very reluctant to let him go on this journey across the continent. On October 6 he had reached the coast—it was his 46th birthday.

Aunt Dell arrived from Boston, Adelaide I saw every day, and Mary Stone and Dora Bartlett very often. My anxiety about the baby increased, and Dora suggested that Dr. Cary call Dr. Walls in consultation—the pediatrician who had done so much for Clay. He came and gave him another formula, but there was no great change for the better. Aunt Dell left for New York. She was to sail on the 13th. I think her courage had failed her—she knew what the near future held for my mother, and could not face it. Dr. Newell's nurse returned to Boston, and her place was filled by Miss Hayes, who was to be with the baby for many months.

On October 20 Albert returned from his long and arduous trip. He was very hoarse and tired. The next night he spoke at Orchestra Hall before an enthusiastic crowd.

Now that Albert was in Chicago for a few days, I decided to go to New York to see my mother, who was at the Plaza. My father and little Pierrot met me, and I found my mother looking better. She had been cheered in her mind by a Miss Young, a Christian Scientist, and a very intelligent, helpful person.[124] I only stayed a day. We did some shopping together, and I left for Chicago. My mother and father were on their way to Baltimore to see Dr. Kelly, of Johns Hopkins.

I found the baby looking very pale and thin. Dr. Walls came a few hours later and said we must have a wet nurse—they could do no more with the milk. Alas! Had I been encouraged in the beginning to continue nursing the baby, all would have been well. I have often

[123] The Hotel Touraine, at the corner of Boylston and Tremont near Boston Common.

[124] Abby relied on Christian Science "helpers" during her final illness.

thought that perhaps Dr. Newell, who knew of my mother's condition and realized what the future held for me, had perhaps purposely discouraged me. At all events, something had to be done now. A wet nurse was found, healthy and young, and Miss Hayes watched her every mouthful, regulated her outdoor exercise and kept her busy cleaning and working in the house.

Catherine with Albert Jr.

Just at this time my dear Adelaide lost her baby by a miscarriage. She was very ill and very sad. But in spite of this disappointment bright years lay ahead for her — Ned's success and fame as a surgeon, her interest in his profession, and, above all, their happy life together.

Albert had closed the campaign by a memorable speaking trip through Indiana. A special train was chartered that carried him over the state. With him, among others, was the faithful Rothschild, and Henry Pettit, Sam Blythe, John McCutcheon and, for a day, George Lorimer. There was a McCutcheon cartoon in the *Tribune* — "The Whirlwind Finish in Indiana." On November 2 Albert telephoned me to come that day to Indianapolis. We spent the night at the Dennison, and the next day, Tuesday, I went to the polls with him in Washington Township. From there we went to see our house that was nearing completion.

I say in my diary that I was pleased and that it was "really charming," but I remember my disappointment in the small entrance hall that worries me to this day.[125] That afternoon I returned to Chicago. Taft was elected, but Indiana went Democratic.

For the next five weeks we were in Chicago, with short visits to Indianapolis, and one flying trip that I made to see my mother in Washington. Albert was exhausted by the campaign, and slept as much as possible.

[125] Abby had been anxious on this point, writing to Catherine just a few weeks before her death: "About your hall — it's so important to have a good entrance."

The baby improved and began to gain, and a little color came into his cheeks. I saw Helen constantly, and Adelaide, who was well again, Cousin Mollie and the Bartletts, and many of my old friends. But my heart was heavy, for my mother had not improved, and I must have known what it meant.

She had been in the Washington apartment for some weeks, but had made up her mind to take another apartment at 2339 Massachusetts Avenue, near Sheridan Circle, for the winter. It was large and dreary, and not like her lovely surroundings.

We reached Washington with the baby on December 9. My father met us. I went at once to see my mother, and found her very depressed.

While we were in Chicago Dr. Hardin had sent her a nurse, who was to be with me so often in the years to come—Miss Parrish. She was young and sweet-looking, with reddish gold hair and a gentle manner that comforted and helped my mother. The baby was brought to my mother's apartment, and even stayed there for a day or two while I was in New York with Albert. I like to think of "him one morning lying on her bed while she had her breakfast tray. In fun she offered him a little piece of muffin and I jumped forward to prevent it. She laughed her gay little quizzical laugh at my young solicitude. "Did you actually think I would give it to him?"

On the 26th we had a theatre party for Carrie Louise Munn, who was making her debut that winter. As we rose from the table someone said to me that Mrs. Munn was in the hall and wanted to speak to me. She was in evening dress. She said, "Catherine, your mother is very ill. I will go to the theatre in your place. Hurry—the car is ready to take you." They threw something around my shoulders. I flew down the stairs. In a few moments I was in my mother's room. Dr. Hardin, Miss Parrish, Jenny, and my father were there. After all these years I can feel and remember the passion of grief that engulfed me. I remember the bells and sirens of that New Year, and how Dr. Hardin went over to the window and closed it. Aunt Dell arrived the 2nd of January, a few hours before my mother's death.

Abby Eddy

Released for afternoon papers Aug
Speech of Albert J. Beveridge
as Temporary Chairman of the Nat'l
Progressive Convention at Chicago,
Monday, Aug. 5.

"We stand for a nobler America. We stand for a united
Nation
Republic undivided by sectionalism. We stand for a broader
liberty, a fuller justice. We stand for social brotherhood
as against savage individualism. We stand for intelligent co-operation instead of reckless competition. We
stand for mutual helpfulness instead of mutual hatred. We
stand for equal rights as a fact of life instead of a catch-
word of politics. We stand for the rule of the people as
a practical truth instead of a meaningless pretense. This
is no political adventure. This is a battle for the
rights of men. Ours is a battle we raise the
standard of the forward movement

To carry out our principles we have a plain program
of constructive reform. We mean to tear down only that which
out of date
is wrong and obsolete; and where we tear down we mean to
the future
build what is right and fitted to the times. We harken to
We give heed our
the call of the present. We mean to make laws fit condition
& will be. We mean to meet the need
as they are — to meet the needs of the people who are on earth
& to prepare for the needs of
today. That we may do this we found a party through which
their children
all who believe with us can work with us; or rather we declare
our allegiance to the party which the people themselves have
founded.

For this party comes from the grass roots. It
has grown from the soil of the people's hard necessities.
It has the vitality of the people's strong convictions.
The people have work to be done and this party is here to do
that work. Abuse will only strengthen it, ridicule
only hasten its growth, falsehood only speed its victory.

Albert's 1912 speech at the Bull Moose Convention

AFTERWORD
Albert J. Beveridge III

Since Catherine is only twenty-seven years old when the diary ends, readers might like to have some idea of what happened to her during the sixty-one years that remained in her life.

The Senator had two years left in his term. They were turbulent years characterized by a growing estrangement between him and the new Taft administration exacerbated by differences over the Payne-Aldrich tariff and the dismissal of his friend Gifford Pinchot. Not only was he frustrated in the Senate, but his political prospects were dimming back home in Indiana. The tariff bill was extremely unpopular in the state, and in the 1910 election the Democrats won back the state legislature, meaning Beveridge's Senate term would not be renewed. Beveridge never gave up his political ambition, however, running for governor in 1912 and for the Senate in 1914 on the Progressive Party ticket and in 1922 as a Republican. Although he won the 1922 primary, it was a bitter contest, and the more conservative elements of the party were never reconciled to his candidacy. He lost the general election.

Probably his finest political moment after he left the Senate came in 1912 as the keynote speaker at the Progressive Party convention in Chicago that nominated Teddy Roosevelt. In that address he is credited in *Safire's Political Dictionary* with adding the term "grass roots" to the political lexicon. The keynote, according to his biographer, Claude Bowers, was "one of the most remarkable speeches ever addressed to a party convention." It began without the customary preliminaries: "We stand for a nobler America. We stand for an undivided nation. We stand for a broader liberty, a fuller justice," he declared. Then, after dismissing charges that the Progressives were only spoilers intent on defeating Taft, he went on: "For this party comes from the grass roots. It has grown from the soil of the people's hard necessities. It has the vitality of the people's strong convictions. The people have work to be done and our party is here to do that work." It was quite a speech; and the auditorium went wild as he finished by quoting *The Battle Hymn of the Republic*: "He has sounded forth the trumpet that shall never call retreat…." Chauncy M. Depew would write him afterwards, "I have read your speech…. You and I are as far apart as the poles in the present campaign, but I admire a good speech… it is the best of your life. It is a masterpiece, and your statements are put with epigrammatic force…."

But politics took less and less time as the years went on, for the Senator had found a new and increasingly satisfactory pursuit in the writing of biography. Since he was not forced to earn a living because Catherine, and, more importantly, her aunt Delia, could support him, he devoted most of his time to research and writing with the same intensity he had displayed in his political career. The result was a masterful four-volume *Life of John Marshall*, that won the Pulitzer Prize in 1920 and a two-volume *Abraham Lincoln* that was uncompleted when he died of a heart attack in Indianapolis on April 27, 1927, at the age of sixty-four. The Senator inspired two biographies himself: *Beveridge and the Progressive Era* (1932), by Claude Bowers, and *Albert J. Beveridge, American Nationalist* (1971), by John Braeman.

For Catherine these were the happiest years of her life. She admired intellectual more than political pursuits, and she knew that her discriminating literary judgments were appreciated by her husband. In 1912, Catherine had purchased a large beaux arts house in Beverly Farms, Massachusetts, near the home of Oliver Wendell Holmes, a friend, and the couple split their time between Indianapolis and Beverly Farms. From the accounts of friends, it was evident that her main goal at this point in her life was to make life comfortable and interesting for the Senator. There was only one subject that produced discord, and that was her husband's chain-smoking. Catherine detested the habit, but it did not impair an otherwise close, even passionate, relationship. The family grew in 1910 with the birth of a daughter, Abby,

Catherine's daughter Abby and son, Albert Jr. ca 1914.

named after Catherine's mother. Catherine would have liked to have had more children, but Abby's birth was difficult and she was warned by the attending physicians that another child would probably cost her her life.

Catherine was not lucky with her children—Albert Jr. experienced the unhappy coincidence of being spoiled as a youth and at the same time pressured to live up to his father's reputation. It proved too much for him. He graduated from a good preparatory school, St. Mark's, but was forced to withdraw from Harvard after his freshman year because of poor grades. In 1932 he graduated from his father's alma mater, DePauw. The following year he was married to Elizabeth Scaife, the daughter of Roger and Ethel Scaife of Milton, Massachusetts. Scaife was, successively, a senior editor at Houghton Mifflin, the firm that had published Beveridge's *Marshall* and *Lincoln*, vice president at Little, Brown, and finally, president of Harvard University Press. The couple had three children: Albert (b. 1935), Elizabeth, known as Elissa (b. 1937), and Franklin (b. 1940).

Shortly after graduation from Depauw, Albert Jr. founded a monthly magazine of political commentary entitled *The Pulse of the Nation*, but it did not prosper. He then began a short career as a broadcaster and journalist and entered local politics by winning a seat in the Indiana Senate. After the war, he ran unsuccessfully for Congress against an entrenched Democrat, Louis Ludlow, and after this defeat his life came apart. He fell victim to alcohol, was divorced from Elizabeth, and for about a decade became the principal worry of his mother. He finally conquered his alcoholism, married Virginia Ryan Baring, a daughter of Thomas "Fortune" Ryan and settled down to

the life of a gentleman whose principal interest was deep-sea sport fishing. But it was to be for only a short period, as he died in 1964 at the age of fifty-six.

Catherine's daughter, Abby, brought her even less joy. By all accounts she was a striking, vivacious, headstrong woman who frequently clashed with her mother. In the 1930s, when in Berlin, she fell in love with Franz Baum, whom Catherine disapproved of as a suitor because she considered him an opportunist. Abby married Baum anyway, under circumstances that led to a permanent rupture between Abby and her mother. Abby had three children with Baum: Franz (b. 1937), Ziska (b. 1938), and Valerie (b. 1941). In the late 1940s, they divorced. Abby was to remarry, again unsuccessfully, and died in 1968.

With one exception, the rest of Catherine's immediate family appear to have drifted apart after the death of her mother and their removal from Chicago. Her father, who seldom went to Europe with the family during Catherine's youth or seemed to participate in the family's social life, spent the remaining years of his life in Paris, where he pursued his artistic bent. He died on June 23, 1921. The *Chicago Tribune* reported in his obituary that after his wife's death "he went abroad to live, discovering in himself a latent talent for art, which he practiced on the left bank of the Seine. He maintained a fine studio in the Latin Quarter. In his twelve years of residence in Paris, he became a popular leader in art circles and a familiar figure at the opera and the races."

Catherine's brother, Spencer, resigned suddenly and unexpectedly from the foreign service in 1909 when he was only thirty-nine, divorced Lurline Spreckels in 1923, and married Viola Cross in 1932. Catherine did not like Viola

Catherine's grandchildren, Albert III, Franklin and Elissa.

and, accordingly, grew distant from her brother, who also lived much of the time in Paris, supported undoubtedly by Delia, leading a life of modest gentility.

The one family member who continued to provide support and comfort to Catherine was her aunt Delia. Dell, as she was called, moved to Washington, D.C., shortly after Marshall Field's death. There she purchased a large house at 2600 on then fashionable Sixteenth Street (called the "Pink Palace"—now the headquarters of the Pan-American Development Foundation). In Washington, Delia continued the lifestyle she had become accustomed to in Chicago. She entertained frequently and lavishly. Her menus reflected the eating tastes of the turn of the century, with six to eight courses at a typical dinner. Her guest list included ambassadors, senators, cabinet members, members of the Supreme Court, and society members. Not infrequently there would be entertainment by visiting artists like Fritz Kreisler. In the summer, it was her practice to rent a house near her niece on the North Shore of Massachusetts. There she died at the home of Catherine's friend Eleo Sears in the summer of 1937.

During the forty-odd years of her widowhood, Catherine concentrated on three principal activities: keeping in contact with her friends and their children, making sure that her Beveridge grandchildren lived up to their grandfather's standards, and supporting philanthropic organizations, especially art museums. As one might deduce from her diary, Catherine was devoted to her friends. Throughout her life she remained in constant contact through letters, telephone calls, and visits to many of the persons who are mentioned in this book: Adelaide Ryerson, Olivia Thorndike, Eleo Sears, Katherine McCormick, and Julia Brambilla, the former Julia Meyer. But friendship frequently meant more than occasional contact. For example, in the 1950s she purchased a small piece of land from Frederic Bartlett adjacent to his home, in Fort Lauderdale, Florida, Bonnet House. There she spent the winters, in part because of the weather but primarily so that she could be near Frederic and his wife and her great friend, Evelyn. Similarly, each summer during the late 1950s and through the 1960s she spent in or around Zurich and the Engadine. She liked Switzerland, no doubt, but the principal attraction was the proximity to the children of her friend and youthful companion Elsie Porter.

Finally, Catherine devoted considerable energy to philanthropy, especially museums of art. She was an important benefactor of the National Gallery in Washington, the Art Institute in Boston, the Herron Art Institute in Indianapolis, and above all the Chicago Art Institute. To the latter she gave Mary Cassatt's *On a Balcony*, one of the museum's most popular paintings, in honor of her aunt Delia.

Catherine died on May 28, 1970, in Fort Lauderdale. She is buried with her husband and son at Crown Hill cemetery in Indianapolis.

Mary Cassatt, On a Balcony, *The Art Institute of Chicago.*

Catherine Spencer Eddy was born June 29, 1881, at her family's home at 1601 Michigan Avenue on Chicago's south side. Her father, Augustus Newland Eddy, was a thirty-three-year-old businessman; her mother, Abby Louise Eddy, a woman of fashion and the daughter of a successful merchant. Both sides of Catherine's family were well known socially, though her father's was a prominent ecclesiastical family, while her mother's was wealthy and worldly.

The maternal side of the family dominated. The most influential figures in Catherine's young life were her mother, Abby, and Abby's sister, Delia Caton. Abby and Delia were leading socialites, two charming sisters who had grown up in Chicago, the only surviving children of Franklin Fayette Spencer and his wife, Rachel. Spencer was a genial, generous man whose business success enabled him to enjoy an ample, cosmopolitan lifestyle, setting a pattern that his daughters and their families would subsequently follow.

Spencer was born in New York State in 1817. He grew up in the town of Gowanda, near Buffalo, where his father was a merchant and he was educated at a local academy. Accounts of his early life differ, but he may have made

his first foray into Illinois as early as 1838, when he is rumored to have staked out a claim on the Rock River and to have "led the somewhat wild and adventurous life natural to that place and time." In 1839, however, Spencer returned to Gowanda to settle his father's estate, which was encumbered by substantial debts, which Spencer worked hard to pay off. According to one report, he did so by driving cattle from Buffalo to Philadelphia and trading in various goods along the way.[1]

By 1843 Spencer's affairs had moved into the black, and he took advantage of this favorable circumstance by marrying Rachel Gifford Macomber, age twenty-three. She came from a respectable New England family. Her parents, native to Massachusetts, had moved to Gowanda eight years earlier; then, five years later, her mother had died. Rachel's father was an inn- or tavern-keeper, a respectable, quasi-public position of some importance in towns of this time. Her only sibling, Charles, became

[1] "Death of Franklin F. Spencer," *Chicago Tribune*, November 2, 1890; "Gone to His Reward: Chicago Loses a Good Citizen by the Death of Franklin F. Spencer," *Chicago Inter Ocean*, November 2, 1890; "F. F. Spencer Is Dead," [*Chicago Times*, November 2, 1890]; "Franklin F. Spencer," *Gowanda Herald*, November 14, 1890; "Frank F. Spencer," *Gowanda Herald*, December 12, 1890; "Funeral of F. F. Spencer: Imposing Ceremonies at the First Presbyterian Church," unidentified Chicago newspaper, n.d. [November 4, 1890], Album 2.

Abby (age 28) and Delia (age 24) Spencer in 1878.

a well-known politician in New York State, a lifelong friend and backer of Grover Cleveland.[2]

Franklin and Rachel moved to Chicago in 1855, when Spencer became the representative of Jewett & Root stoves, manufactured by his sister's husband in Buffalo. Stoves were then the principal means of heating businesses and homes. Spencer remained in the business for about ten years, becoming very successful as a stove dealer. He operated first from a location on Chicago's Water Street, relocating to River Street after a fire. Agents of the R. G. Dun Company, who as early as the 1840s had begun to formulate their gossipy credit reports on individuals and businesses, were admiring. In 1862 they regarded Spencer's business as "sound, strong, and reliable," and in 1865 an agent wrote simply, "he is [a] first-class businessman and must succeed." Franklin's work selling stoves gave him a broad acquaintance throughout the Midwest, which he continued to extend throughout his career.[3]

HIBBARD, SPENCER & BARTLETT

It was only in 1865, when Spencer was forty-seven years of age, that he established the firm

that generated a lasting fortune for his family. He struck up a friendship with William Gold Hibbard, a hardware man who was like himself from New York State. Like Spencer, Hibbard was a merchant's son and had married a woman, Lydia van Schaak, from a politically active New York family. The two men bought out the other partners in the hardware firm of Tuttle & Hibbard, with which Hibbard had been associated for nearly a decade. The new firm of Hibbard & Spencer was formed at an auspicious time, as the city's population was rapidly booming.[4]

[2] "Death of Mrs. Spencer," unidentified Chicago newspaper, n.d. [March 19, 1887], Album 2; handwritten notes in family register (Beveridge Family Papers); "Death of Z. A. Macomber, Esq.," unidentified Buffalo newspaper, n.d., Album 2; "Charles S. Macomber Dead: An Old Friend of President Cleveland Passes Away," unidentified newspaper, August 23, 1887, Album 2.

[3] "Sherman S. Jewett & Co.," Alfred T. Andreas, *History of Chicago: From the Earliest Period to the Present Time*, 3 vols. (Chicago: A. T. Andreas, 1884-1886), 3:483; "Hibbard & Spencer," *Illinois*, vol. 28, p. 210, December 23, 1862, and February 28, 1865, R. G. Dun & Co. Collection, Baker Library, Harvard Business School.

[4] Addie Hibbard Gregory, *A Great-Grandmother Remembers* (Chicago: A. Kroch, 1940); Maxwell Bloomfield, "Peter van Schaak and the Problem of Allegiance," *American Lawyers in a Changing Society*, 1776–1876 (Cambridge, MA: Harvard University Press, 1976), 1–31.

WILLIAM GOLD HIBBARD 1825 — 1903

FRANKLIN FAYETTE SPENCER 1817 — 1890

ADOLPHUS CLAY BARTLETT 1845 — 1922

Hibbard and Spencer's partnership was an immediate success. By 1870 theirs was regarded as "one of the strongest firms in business in this city." In 1872, the year after the Chicago fire, the net worth of the company was estimated as $500,000, while its principals were looked upon as "first class merchants" who "stand high socially." Enjoying the bond of friendship, the two men had talents that were complementary. Hibbard did the purchasing and ran the administration. Spencer was in charge of credit. His quick judgments, often based on a moment's conversation with a customer, were "uncannily dependable." While generous in extending credit, the store was regarded as highly reliable by its creditors. This perception of its underlying soundness was crucial in helping it weather crises such as the Great Fire of 1871 and the Panic of 1873. [5]

In 1882, Hibbard and Spencer invited into their partnership Adolphus Clay Bartlett, a much younger man who had been with the firm since its earliest days, first working in the stockroom and gradually assuming responsibility for all the firm's sales. He was young enough to be Spencer's son, and his children and Spencer's grandchildren were close in age. A sense of close kinship grew up between the two families.

By the 1880s, Hibbard, Spencer & Bartlett had become one of the nation's largest hardware companies, a position it retained well into the twentieth century. It benefited from the same economic conditions that catapulted many other Chicago companies to eminence at the time: rapid urban population growth, a concentration of capital and enterprise in the city, and

a great rural hinterland that purchased many of its necessities from Chicago with the aid of traveling salesmen and spreading rail lines. [6]

The firm's first crisis was the terrible fire that swept the city in 1871. The blaze destroyed nearly all the firm's stock. [7] Though the firm's immediate losses were staggering, the huge demand for building material that the fire created more than offset them. After the fire, Hibbard & Spencer remained open for business, operating first for a brief period from Mr. Hibbard's home, then from a speedily constructed shed on the lakefront. What saved the firm, apart from energy and hard work, was its

---

[5] "Hibbard & Spencer," *Illinois*, vol. 28, pp. 63 and 149, May 21, 1872, and October 3, 1873, R. G. Dun & Co. Collection; Fred C. Kelly, *Seventy-Five Years of Hibbard Hardware, 1855–1930: The Story of Hibbard, Spencer, Bartlett, & Co* (Chicago: privately printed for Hibbard, Spencer, Bartlett & Co., 1930), 31.

[6] William Cronon, *Nature's Metropolis: Chicago and the Great West* (New York: W. W. Norton, 1991).

[7] Kelly, *Seventy-Five Years of Hibbard Hardware*, 65–66.

Franklin Spencer

credit rating, which permitted it to borrow to replace stock and construct new facilities. In addition, it had prudently insured itself against such a casualty, though not for full replacement value. As it recovered, the firm built a larger five-story building on the corner of Lake and Wabash. By 1884, it had extended its business into several adjacent buildings, occupying all the space from 16 to 32 Lake Street. It remained in this location for thirty years, until it moved, in 1903, into impressive new quarters: a ten-story building block located at the State Street Bridge. By this time the firm had withdrawn from the retail trade and sold to wholesalers exclusively. The firm remained at the State Street location until 1924, when, as a consequence of the City Beautiful movement, the building was condemned to make way for the construction of Wacker Drive.[8]

Having surmounted the great challenges of the 1870s, Franklin Spencer enjoyed unbroken and increasing prosperity. Around this time, he built a house at the corner of Michigan Avenue and Sixteenth Street that would remain home to his family until after the turn of the century.

Personally, Spencer was an affable character. In his business dealings and personal life, he was steady and kind. Described as "genial, warm-hearted, and generous," he was apt to invite others home to share some delicacy, a common occurrence as he lived "somewhat luxuriously for those days." Rachel and he were Presbyterians. They gave generously to the First Presbyterian Church and to the Presbyterian hospital. They also retained their ties to Gowanda, giving money needed to build a new Presbyterian church in the town. Franklin also contributed to the founding of the American Church in

Paris, though when he later visited it he was offended by the style of worship that he found. No doubt there were other charities, of which no specific record survives.[9]

Spencer was also an affectionate father who doted on his daughters and young grandchildren. Letters to his daughters while in school counseled them to learn, but also to benefit from and enjoy the many riches life had to offer. For a dignified man, he had a puckish side. He had a photograph taken of himself holding hands with his dog, and on some of his stationery there was engraved the image of an extended hand exhibiting the word "Shake!" There is no mistaking the great fondness he felt for his only granddaughter, Catherine. Preserved in her family scrapbook is an early letter from him, addressing her as "My dear charmer"; she was three years old at the time. The letter is illustrated with a pencil sketch of ducks and ducklings swimming across a pond to get crackers from "Aunt Catherine." Her first telegram, which she received while in New York with her parents when she was eight, was a loving message from her grandfather telling her that the pansies and crocuses in the yard were waiting to welcome her home. Alert and active until the end of his life, Spencer died at age seventy-three, when Catherine was nine.

[8] Gregory, *A Great-Grandmother Remembers*, 50–56. When forced to move from the State Street building, Hibbard, Spencer & Bartlett commissioned the architectural firm of Graham, Anderson, Probst & White to design a new building for a riverside site on North Water Street. The resulting fourteen-story building was a state-of-the-art facility with just under one-million square feet of floor space. It was a riverfront landmark until its demolition in the 1980s. The NBC building now stands on the site.

[9] Kelly, *Seventy-Five Years of Hibbard Hardware*, 32; "Dedication of Presbyterian Church at Gowanda," Album 2; *Catalogue of the Mary Spencer Library* (Gowanda, NY: Presbyterian Church, 1890), Album 2; "Mrs. Franklin Spencer," [*Gowanda Herald*], n.d., describing dedication of memorial window. Obituaries noted Spencer's penchant for anonymous giving.

He left an estate valued at $1.5 million, including shares of Hibbard, Spencer & Bartlett stock, which Abby and Delia inherited equally.[10]

THE SPENCERS' LIFESTYLE

Like the Blairs and the Newberrys, the Spencers belonged to a class of Chicagoans who had accumulated considerable wealth before the Great Fire. As Janet Ayer Fairbank and Helen Ayer Barnes note perceptively in their introduction to *Julia Newberry's Diary*, "It is difficult for anyone not born a Chicagoan to believe that the city of even the late Sixties or early Seventies could have been anything more than a frontier town, a trading post on the edge of the wilderness," yet it was "a place where delightful people lived with elegance, in close touch with the culture and civilization of the Atlantic seaboard, from which many of them had lately come."[11]

The Spencer girls were certainly raised in this style. Whether Franklin and Rachel found the educational opportunities for girls in Chicago inadequate, or they wanted their daughters to

[10] Franklin F. Spencer, last will and testament dated May 1, 1878, record no. 5-5235, Cook County Circuit Court Archives, Chicago; unfortunately the probate record itself has been lost.

[11] *Julia Newberry's Diary*, with an introduction by Margaret Ayer Barnes and Janet Ayer Fairbank (New York: W. W. Norton, 1933), vi–vii.

Thomas Mears Eddy

acquire a finish that midwestern schools could not give, Abby and Delia were sent to Boston to attend the Pemberton Square School. Abby graduated in 1868 at the age of eighteen, while Delia, who was then only fifteen, went on to complete her studies in Troy, New York, where she probably attended Emma Willard's.[12]

By their teens, the girls had begun to exhibit a flair for dress that would remain a passion throughout their lives. They were known for their contrasting styles of beauty. Delia was dark-haired, tall, and thin, with soulful dark eyes that could shine with imperiousness or humor. Abby was blond, with flawless skin and a serene and innocent demeanor. Whereas Delia's costumes were likely to be florid or dramatic, Abby's tended to be simple, hinting of the picturesque or the bohemian. Both girls had pierced ears and wore long, elegant dangle earrings. Abby often wore a very large, plain cross, reflecting a spiritual seriousness characteristic of her.

After her graduation from Pemberton School, Abby took up her place in Chicago society. Contrary to the conventional belief that respectable women were seldom written about in the nineteenth-century press, her appearance and activities, as well as those of her friends, were routinely reported in the Chicago papers. In fact, judging from her careful preservation of newspaper clippings about herself, Abby was rather mindful of publicity. Her family's prominent position, its connection with families who ran Chicago's newspapers, and Abby's long-time friendship with Caroline Kirkland, who became a society writer—publishing under the moniker "Madame X" in the *Chicago Tribune*—all ensured that her family's doings would be

reported, albeit in a generally respectful and admiring way. Such reportage gives us our earliest glimpses of Abby. In the spring of 1870, she is described in the *Chicago Sunday Times* as a "very sprightly" young lady, "a perfect blond with blue eye[s]" who "dresses a great deal, and not only expensively but in good taste," "sings well, and is passionately fond of flowers." She had a little phaeton and pony, which she was frequently seen driving around town.[13]

THE EDDY FAMILY

In the 1870s, both Abby and Delia married and came into their own socially. On June 27, 1872, Abby became the wife of Augustus Newland Eddy, son of a well-known ecclesiastical family. Both his grandfather and his father were prominent Methodist ministers. His grandfather, the late Augustus, had been one of the pioneering elders of the church in the Ohio River valley, helping to establish congregations in the then newly settled regions around Cincinnati. His father, Thomas Mears Eddy, had likewise spent the early part of his career laboring to bring the gospel and the Methodist faith to the isolated inhabitants of the frontier. Having experienced conversion during the wave of revivals known collectively as the Second Great Awakening, he embarked on a career as a circuit preacher while still in his teens. It was an arduous calling that entailed long days in the saddle, sheltering in the often crude homes of believers, and preaching, eating, and being paid as the occasion

---

[12] Pemberton Square School, commencement announcement with notes, Album 3.

[13] "Merry Matings," unidentified Chicago newspaper [May 11, 1870], Album 3; "Our Young Ladies," unidentified Chicago newspaper, July 24, 1870, Album 3; "Peck-Spaulding: A Grand Wedding at Trinity, Yesterday Evening," *Chicago Re[cord-Herald?]*, [November 18, 1870], Album 3.

offered. (His earnings in the early years of his career were $60 one year, and $55 another.)[14]

Though never in good health, Rev. Eddy was tireless and, as he took up post after post in the Midwest, he gathered a reputation for his sensibility, wit, and fervor. He was a captivating speaker and, while still in his twenties, began to write eloquent essays on spiritual and controversial subjects for the denominational newspapers. Though he never became wealthy, Eddy was widely known throughout Ohio, Indiana, and Illinois because of his family's contributions

to Methodism, and he enjoyed that special sort of respect bestowed on outstanding nineteenth-century clergy. Visiting Cincinnati in the summer of 1843, where his family had once lived, Eddy met a former friend from childhood, Anna White, and fell in love with her. After their wedding in 1845, they moved to Rising Sun, Indiana, where they first made their home with a friend, Rev. Elijah Newland. When Catherine's father was born in 1848, his name, Augustus Newland, honored both Thomas's father and his hospitable friend. The Eddys had several children besides Augustus, and their offspring were distinguished. On the Eddy side of the family, Catherine's cousins included the noted architect Thomas Eddy Tallmadge (1876–1940) and diplomat Hugh Root Wilson

---

[14] Date of wedding from handwritten family register, Beveridge Family Papers; Charles N. Sims, *Life of the Reverend Thomas Mears Eddy, D.D.* (New York: Phillips & Hunt; Cincinnati: Walden & Stowe, 1884); John Carbutt, "Thomas Mears Eddy," *Biographical Sketches of the Leading Men of Chicago* (Chicago: Wilson & St Clair, 1868). The latter contains a fine engraved portrait.

Young Augustus Eddy and Abby Spencer

(1885–1946), who was the last U.S. ambassador to Germany before World War II.[15]

Rev. Eddy's career entered an exciting new phase when in 1856 he was named editor of the *Midwestern Christian Advocate*, a widely read and influential Methodist newspaper based in Chicago. The appointment marked a turning point for the Eddy family. It placed the reverend in a position of great visibility and influence, which he used over the next fifteen years to attack the evils of slavery and to espouse the cause of the Union in the American Civil War. It also brought him a larger and more reliable income, access to more worldly and sophisticated acquaintances, and the opportunity to spend more time with his family. In the center of one of the nation's great cities, both he and his children found new intellectual and social opportunities. By the time he resigned the editorship in 1865, he had become one of the ablest leaders of his denomination. His merits were acknowledged in several enviable appointments, first as pastor of the Charles-Street Church in Baltimore, where he was responsible for the construction of the Mount Vernon Place Church, and then as pastor of the Metropolitan Church in Washington, D.C., where President Grant was among his parishioners. Finally, in 1872, Thomas Eddy was called to New York City to serve as missionary secretary of the denomination; he died there in 1874 at age fifty-one.[16]

Catherine's father appears to have had some difficulty defining himself in relation to this powerful clerical figure. He was eight when his family moved to Chicago, and he received his education in Chicago's schools. After graduating from high school, he attended the new "Douglas University," the name familiarly given to the liberal arts college the Baptists had founded on the South Side, forerunner of the present-day University of Chicago. Rejecting the family's pastoral calling, Augustus joined the leading retail firm of Farwell, Field, and Co., one of the early partnerships of Marshall Field. When he married Abby Spencer in 1872, he was regarded as a rising young businessman and may have become a member of the Board of Trade. He was not a merchant at heart, however, at least not by Chicago's standards. If Henry Blake Fuller was correct when he described Chicago as "the only great city in the world to which its citizens have come for the one common avowed object of making money," Augustus was an odd man out. Though he continued to be active in business, sharing an office with his brother-in-law, Arthur Caton, and starting an industrial metals firm, he was never successful, and the firm eventually went bankrupt.[17]

In a similar manner, early in his career Augustus took part in several notable civic enterprises before his enthusiasm petered out. In 1878, he was among the group of young men who founded the Calumet Club, which was located

[15] Sims, *Life of Reverend Eddy*; Sharon Irish, "Tallmadge, Thomas Eddy," *American National Biography* (New York: Oxford University Press for the American Council of Learned Societies, 2000), hereafter cited as *ANB*; "Hugh R. Wilson Dies," *New York Times*, December 30, 1946. Genealogical information tracing the connection of the Wilsons to the Eddys is preserved in the Tallmadge Family Scrapbook, box 1, folder 21, Thomas Eddy Tallmadge Papers, Newberry Library, Chicago.

[16] The Tallmadge Papers preserve additional information about Rev. Eddy's later years. His death received national press coverage.

[17] "Augustus Eddy, Ex-Chicago Merchant, Social Leader, Dies," *Chicago Tribune*, June 27, 1921; "Augustus Newland Eddy," *The Book of Chicagoans* (Chicago: A. N. Marquis, 1905); on "Douglas University," see Bessie Louise Pierce, *A History of Chicago*, 3 vols. (Chicago: University of Chicago Press, 1937-57), 2:297; Henry Blake Fuller, *With the Procession* (New York: Harper & Brothers, 1895); 1908 bankruptcy record of Imperial Expanded Metal Co., case no. 16117, National Archives Records Administration, Chicago.

in the Prairie Avenue district and drew its membership from that community. The club was known for its receptions and art exhibitions, feting General and Mrs. Ulysses S. Grant in 1879, for example, on their return from their famous trip around the world. Augustus was also a member of the executive committee that planned the 1880 Republican convention in Chicago. But these early endeavors were also his last. More enduring were his artistic inclinations—vague talents at drawing and writing that he never properly developed. Despite his kindness and ready execution of any family responsibility, Augustus Eddy did not flourish, and it does not seem that he was happy.[18]

He remains an indistinct figure in Catherine's chronicle. While Catherine mentions her mother frequently, her references to her father are infrequent and wistful. There was obviously a bond between them, however, for Augustus seems to have afforded Catherine a refuge from the more demanding lifestyle of her mother. His presence in her life is documented in another record that Catherine left behind, her 1901 engagement calendar, where he appears as her daily companion—often her sole companion—during her mother's frequent bouts of ill health. During such periods, Catherine and her father attended church together, paid visits, took long walks about the neighborhood, and kept one another company at the dinner table. Conscious of her father's unhappiness and unrealized talents, Catherine would probably have concurred with Edith Wharton's feelings regarding her own father: "I imagine there was a time when his rather rudimentary love of art might have developed had he anyone with whom to share it.... I wondered what stifled

cravings had once germinated in him and what manner of man he was really meant to be. That he was a lonely one, haunted by something always unexpressed and unattained, I am sure."[19]

Following a custom common at the time, Abby and Augustus took up residence at the Spencer home at 1601 Michigan after they were married. Abby assumed greater responsibility for running the household as her mother aged, becoming its absolute mistress in 1887 when Rachel died.

DELIA AND THE CATONS

While Abby's marriage to Augustus united the Spencers with a highly respectable ministerial family, Delia's marriage four years later, to Arthur J. Caton, connected them to one of the wealthiest and most prominent families in town. Arthur was the only son of prominent jurist and millionaire John Dean Caton, who had arrived in Chicago, poor and untested, in 1833. Born in 1812 to a large, impecunious family, Judge Caton had led a picaresque, eventful life, reflecting both his manifold interests and evanescent aspects of Illinois in its earlier days.[20]

After a hard upbringing in New York State, he migrated to Chicago at age twenty-one with

[18] Augustus's involvement in the Calumet Club and the Republican convention are documented in Andreas, *History of Chicago*.

[19] Catherine Eddy engagement book, 1901 (Beveridge Family Papers); quotation appears in R. W. B. Lewis, *Edith Wharton: A Biography* (1975; repr., New York: Vintage, 1993), 24. After his wife's early death in 1909, Eddy moved to Paris, where he dabbled in the arts.

[20] Sketches of John Dean Caton appear in Steven Caton, "'Worthy Lady . . .': Dilemmas of Love and Language in Early Chicago" (paper presented at the Ethnohistory Workshop at the University of Pennsylvania, Philadelphia, May 4, 2000), and Wayne C. Townley, *Two Judges of Ottawa* (Carbondale, IL: Egypt Book House for the McLean Historical Society, 1948); see also Robert Fergus, *Biographical Sketch of John Dean Caton, ex-Chief-Justice of Illinois* (Chicago: Fergus Publishing, 1882).

only rudimentary training as a lawyer. That proved no impediment, as he was one of the first of his profession to arrive in the city. He soon became deeply involved in forming city government and the state's legal system. Arriving just as Cook County was being incorporated, he argued the very first case in its court. The city's other lawyer—with whom he shared an office—represented the other side. Caton became a justice of the peace and the city's first corporation counsel; in the city's first election, he was elected third-ward alderman. At the age of thirty, he was appointed to fill a vacancy on the state supreme court, on which he served from 1842 to 1864, occupying the position of chief justice for the last six years.

Caton was fortunate in his marriage. His wife was Laura Adelaide Sherrill of New Hartford, New York, whom he had met before leaving the state. He wooed her by letters, and in 1835 they were married. Laura's sister, Emily, also married a Chicago man, Frederick Eames, and settled in Chicago as well. Eames, a banker, headed the firm that would evolve into the Continental Bank of Illinois. The Eameses' daughter, Emily, a lifelong friend of Abby and Delia, married Franklin MacVeagh, originally

Arthur Canton and Delia Eddy around the time of their maarriage.

a native of Pennsylvania. He was a wealthy Chicago wholesale grocer active in politics who eventually became Taft's treasury secretary. Franklin's brother Wayne MacVeagh, who had remained in Pennsylvania, became U.S. attorney general under Garfield and later ambassador to Italy; in turn, he was connected to the politically powerful Cameron and Sherman families. Thus, through Laura Sherrill, the Catons were allied with a number of other families prominent in Chicago and beyond. In the 1830s and 1840s, however, these reputations lay in the future.[21]

Caton was also fortunate that being a judge, even on the state supreme court, did not then preclude active business involvement. While on the bench, Caton became involved in the telegraph business, an enterprise that made him very wealthy. In 1849, he became a stockholder and director of the languishing Illinois and Mississippi Telegraph Company. Stung by the loss of some earlier wealth (from real estate) in the downturn of 1837, Caton drove the company to profitability. He improved both the reliability and extent of the telegraph lines, supplementing company lines with those he himself established and owned. Having secured valuable Morse patent rights and executing one of the nation's first contracts to use the telegraph to coordinate railroad traffic, Caton in 1866 leased the lines in perpetuity to Western Union. This brought him a personal income of over $70,000 a year, considered an immense sum at the time. By the time he died, he was understood to have made a "colossal fortune," which, after his retirement from the bench, he lived for thirty years to enjoy.[22]

Many of Caton's activities during his "retirement" were intertwined with his life in Ottawa, Illinois, where he had established a country estate. Recalled today as a site of one of the Lincoln-Douglas debates, Ottawa stands in an area where the Illinois River, burrowing deep into sandstone fields, has cut picturesque and occasionally dramatic bluffs. Caton bought a large tract of land lying atop one of these bluffs and built a house on it. It was in Ottawa that Arthur Caton was born and grew up. When the Catons' house was destroyed by fire in 1886, the judge replaced it with a much grander structure. This was "the Ottawa house" to which Catherine refers: a twenty-eight-room Queen Anne–style mansion that took in lovely views of the countryside while proudly offering itself to the view of the town below. It was made of red brick, its "castle-like bulk" topped with gables and punctuated by "great round bays, dormers, a spacious veranda, and tall chimneys." Inside, the rooms were "trimmed in fine woods and adorned with marble and tile fireplaces, parquet floors, and highly ornamental built-in cabinets." From the ceilings hung brass and copper chandeliers, one "embellished with opalescent and ruby glass."[23]

In Ottawa, Caton lived the life of a gentleman. He was a backer of numerous town enterprises, including a starchworks, glassworks, waterworks, copper mines, and coal mines. The fledgling Ottawa Academy of Sciences bore his stamp,

[21] Charles H. Sherrill Jr., *The Descendants of Samuel Sherrill* (New York: privately printed, 1894); "Death of Mrs. Caton," *Ottawa Free Trader*, November 26, 1892; "Laid in the Tomb," *Ottawa Free Trader*, November 26, 1892; Steven Caton, "'Worthy Lady . . .'"; on the MacVeaghs, see Amelia Gere Mason, *Memoirs of a Friend* (Chicago: Laurence C. Woodworth, 1918); Robert S. La Forte, "MacVeagh, Franklin," *ANB*; Robert C. Olson, "MacVeagh, Isaac Wayne," *ANB*. Simon Cameron and his son Donald were U.S. senators from Pennsylvania. The Shermans were an Ohio family whose most famous members were General William Tecumsah Sherman and his brother U.S. senator John Sherman.

[22] Townley, *Two Judges of Ottawa*, 38–41. The rights were eventually sold to Western Union for $1.7 million.

[23] John Drury, *Old Illinois Houses* (1948; repr., Chicago: University of Chicago Press, 1977), 165; Herma Clark, "When Chicago Was Young," *Chicago Sunday Tribune*, March 24, 1946. The house was demolished in 1946.

for he was avidly interested in natural and local history. He wrote works on such subjects as artesian wells, the life of various Native American tribes, and the origins of the prairie. He accumulated a fine library. He had such a passion for deer that he wrote a four-hundred-page book, *The Antelope and Deer of America*, and established an extensive park for deer and elk on his land. He and Mrs. Caton traveled widely—to Europe, the Far West, and Asia—bringing back plants and decorative objects that were given a place at their Ottawa home.

Judge Caton's son, Arthur, stylish and self-possessed, was the ornament of all his father had achieved, but little more. Arthur lacked his father's drive, his curiosity, his interest in the material world. Born in Ottawa in 1851, Arthur was schooled at Phillips Exeter Academy, in Andover, Massachusetts, and at Hamilton College, in New York, receiving his bachelor's degree in 1873. He was admitted to the bar and practiced for a while in Chicago, but work not being a necessity, he did less and less of it as time went on. Sociable and athletic, venturesome in a conventional sort of way, he scouted the world from the sturdy bastion his father's success afforded. After his marriage to Delia, his time was given over to travel, society, and club life. Being openly and exclusively a man of leisure made Arthur unusual among Chicago men of his time.[24]

As if to compensate, he took his pastimes very seriously. He was one of the leading sportsmen of his time, helping to establish in Chicago such distinctively upper-class leisure activities as polo, golf, horse racing, and coaching. He bred dogs and horses on his Ottawa farm and was one of the leading advocates of the hunt.

He had a role in creating the Washington Park track and was a standout participant in its crowning ritual, American Derby day. He served for six years as president of the prestigious Chicago Club, a tribute to his popularity.[25]

Arthur's dedication to fine horses and coaching—well documented in the pictures of him that survive—was perhaps the outstanding feature of his personality. His splendid coach and four, with its perfectly matched horses and smartly dressed attendants, were often pressed into service to carry about visiting dignitaries. Only a handful of Chicagoans had the wealth to maintain a coach or the expertise needed to drive one well. Arthur on the box cut an elegant and impressive figure. He frequently exhibited his horses in the New York Horse Show and was considered one of the leading whips in the country.[26]

On Wednesday evening, May 10, 1876, Arthur and Delia were united in a lavish wedding. The hoopla surrounding the event was characteristic of the excitement that Delia habitually generated. The evening ceremony at the First Presbyterian Church, followed by a large reception at the Spencers' home, was extensively reported in the newspapers, which touted the event as arousing "widespread interest" as "the

[24] "Arthur J. Caton Dies Suddenly in New York Hotel," *Chicago Inter Ocean*, November 19, 1904; "Arthur J. Caton Dies," *Chicago Daily News*, November 19, 1904; "Arthur J. Caton Dies Suddenly," *Chicago Daily Tribune*, November 19, 1904; Carrol H. Quenzel, "'Society' in New York and Chicago, 1888–1900" (Ph.D. diss., University of Wisconsin, 1938), 21–25.

[25] Illinois Office of the Secretary of State, *Certified List of Illinois Corporations* (Springfield, IL: Secretary of State, 1903), lists Arthur as president of two corporations, the Macsoutah Kennel Club and the Caton Stock Farm; "Arthur J. Caton to Succeed Himself as President of the Chicago Club," *Ottawa Journal*, February 6, 1899.

[26] According to Quenzel ("'Society,'" 128–29), there were only five coaches in all of Chicago in Arthur's time.

most stylish and fashionable wedding" occurring in Chicago for a very long time. The high
fashion on display at the church also made the
event slightly risqué. In the hours before the
ceremony, the street in front of the church was
packed with carriages waiting to deposit "their
gaily-attired occupants." The ladies who
descended "were richly and elegantly attired,
many in full evening dress." As night fell, they
entered the church, which was brilliantly illuminated and lavishly decorated with huge
stands of flowers. "Many of the fairest members
of the *elite* of society graced the occasion, and
many of the full-dress costumes were elegant in
the extreme." "Silks and laces, ravishing bon-
nets, and brilliant and costly jewels, contributed to an unusually varied scene." Among
the guests were U.S. senator Lyman Trumbull
(a contemporary of Lincoln who had sat with
Caton for years on the bench), former Chicago
mayor and U.S. congressman John Wentworth,
General Philip Sheridan and his wife, members of the Farwell family, the Potter Palmers,
and the Marshall Fields.[27]

Afterwards, the crush shifted to the vicinity of
the Spencer home at the corner of Sixteenth
and Michigan. In honor of the occasion, the
façade of the residence was brightly illuminated, bathed in the jet of an "electric lime light
that shed a brilliant lustre on the surroundings."
It lit up the hectic scene on the street, caused
by "the dense line of carriages that fairly
blocked Michigan Avenue and Sixteenth for
squares." A half dozen policemen were on the
spot, keeping back spectators so that guests
could easily make their way to the house.
Inside, the rooms

> were ornamented with the utmost
> taste. The bride and bridegroom

received the congratulations of hundreds of their friends standing under a
superb canopy of the choicest flowers.
Pictures, mirrors, vases, in fact everything that taste could suggest or wealth
procure had been availed of to make
the ornamentation of the rooms all
that the most fastidious could expect.
The salon was crowded for hours, and
by a bevy of beauty elegantly framed,
such as is seldom witnessed even in
the most fashionable circles of
Chicago. Some of the costumes were
superb, violet and white satins, orange
and black silks, rose-colored and lavender silks veiled in folds of the most delicate laces of all colors of the rainbow,
and every description of fabric from
those as massive as velvet, to web-like
gossamers delicate and fleecy as a
cloud. All these various tastes and
styles in dress contributed to a general
effect that was brilliant in the
extreme.[28]

The achievement the evening represented did
not belong only to Delia or the Spencers but to
the whole of Chicago. In a city recently founded
and even more recently incinerated, the display
of taste and fashion Delia's wedding inspired
was reassuring. Though about to blossom into a
sophisticated metropolis, Chicago was at this
time still a "new Western city," just emerging
from a "primitive, crude, provincial period."
Despite the elegance of which Julia Newberry's

---

[27] "Caton-Spencer," *Chicago Inter Ocean*, May 13, 1876;
Herma Clark, "When Chicago Was Young," *Chicago Sunday
Tribune*, n.d., Album 3.

[28] "Merry Matings: Caton-Spencer," unidentified Chicago
newspaper [May 13, 1876], Album 3.

descendants wrote, Chicago was a town of "wide, dusty, ill-paved streets," with "homes set in pleasant gardens, a noisy business center with farm teams hitched along the principal thoroughfares, [and] enormous energy." It was a "healthy and wholesome" environment, as Caroline Kirkland observed—but scarcely dignified or polished. Chicagoans knew this and were eager to emulate those who set high standards of dress, entertainment, interior decoration, and arts patronage. For the next twenty-five years, "the Spencer girls," as they continued to be known, were among the ladies who filled this need, whose outfits and parties were breathlessly written of in the papers, and who were regarded gratefully and admiringly as satisfying some urgent collective longing or requirement. "Many Clamor for a Single Look at Mrs. Arthur Caton" proclaimed one headline the day after a charity bazaar. Simply by getting dressed in the morning, traveling incessantly, and buying what they wanted, Abby, Delia, and their ilk contributed to the growing material and aesthetic refinement of Chicago.[29]

Throughout their adult lives, Abby and Delia spent substantial amounts of time in Europe. Back home in Chicago, this experience showed. Abby was admired for her subtle yet unerring sense of taste, her exquisite Parisian clothes elevating fashion "above mere mode." She was "ever a vision" in the loveliness of her garments, a close friend remarked, "for dress with her was really a fine art." Similarly, Abby's entertainments were known for their "quiet sumptuousness," for their freedom from any hint of novelty, ostentation, or extremism. Her evenings combined what was admirable and excellent with a gracious, unpretentious hospitality. Over the years, she and Delia hosted

many outstanding artists, including James Russell Lowell, Mrs. Patrick Campbell, Paderewski, Fritz Kreisler, and Ethel Barrymore. Elaborate arrangements were made on such occasions, as when, in 1899, Isadora Duncan came to dance at the Eddys' home. Tapestry screens and chandeliers were removed from the dining room and a temporary stage, constructed at one end, was decorated with greenery, flowers, and special lights to create the effect of a woodland scene. "Miss Duncan was a great success," the guests sat down to a marvelous supper, and Abby "went to bed at 1:30 pleased."[30]

Meanwhile, Delia was evolving into a brilliant social leader. The station she enjoyed as Mrs. Arthur J. Caton suited her exactly. In addition to being good-looking and rich, Delia possessed great energy and vivacity and an independent spirit that allowed her to enjoy the advantages of her position fully. Her tall graceful figure, beautiful coloring, and gorgeous wardrobe were only part of her appeal. She was also witty and inventive and as a hostess understood how to surprise, charm, and harmonize people. She possessed great dash, and it showed in her guest list, her cuisine, and her style of speaking. After posing dutifully for an hour in a tableau vivant for the sake of charity, Delia was the sort who would toss her tiara to a maid and run off in a twinkling. She did everything in a large and fearless way. Yet, though widely admired and eager to retain the good opinion of others, Delia at the same time quietly did what she

[29] Remarks of Caroline Kirkland, *Abby Spencer Eddy: In Memoriam and Three Appreciations* (Chicago: privately printed, 1909); "Many Clamor for a Single Look at Mrs. Arthur Caton," *[Chicago] Sunday Chronicle*, February 1, 1903.

[30] Remarks of Emily MacVeagh in *Abby Spencer Eddy*; Abby Eddy to Catherine Eddy, postmarked March 8, 1899, Beveridge Family Papers.

pleased. Considered the leader of the city's "ultra-smart set," she did not always please her more sober-minded neighbors, and pious ladies were sometimes known to frown at her ways.[31]

Under Delia's direction, the Caton residence at 1910 Calumet Avenue became one of the most fashionable in the city. Though unremarkable on the outside, it was thought to surpass all others in interior beauty. In 1898, Delia had the house remodeled to make it more suitable for large entertainments, adding a dining room large enough to accommodate seventy-five comfortably. Guests were likely to be greeted by their hostess, dressed perhaps in pale blue velvet or silver-gray silk, standing before a large mirror in a splendid red apartment furnished in the French style and adorned with old tapestries, its floor gleaming like ebony. In the dining room, guests found the tables shining with museum-quality porcelains or, more famously, with solid gold plates. Every object in sight was a rare bibelot. The room itself was finished in dark oak, its walls completely covered with old tapestries, except at one end, where two old paintings of great size were hung. Observers wondered whether Delia had ransacked the palaces and museums of Europe, but of course

such a thing had not been necessary. The power of her purse was considerable. Rare was the nineteenth-century American woman who had her own R. G. Dun credit report, but Delia did. On the strength of her connections and wealth, it concluded that, though she was in "no business whatever, . . . we should consider Mrs. C. good for anything she would be apt to buy."[32]

Despite their obvious differences, nothing altered the close relationship between Delia and Abby. Acting in concert throughout their lives, they remained extremely close, in many ways more important to one another than either was to the man she married.

Such was the family circle into which Catherine was born. It was a thoroughly adult world. Fortunately for Catherine, there was one other youthful figure on the scene: her brother, Spencer Fayette Eddy, who was her elder by eight years. Doted on by his mother and aunt, Spencer was bright, very self-assured, and—if a little bit spoiled—very charming. Always debonairly dressed, he had, as a young man, the air of someone who had always been grown up but would never be old. Fond of the high life, Spencer often alarmed his parents, who feared he was extravagant and too easygoing. Yet by the time Catherine was in her teens, Spencer was launched on a promising career in the diplomatic corps. Since Delia and Arthur remained childless, the family's hopes for the future rested entirely on Spencer and Catherine.

Prairie Avenue

Although Chicago was one of the nation's most dynamic cities, Catherine lived in a small, sheltered community. Her family lived in the

[31] Arthur Bissell, "The Original Gold Coast: A Mature Consideration of Old Prairie Avenue Days," *The Chicagoan*, September 8, 1928, 12–13. Arthur Meeker, *Chicago, with Love: A Polite and Personal History* (New York: Knopf, 1955), 57–59. Quoted phrase from "Mrs. Field Was There," unidentified newspaper clipping, n.d., loose newspaper clippings, Beveridge Family Papers. One of the Catons' Ottawa neighbors used to send her grandchildren to call on Delia but would not call on her herself (Robert Jordan, personal communication, Ottawa, December 2000).

[32] "Dinner-Giving Increasing in Popularity in Chicago," *Chicago Sunday Tribune*, February 16, 1902; Mme. X, "In Society: The Art of Dinner-Giving," *Chicago Sunday Tribune*, January 16, 1910; "In the Society World: Mrs. Arthur Caton Gives a Dance for Mr. Spencer Eddy," *Chicago Tribune*, December 28, 1898; "Mrs. Arthur Caton's Bal de Tete," *What-To-Eat* [New York], January [15?], 1903; "In the Society World: Young People at First Dinner Dance of the Season," *Chicago Tribune*, December 18, 1901. On Delia's financial status, see "Delia Caton," *Illinois*, vol. 43, p. 252, January 2, 1879, R. G. Dun & Co. Collection.

Prairie Avenue district along with many of their relatives and friends. This was late-nineteenth-century Chicago's most fashionable neighborhood, but when Catherine's parents were married in the early 1870s, its character was still to be formed. Before the fire of 1871, Prairie Avenue was, in Arthur Meeker's words, "little more than a cow-track across sand dunes shaded by cottonwood trees." Amid corn patches stood a few scattered brick houses on bare city blocks.[33]

Soon, however, the neighborhood blossomed into an elegant community. Located along the lakefront less than a mile south of the city, it represented a complete contrast to the bustle, congestion, and grime of downtown. Its wide, clean streets were shaded with rows of beautiful elm trees, behind which rose houses built in an astonishing array of architectural styles. Impressive homes sat behind ornamental stone copings and spiked iron fences, the older houses, made of wood, with their generous verandas; the newer houses, made of stone, looming up massive and severe. Aside from the rumble of trains along the lake—then considered a romantic sound—the atmosphere was soothing and quiet.[34]

The formality of the neighborhood belied its essential intimacy. Behind the imposing facades that lined Calumet, Prairie, and Michigan Avenues lived families connected by a welter of marital, business, and intergenerational ties. In the late 1870s, nearly all the fami-

lies who would matter to Catherine in the years ahead lived nearby. The blocks were crowded with families who, singly or in combination, had made their money in the law, banking, railroads, real estate, stockyards, extractive industries, or newly emerging utilities. Robert Todd Lincoln, the young Robert Allerton, various members of the Armour clan, and the family of Wirt Dexter were among those Catherine and her family saw most frequently. Prairie Avenue was a true elite, insofar as its members were closely connected and powerful not only in business but in government and philanthropy.[35]

On Calumet, the street nearest the lake, the Catons had a regular colony. There, the judge had bought several parcels of land on which to build residences for himself and his family. The home that he and his wife occupied at 1900 Calumet was joined by a large house immediately to the south, designed by Burnham and Root, into which Arthur and Delia moved when they were married. The house at 1910 Calumet was Delia's home for the next quarter century. To the north of Judge Caton's were the homes of Arthur's two sisters—Caroline, who had married prominent attorney Norman

[33] Arthur Meeker, *Prairie Avenue* (New York: A. A. Knopf, 1949), 28; Adeline Hibbard Gregory, *Reminiscences of Lydia Beekman Hibbard* (Chicago: privately printed, 1929), 35.

[34] Arthur Bissell, "The Original Gold Coast," *The Chicagoan*, August 11, August 25, and September 8, 1928; Meeker, *Prairie Avenue*, 28.

[35] Among them were a number of families who would soon move to the north side. Early residence in Prairie Avenue was the foundation of many north-south ties. The Eddys remained close to Mrs. Robert Patterson and Mrs. Robert S. McCormick, the two daughters of Joseph Medill, who grew up on the same block with the Catons. Among the Chicagoans with whom Catherine regularly socialized, only a handful—such as the Potter Palmers, the Bryan Lathrops, and the Deerings—lacked a historical connection to the Prairie Avenue district. The *Chicago Society Directory and Ladies' Visiting and Shopping Guide* (Chicago: Ensign, McClure & Co. and W. B. Keen, Cooke & Co., 1876); *The Bon-Ton Directory* (Chicago: Harris & Morrow, 1879-80); the *Chicago Blue Book* (Chicago: Chicago Directory Co., 1902); "Street and Avenue Guide," *The Lakeside Annual Directory of the City of Chicago...1875–6* (Chicago: Donnelley, Loyd & Co., 1875), 82; George Washington Bromley, *Atlas of the City of Chicago* (Philadelphia: G. W. Bromley & Co., 1891); and Sanborn Map Company, *Insurance Maps of Chicago, Illinois* (Pelham, NY: Sanborn Map Company, 1901-1911), were used to reconstruct where people in the neighborhood lived.

Williams, and Laura, who became the wife of Charles A. Towne.

Just to the south of the Catons on Calumet in the 1870s lived the Joseph Medills and the Levi Leiters. Mrs. Arthur Meeker, whose son would grow up to write a novel about Prairie Avenue, was also a near neighbor. Further down the street lived Mrs. Philip D. Armour (Belle Ogden Armour), whose sister-in-law Mrs. Joseph F. Armour, later the wife of Charles A. Munn, became one of Abby's dearest friends and traveling companions.

The principals of Hibbard, Spencer & Bartlett also settled down in the neighborhood to raise their families. Franklin Spencer's partner William Gold Hibbard, one of the neighborhood's earliest residents, built an expensive Italianate house for his large family at 1701 Prairie. He built other homes nearby for his six daughters and son as they reached their maturity and married. Spencer's younger partner, Augustus Bartlett, moved into the neighborhood a little later, where he lived first at 2222 Calumet before settling down at 2720 South Michigan.

The partners, who had combined so successfully in business, showed their like-mindedness in other domains. Relations among the families

were maintained through decades of cordial and affectionate exchange. Stoked by their commercial success, all three partners cultivated their interest in the arts. Family life was devoted to the careful rearing of children but also to international travel and art collecting. A picture of Will Hibbard late in life, resting at home on a banquette beneath ranges of European paintings acquired in the course of extensive travel, epitomizes the cultured and cosmopolitan style of these families.

The family of Adolphus Bartlett had the strongest cultural proclivities. Adolphus, himself a man of broad professional and philanthropic interests, encouraged his children's artistic interests in a systematic and unapologetic way. Of the four children he had with his first wife, Mary, three became noted art collectors and helped found museums. One of their daughters, Florence Delia Dibell Bartlett, became an avid collector of indigenous art and founded the Museum of International Folk Art in Santa Fe. Another daughter, Maie Bartlett, who married Dwight Bancroft Heard, founded with him the Bartlett Heard Museum in Phoenix, where the Bartletts were early investors in real estate.[37]

The best known of the Bartlett children, however, was artist Frederic Clay Bartlett, who was destined to become one of Catherine's lifelong friends. Frederic, who was Spencer's age, had gone to boarding school with him before going abroad to study art in Munich and Paris. While abroad, Frederic met the first of his three wives, the artistically inclined Dora Tripp of White Plains, New York, and in 1898 they were married. Catherine was very fond of Frederic and Dora, who, while personifying the single-minded pursuit of beauty, remained spontaneous

---

[36] By the time Catherine was grown, the Leiters had moved to Washington, D.C., as had the Munns.

[37] The Bartletts actually had six children, two of whom did not live to maturity. Their fourth adult child was Frank Dickinson Bartlett, who died in 1900 at the age of twenty. Bartlett Gymnasium at the University of Chicago, created in his memory, is adorned on the inside with murals by his artistic brother, Frederic. The first Mrs. Bartlett died in 1890. Adolphus remarried and had one child by his second wife. "Adolphus Clay Bartlett," *Who's Who in Chicago and Illinois* (Chicago: A. N. Marquis, 1911); "Adolphus Clay Bartlett," *National Cyclopedia of American Biography*, vol. 305; "Adolphus Clay Bartlett," *Encyclopaedia of Biography of Illinois* (Chicago: Century Publishing & Engraving Co., 1892-1894); Bartlett Heard Museum Web site, http://www.heard.org/about-history.php.

and fun-loving. By the turn of the century, Frederic had begun to execute the first of the commissions that incorporated his stately murals into Chicago buildings. He and Dora began to plan Dorfred House, the distinctive residence they built for themselves at Twenty-ninth and Prairie. With architect Howard Van Doren Shaw, Frederic and his father also built an elegant country estate, the House in the Woods, which stands on the shore of Lake Geneva. Though Frederic's early career had a pronounced civic and institutional aspect—his work graced such buildings as the Second Presbyterian Church, the University Club, and the Burnham Library of the Art Institute—he reveled in the private use of his talent, creating exuberantly decorated settings and objects for himself and others he knew.[38]

The remarkable family of Hugh Taylor Birch was also very dear to the Eddys. Beyond Catherine's immediate family, few people meant more to her than her friend Helen Birch and Helen's mother, Maria Root Birch, known within the family as "Cousin Mollie." Hugh Taylor Birch was a corporation lawyer who made a second fortune in real estate, and his wife was the first cousin of Abby and Delia. Her father, Francis H. Root of Buffalo, had married Franklin Spencer's sister and given him his start selling Jewett & Root stoves. Growing up in Buffalo, Mollie visited back and forth with Abby and Delia, and on one such trip to Chicago met Hugh Taylor Birch, who in the 1870s was an assistant state's attorney. In 1876, they were married and settled down at 1912 Michigan Avenue, just a few blocks south of the Spencers, in a house Mollie's father had given her as a wedding present. In the succeeding years, Hugh became general counsel of

Standard Oil and used his money to buy large tracts of land along the Florida coast, eventually owning a large section of Fort Lauderdale's beach. An avid naturalist and conservationist, he eventually gave much of this Fort Lauderdale land to the state for use as a park and nature preserve. Similarly, he created an extensive nature preserve around Antioch College, his alma mater, which was founded by a family friend, Horace Mann.[39]

Hugh and Mollie's daughter, Helen, was about Catherine's age. First cousins once removed, Helen and Catherine were like sisters, the fondest of friends from an early age. They were always together in Chicago, and, though both went away a great deal, they met up with each other whenever possible when traveling in Europe. Mollie also had a sister, Ella, whom the Eddys loved, though Ella lived mostly in Europe as an adult.

The Birches were an extremely private family, far more so than the Catons or the Eddys. By 1900 the Birches were probably as wealthy as

[38] Erne R. Frueh and Florence Frueh, "Frederic Clay Bartlett: Chicago Painter and Patron of the Arts," *Chicago History* (Spring 1979), 16–19; "Frederic Clay Bartlett," *National Cyclopedia of American Biography* vol. 43; "Mrs. F. C. Bartlett," *Chicago Tribune*, March 4, 1917; "Mrs. F. C. Bartlett Funeral," *Chicago Daily News*, March 5, 1917; "Daniel J. Tripp," *Westchester News*, April 19, 1886; "Bartlett-Tripp," *Westchester News* [October 5, 1898]; J. Thomas Scharf, *History of Westchester County*, New York, 2 vols. (Philadelphia: L. E. Preston, 1886), 1:588; Isabel McDougall, "An Artist's House," *House Beautiful* 12:4 (September 1902), 199–210; "Some Recent Work of Mr. Howard Shaw," *Architectural Record* 22:6 (December 1907), 421–52; "The New University Club in Chicago," *Architectural Record* 26:1 (July 1909), 1–23; Jayne Rice and Tony Branco, *Reflections of a Legacy: The Bonnet House Story* (Fort Lauderdale, FL: Bonnet House, 1989).

[39] "Hugh Taylor Birch," *New York Times*, January 9, 1943; "Hugh Taylor Birch, 95, Native of Lake County, Dead," *Chicago Tribune*, January 8, 1943; "Hugh Taylor Birch," *Who's Who in Chicago* (Chicago: A. N. Marquis, 1911); Lucy G. Morgan, *The Story of Glen Helen: The Enlarged Campus of Antioch College* (Yellow Springs, OH: Antioch Press, 1931); Maria Root Birch will dated July 10, 1908, docket 137, p. 79, no. 13529, Cook County Circuit Court Archives. Hugh was introduced to the Spencers by the sister of Professor Orton, one of Hugh's teachers at Antioch. William Albert Galloway, *The History of Glen Helen* (Columbus, OH: F. J. Heer, 1932).

Hugh Taylor Birch

Frederick Bartlett and Helen Birch

the Catons, but they lived far more simply. Unlike their cousins, the Birches did not aim for social prominence. Though highly cultured and devoted to cultural philanthropy in Chicago, they spent only a small part of their year there, preferring to stay in Florida or Europe. All three of the Root women—Cousin Mollie, her sister, Cousin Ella, and Mollie's daughter, Helen—were talented, serious, and cultivated. All three had musical gifts that had been carefully nurtured, and all engaged in the arts in serious ways. When Mollie died, she was described as having been "a friend of all struggling artists" and "for many years one of Chicago's leaders in music." As Catherine recalled in a family album, Mollie was "very musical and had studied the piano in Germany. Various members of the [Chicago Symphony] orchestra would come to her house to read chamber music with her—She was gifted and charming." Theodore Thomas, founding conductor of the Chicago Symphony Orchestra, was a personal friend, and Mollie gave liberally to the orchestra. Elsewhere Catherine identifies Mollie as among the patrons who helped the great diva Mary Garden get established.[40]

As for Ella, after a brief unhappy marriage to Methodist bishop John Fletcher Hurst (a much older man whom Ella had married to please her father), she married Theodore Byard, a singer of English nationality well known both in England and on the Continent. Byard owned a villa in Venice, and after their marriage Ella lived abroad, dividing her time between Venice and London and frequenting the musical circles in both cities.[41]

Of Mollie's daughter, Helen, a friend wrote that words could not do justice to the richness and radiance of her personality. "She was

Elizabethan in splendor," wrote the friend, Harriet Monroe, legendary editor of the modernist journal *Poetry*. Like her mother, Helen was an accomplished pianist; before her early death, at age forty-two, she wrote several sonatas and a book of poetry. She remained single into her thirties, when she married Frederic Bartlett, after Dora died in 1917. Though Helen lived only eight years after her marriage, she and Frederic were responsible for two significant cultural achievements. First, on her family's land in Fort Lauderdale, they built the very American Bonnet House, now a historic house museum. Second, they began collecting post-Impressionist art at a time when few Americans perceived its beauty. They eagerly bought canvases by Matisse, Gauguin, Picasso, Van Gogh, and Modigliani. After Helen's death, Frederic gave this collection, including Seurat's *Sunday Afternoon on the Island of La Grande Jatte*, to the Art Institute in her memory. Though little valued at the time, the paintings constituting the Birch-Bartlett collection have come to be regarded as among the greatest the Art Institute owns.[42]

Marshall Field was another Prairie Avenue resident who bore a special relation to the Catons and the Eddys. Field lived at 1905 Prairie Avenue, directly behind Arthur and Delia. There, in an outwardly severe but inwardly opulent house designed by Richard Morris

[40] Catherine's notes on Mollie, Album 2; "Musicians' Friend, Mrs. Birch, Buried," *Chicago Inter Ocean*, July 25, 1913.

[41] "Bishop Hurst Married," *New York Times*, September 6, 1892; "Francis H. Root," *New York Times*, September 8, 1892; "Bishop Hurst Dead," *New York Times*, May 4, 1903; "Theodore Byard Dead," *New York Times*, September 24, 1931.

[42] Harriet Monroe to Frederic Clay Bartlett, May 27, 1927, Album 3; "F. C. Bartlett's Wife, Noted as Musician, Dies," *Chicago Daily Tribune*, October 26, 1925; "Mrs. F. C. Bartlett, Artist's Wife, Dead," *New York Times*, October 26, 1925; *Reflections of a Legacy*; Helen Birch Bartlett, *Capricious Winds*, with an introduction by Janet Fairbank and an appreciation by Harriet Monroe (Boston: Houghton Mifflin, 1927).

Hunt, he lived with a staff of eleven servants. Otherwise, Chicago's wealthiest citizen lived alone. His first marriage, to Nannie Scott, had not been happy; it ended with her death in 1896. Nannie was referred to as an invalid, a designation that sometimes cloaked the reality of mental illness or alcoholism. Her moodiness, with fits of defiance and patent unconventionality, grated on Mr. Field, who liked to maintain a reserved demeanor and strictly decorous life-style. Mrs. Field spent most of her time in Europe beginning in the 1870s; it was there, in the main, that the Fields' two children, Ethel and Marshall Jr., were raised. Whereas Ethel married and settled in England, Marshall Jr. married a Chicago woman and settled down right next door to his father.[43]

In his estranged state, the elder Field spent much of his time with the Catons and became intimate with Delia. After the death of his wife, Field "was almost always in the Caton company, in their box at the opera and horse shows, and traveling with them." Though never acknowledged openly within their social set— for that would have been scandalous—it was understood that Delia and Mr. Field were having an affair. When the young Arthur Meeker asked his mother whether she found it odd that "the woman you looked up to as your leader, married to one man, was generally supposed to be another man's mistress," she responded, "Why, no, dear, we didn't find it odd; we never thought about it at all." The couple scarcely

expected the press to be as accepting, and as early as 1899 they used diversionary tactics to protect their relationship from publicity.[44]

DOMESTIC LIFE

All of this mattered little to Catherine when she was a child. Her days were centered on her family's dear gray house, her colony of dolls, and Salem the cat, the first of many pets that she would own. Her parents' household was cosy and sociable, including not only her mother and father, but her grandparents, Franklin and Rachel Spencer, the family servants, and her brother. There was always companionship and the bustle of activity, even when Spencer went away to school or Abby traveled for the sake of her health. When the charms of the household paled, Catherine found diversion with her best friends, Helen and Adelaide— Adelaide being another neighbor-girl, the daughter of David G. and Mary Kendall Hamilton. Catherine and Helen were often sent out with the coachman, Edward Pender, for rides in the carriage or dressed up in little-girl finery to have their pictures taken.

Catherine went abroad with her family at an early age. A handwritten chronology she drew up in her maturity discloses that she made her first trip to Europe when she was three, traveling with the entire family to Schwalbach, a German spa town that was a favorite of theirs. When Catherine was small, she went to Europe in the fall every third or fourth year, after spending the summer in the East, usually in the Massachusetts resort town of Manchester. Once she reached seventeen, she went to Europe every year. Typically, she and her mother met up in Europe with Delia or with close friends, such as the Dexters or Munns.

---

[43] *Twelfth Census of the United States*, 1900, Schedule No. 1 ("Population"), Illinois, vol. 15, sheet 4, line 34 (Marshall Field residence); Meeker, *Chicago, with Love*, 56–57; see also Arthur Meeker's compassionate fictionalized portrayal of Nannie Field as Corinne Kennerly in *Prairie Avenue*.

[44] Mrs. Field Dies of Pneumonia," *New York Sun*, July 24, 1937; Meeker, *Chicago, with Love*, 59; Abby Eddy to Catherine Eddy, postmarked March 8, 1899, Beveridge Family Papers.

Catherine was taught from an early age to be feminine and pleasing. Abby, an affectionate but watchful mother, reminded Catherine to be thoughtful always. She charged her with small responsibilities around the house and reminded her of her duty to her family. While away on an extended trip in 1889, Abby instructed her eight-year-old daughter to "[b]e a sweet little daughter to your papa; always be ready to go to table with him, and tell Anna to get birds or chicken or beef for him, as he does not like chops, or lamb, or mutton." A few days later Abby reminded her to "[k]eep your hair nicely brushed and never allow your hands to be dirty very long" and to write Spencer "a nice letter once a week so that he will know you are thinking of him." To shape Catherine into a woman who would be a credit to her family was Abby's chief aim.[45]

The lifestyle of the Eddys and Catons, though offering many pleasures, was not an easy regimen to maintain. Behind the outward show of ease and fashion lay a world of work and responsibility. Abby's letters show her to be a diligent head of house, attentive to the innumerable details that running a large turn-of-the-century establishment entailed. She was eager to transmit an understanding of these duties to her daughter. Seeing that all the household goods were properly cared for; superintending the arrangement and decoration of the rooms; having her own clothes and those of everyone else in the house brought constantly up to date; seeing to the marketing, cooking, and cleaning; and making sure that the servants were properly trained and cared for was a demanding, full-time occupation. As Abby's health began to fail when Catherine reached adulthood, Abby tried all the harder to teach Catherine everything

she knew. By the time Catherine reached her mid-twenties, she was running the large household at 1910 Calumet Avenue.

Though highly dependent on her servants, Abby was a woman of liberality who was sensitive to their needs. In her letters to Catherine regarding household management, Abby urged Catherine to learn all she could about her servants' work. She pressed her to spend time in the kitchen, laundry, sewing room, and nursery, familiarizing herself with the attendant chores. Abby encouraged Catherine to be personally involved with her servants, making sure they were given things that would make them feel well cared for. The valuable nurse Miss Hayes was to be given plenty of time off to ride out in the carriage, for example, and the servants' kitchen outfitted so that its occupants would find it a pleasant place to read.[46]

Although the 1900 census records establish that the Eddys had two maids, Jenny Byrne and Delia McGarry, and a coachman, Peter Rasmusen, the reality was more complicated. This permanent staff was supplemented by an ever-shifting cast of characters. Because Abby and Delia were so close, and their lives were so intertwined, they were constantly sharing goods, houses, and servants. Delia maintained a large staff, including several English menservants, whom she was always eager to retain. Accordingly, when Delia closed up her house to go east or to Europe, a major reshuffling of

[45] Abby Eddy to Catherine Eddy, from New York, [Spring 1890], Beveridge Family Papers.

[46] Abby Eddy to Catherine Eddy, October 16, 1908, and October 18, 1908, Beveridge Family Papers. Abby's most trusted servants, Jenny Byrne and Delia McGarry, received bequests of $2,500 in her will, which instructed family members to employ and care for the two women for the rest of their lives. Abby Eddy, last will and testament dated October 15, 1907, docket 106, p. 130, record no. 47-8848, Cook County Circuit Court Archives, Chicago.

her staff ensued. Her belongings were packed up for transatlantic shipment under the supervision of her head butler, Churchill. One summer she sailed for Europe with 160 crates of belongings (exclusive of her wardrobe), her maid, a valet, and a car. Maids and menservants left behind were taken up into the Eddys' household or left to tend the Chicago house.[47]

Indeed, Delia's wealth and involvement in her sister's family compensated for and disguised the Eddys' more modest financial position, for her willingness to share extended beyond menservants to money. The disparity between Delia's position and that of the Eddys was not always evident to outsiders, particularly those they met while traveling. Public perceptions of the Eddys' wealth varied, with some journalists describing them as immensely wealthy and others more astutely adjudging them well-off. The most accurate assessment was that of a journalist who wrote that they were "not enormously rich, but moderately so." Certainly many of their friends were wealthier. Yet the perception that Catherine came from "one of the most exclusive and wealthiest families in Chicago" was valid, considering the solidarity that existed between Delia and Abby, Catherine's status as Delia's favorite niece, and the resources at Delia's disposal, especially after her 1905 marriage to Marshall Field.[48]

Although Franklin Spencer's death had left Abby a wealthy woman, finances were for her a constant worry. From the time of her father's death (1890) until her own in 1909, Abby lost roughly $1 million (about $15 million in present-day terms) through a combination of bad management and overspending. Too ignorant and passive to watch over her own wealth, Abby had entrusted the management of her estate

and at least part of its principal, to her husband. When he used her money to go into business, the enterprise languished, and by 1899 Abby was seriously alarmed. Meanwhile, the showy and ambitious lifestyle Abby insisted on for her children was producing results that were worrisome. Of particular concern was Spencer, who, as a single twenty-nine-year-old, was incapable of living within his means, even though, when all sources were taken into account, his income was equivalent to about $92,000 in present-day terms. (There was of course no income tax at the time.) Abby expected Catherine to spare herself anguish by marrying well and managing her money more wisely than her mother had done. Begin at once, Abby admonished Catherine when she was eighteen, "to learn all you can about the business of caring for your money . . . keep your books yourself and take [a] regular course of instruction from some one so you will not be the ignorant person I was." Above all, Abby warned, "never give your money to your husband [or] brother . . . never lend to your relations. . . . Never give your principal to [your] husband for any scheme whatever." Abby urged Catherine to seek the advice of the best authorities in order to acquire a competence in business. It was a big burden for so young a girl.[49]

[47] *Twelfth Census of the United States,* (1900), Schedule No. 1 ("Population"), Illinois, vol. 15, sheet 5, line 97 (Augustus Eddy residence); Abby Eddy to Catherine Eddy, September 15, 1908, and September 17, 1908, Beveridge Family Papers.

[48] Assessments of the Eddys' wealth appeared in the news coverage of Catherine's engagement. See "Senator Beveridge Wins Social Leader and Heiress to Millions," *Indianapolis Star,* June 23, 1907; "Miss Catherine Eddy, Chicago Girl, May Become Mistress of White House," unidentified Chicago newspaper, June 17, 1907, loose newspaper clippings, Beveridge Family Papers; "Beveridge-Eddy Wedding in Fall," *New York World,* June 18, 1907; "Miss Eddy Well Known in Paris," *New York World,* June 23, 1907.

[49] Abby left an estate of $500,000 (about $7 million in today's dollars). She neither mentioned her husband in her will nor left him even a tiny sum. See Abby Eddy, last will and testament, cited above; Augustus Eddy to Delia Caton, May 8, 1903, and Abby Eddy to Catherine Eddy, March 14, 1899, Beveridge Family Papers.

EDUCATION

Though Catherine and Spencer were both carefully educated, their educations had almost nothing in common. Spencer's education was conventional for an upper-class male at the time: educated by a private tutor until he was eleven or twelve, he was then sent to St. Paul's School in Concord, New Hampshire, where he studied for three years, until 1888. He then traveled abroad with his family, studying under a tutor in Berlin and attending the University of Heidelberg. Returning to the states, he entered Harvard, where he rowed and played football, was popular, and made some important friends. He did not apply himself to his work, however. His academic record was scandalously bad. Grades of E and F abounded in his transcript. Only in German did he make a creditable showing, and even there, despite his time in Germany, he earned only a B. His grades were so low that he was twice put on probation. He graduated belatedly in 1896, though belonging to the class of 1895.[50]

Poor grades didn't prevent Spencer's career from getting off to an auspicious start. Returning to Chicago in the fall of 1896, he began working in the family firm and joined the Chicago Club and the Saddle and Cycle. In mid-1897, he went east hoping to obtain a position in the diplomatic corps as private secretary to Horace Porter, who had been appointed ambassador to France. Spencer had strong recommendations, but Porter had a young friend in mind—T. Edgar Scott of Philadelphia—to whom he gave the post instead. Spencer then went to Washington in the hope of being hired by John Hay, ambassador designate to the Court of St. James, with whom Spencer was slightly acquainted. Hay hired him on the spot, and Spencer sailed for England before April was out. He served as private secretary throughout Hay's relatively short stint as American ambassador, accompanying the Hay family and Henry Adams on a six-week trip to Egypt in 1898 and returning to Washington with Hay when he was appointed secretary of state. Having made a powerful friend and proved his fitness for the work, Spencer was appointed third secretary of the American embassy in London early in 1899.[51]

There is little doubt that the profession of diplomacy suited Spencer's urbane, mannered, and cosmopolitan upbringing. He was highly social and charming, to old and young alike. The dyspeptic Henry Adams, who, being thirty-five years Spencer's senior, regarded him as "a young man to play with," mentioned him frequently in letters to Elizabeth Cameron around this time. To Catherine, Spencer was a solicitous and affectionate older brother, writing her charming notes to distract her from boredom and seasickness during an Atlantic crossing when she was a teen. Knowing she was prone to both, Spencer wrote a series of notes to be opened on each day of her eight-day journey. Each tells a story of the mythological character for whom the day was named. In the letter for Wednesday, for example, Spencer amusingly recounts how "Wuodan or Odin," for whom the day was named, "swooped down on a dinner party in the shape of an eagle or gull and carried off all the champagne—only in those days they

[50] "Spencer Eddy Dies; Former Diplomat," *New York Times*, October 8, 1939; "Spencer Eddy Dies Here at 65; U.S. Ex-Minister," *New York Herald*, October 8, 1939; "Spencer Fayette Eddy," *National Cyclopedia of American Biography*, vol. 31; "Spencer Eddy Wedded to Lurline Spreckels," *Chicago Record-Herald*, April 27, 1906; Spencer Eddy grade record (UAIII15.75.10) and alumni record from Quinquennial File, Harvard University Archives. Spencer is depicted as "Wolcott the Magnificent" in Charles Macomb Flandrau's novel *Harvard Stories* (Boston: Copeland and Day, 1897).

[51] "Is Secretary to Ambassador Hay," *Chicago Times-Herald*, April 15, 1897; "Spencer F. Eddy Prepares to Go," *Chicago Tribune*, April 16, 1897; unpublished memoir of Elsie Porter Mende, Beveridge Family Papers.

called it mead. So if you see a gull today you can imagine that it is Odin who is going to carry off your lemonade…." Spencer's urbanity endeared him to members of the Russian imperial family and the cream of English society. His mother and aunt used Spencer's extensive connections not only to advance their social ambitions but to further the glorious plans they had for Catherine.[52]

Catherine's education was idiosyncratic. It differed not only from Spencer's but from that of most other girls she knew. Whereas Adelaide and her other friends were sent to East Coast girls' schools once they had reached a certain age, Catherine, who continued her studies until she was in her twenties, remained with her mother and aunt and was schooled almost entirely by private teachers. Her education reflected a determination on the part of her mother and aunt to mold her into a certain type of woman. The sort of cultivation she received, though unusual and seemingly informal, was very seriously undertaken. The object was not so much to endow Catherine with a specific body of knowledge as to form her character and personality. Information was necessary, but only in relation to an overriding object, which was to fit her to take up a social role—to be an admired hostess and to move comfortably in cosmopolitan society. Extensive foreign travel, observation, and personal instruction from her mother and aunt were, perhaps, just as important a part of her education as the formal instruction she received from an impressive group of paid companions and teachers.[53]

Her studies focused mainly on literature and history and on mastering foreign languages. Stimulated no doubt by the sites she visited during her travels, she had from an early age a keen interest in European history, especially in romantic tales of religion and nobility. From years of sightseeing and concertgoing, she developed an appreciation of fine architecture, painting, and music. Whenever she was in Paris, she went about under the protection of a paid companion, Mlle. Cognier, who presumably instructed her in French culture as well as manners. The few other teachers whose names are known to us were impressive characters. Among them was Robert Herrick, a young English professor at the University of Chicago just beginning his career as a novelist. Another, a German noblewoman named Frudy von Moewis, was a learned spinster whose father who had sat in Bismarck's cabinet. She was a companion to the daughters of several distinguished families. With her, Catherine traveled throughout Italy and Greece, absorbing what von Moewis had to say about ancient art and archaeology. The two spent a winter in New York City, attending the theater and lectures at Columbia University. In the winter of 1899, Catherine studied at Dieudonne—presumably in France or Switzerland. In 1901, she was still receiving weekly formal instruction in French,

---

[52] *The Letters of Henry Adams*, ed. by J. C. Levenson, et al., 6 vols. (Cambridge, Mass.: Belknap Press of Harvard University Press, 1982-1988), 4:734.

[53] If Quenzel's observations on the education of upper-class Chicago girls are correct ("'Society,'" 178–80), the education Catherine received was exceptional. Many of Catherine's friends and acquaintances went to Dobbs; Adelaide attended Miss Porter's (*Directory of the Misses Masters School*, 1877-1907 [Dobbs Ferry, NY: privately printed, 1907]; "Mrs. Edwin W. Ryerson," *Who's Who in Chicago* [Chicago: A. N. Marquis, 1950]). The Hibbard girls, slightly older than Catherine, were educated at Mr. and Mrs. Henry Babcock's School on Eighteenth Street, between Prairie Avenue and Lake Michigan, the Babcocks being "clever Boston people" (Gregory, *Reminiscences*, 65). Catherine's education was more similar to the education Consuelo Vanderbilt described as receiving; see Vanderbilt, *The Glitter and the Gold* (New York: Harper and Brothers, 1952). Mrs. Leiter's education of her daughters, who used to live in Prairie Avenue, may have served as a model for Delia and Abby.

German, and Italian, though by this time she was certainly fluent in German. In news coverage of her engagement in 1905, she was described as "a linguist of rare ability."[54]

The absence of formal schooling may have made her a trifle less sure of herself, for she considered herself shy, but it did not stunt her intellectual curiosity or analytic ability. On the contrary, she was strongly oriented to the world around her and passionately interested in new ideas and theories in virtually any field. In conversation she was bright, amusing, and quick, and she had a host of friends, both men and women in Chicago and on the East Coast, by the time she was twenty.

Because Catherine remained under the watchful protection of her mother and aunt, their influence over her was unusually strong. To the end of her days, she worshipped her mother and adored her aunt, greatly respecting their authority. When her mother and aunt began grooming her in her mid-teens for introduction into the aristocratic societies of Europe, Catherine seemed ready enough to obey. Seizing on the opportunity that Spencer's diplomatic position at London created, Abby arranged in 1898 to have her very young daughter presented at the Court of St. James. It was the beginning of Abby's assault on European aristocracy, a campaign in which, it seemed to one observer, Catherine "bowed before almost every sovereign in Europe."[55] That Abby may have been overeager Catherine acknowledged later in life, when, in

an autobiographical fragment, she reflected on her first odd yet magical presentation at the Court of St. James.

The decision to allow me to be presented was not a wise one. I was far too young, not yet seventeen. I had just been in school at Dieudonne, and had two winters of lessons ahead of me before "coming out" in Chicago. My hair was still in a braid. The reason that prompted my mother to permit it was that it offered the unusual chance of [my] being presented in the Diplomatic Corps and going to court with Spencer. She had thought of being presented herself, but that would have meant my father's presentation at a levee, and he, of course, was in America.

In Paris that April the first thought was to put me into grown-up clothes—but not too many of them, as I would not, because of my extreme youth, go to many parties in London. Worth made my presentation gown. It was heavy white satin, with flounces of white tulle held up by bunches of small white roses. The long white satin court train was fastened at the shoulders. At the first fitting old Mr. Worth came in and said that as I had pretty shoulders he would advise cutting the dress with a Second Empire décolletage. I was slender, but my delicately covered ribs were laced into a tight boned bodice. Mademoiselle Thérèse, Worth's greatest fitter, and Madame Bond, the first vendeuse, did the dress together.

Then came the question of my hair. It was long and heavy and had never been put up. Auguste Petit himself came to do it, and experiments were made. It was finally decided to put it in a knot at the back of my head, and the hair in front was arranged very stiffly

[54] "Books in Old Nursery," typescript, June 1953 (Beveridge Family Papers). Catherine writes of Mr. Herrick, Mlle. Cognier, and Miss von Moewis in her memoir, while her language lessons and studies in New York are documented in her 1901 engagement calendar and her correspondence. Her linguistic abilities are noted in "Beveridge To Meet Fiancee," *New York Press*, June 17, 1907.

[55] "The Whirl of Society," *Chicago Inter Ocean*, June 18, 1907.

Spencer and Catherine at the Court of St. James

(as can be seen in the photographs). It was impossible for me to do it myself, and when we arrived in London a French coiffeur who had been instructed by a letter and drawings by Mr. Auguste, came every day to coif me. We stayed at Brown's hotel in Dover Street.

I do not remember the date of our arrival in London, but the Drawing room took place May 13, 1898. The Princess of Wales ([later] Queen Alexandra), "owing to a cold in her eye," did not hold the Drawing room.[56] *Her place was taken by the Princess Christian of Schleswig Holstein. In my diary I wrote, "Spencer came for me in a carriage at 2:15. The coachman and footman wore the Ambassadorial cockade, and little bunches of carnation and lily-of-the-valley. My bouquet was lily-of-the-valley and white rose noisette. Spencer wore court costume, which consisted of silk knee breeches and a full dress coat. He stuck his stockinged legs into a corner of the carriage to give my dress room and carried his hat. We had a diplomatic pass and did not have to stay in line, but drove directly to Buckingham Palace to the ambassadors' entrance.*

"Spencer said, 'Do you realize where you are?' But I was not a bit nervous. In the cloak room I joined Mrs. Hay and Helen, and when we had left our capes we met Mr. White [the first secretary of the American embassy] and went toward the state rooms....

"The women not presented in the Diplomatic Corps were penned in a room that we passed.... It looked, with the sun coming in the windows, like a bed of flaunting phlox and peonies. Out in the court yard the red coats of the soldiers

brightened the dark, grim walls. The First Life Guards and the First Battalion Coldstream Guard were there in all their glory.

"At the entrance to the room where we were to assemble we were met by Sir William Colville [the Master of Ceremonies], who escorted us in. Helen at once asked him if he would 'canter me over the course,' so I was shown where the Princess would stand. Then I was introduced by Helen to various diplomats as they gathered. Finally Mrs. Hay beckoned me to come and be presented to the Duchess of Devonshire. She was dressed in black and blazing in diamonds. She was very cordial and friendly to us. At last the clock struck three and we were told to stand in line. First came the Duchess of Devonshire, then the Turkish Ambassadress, Mrs. Hay, Catherine Eddy, Helen Hay, the wife of the Danish minister, and someone she was presenting.

"The Duchess of Devonshire started across the adjoining room, two men easing her train as she did so, and spreading it out behind her. Then Mme. Anthropoulo Pasha [the Turkish ambassadress] and Mrs. Hay. As soon as the latter's train was moving I placed myself at the door, and off I went. At the door of the Throne room I made a deep curtsey, and then Mrs. Hay made a motion for me to come forward towards the Princess. I heard her say 'Miss Catherine Eddy,' and to my utter amazement Princess Christian held out her hand to me, something for which I had not been prepared. I took it and made a low curtsey as I did so. Then on to the Duchess of York (later Queen Mary), and another to Princess Victoria of Schleswig Holstein. Then came the Prince of Wales (later King Edward VII). I went down very low to him and then to the Duke of York

---

[56] The queen, Victoria, would not have appeared at a drawing room at this stage of her life. She had withdrawn from society decades earlier following the death of her husband, Prince Albert.

(later King George V). My train was thrown across my arm, and I stood with Helen behind Mrs. Hay, and the Turkish Ambassadress. One by one we saw the English ladies pass by. Some of them looked very pale. They were often mixed up in their trains, gave little rips to their skirts as they went sideways, and walked awkwardly into the arms of Sir Ponsonby Fane [another court functionary], who turned them gently around and set them off in the right direction. The most noticeable women presented were Lady William Beresford, Miss Joan Wilson and Margot Asquith. When it was over the royalties bowed to us and withdrew. At Mrs. Hay's we had tea, but I did not stay long...."

But the great moment for me was the ball at Buckingham Palace, where "I had as good a time as I could have at a state function." Again I went with Spencer in a carriage with footman and Ambassadorial cockades, and "the guards presented arms as we drove to the special entrance." I wore the same dress in which I had been presented, but, of course, without the train. When we arrived "the Hays had not yet come, and I left my cape and followed Spencer toward the great ball room. At the entrance we met the military and naval attaches, and in some manner whip went a tulle ruffle on my skirt, and I had to return to the dressing room and have it sewed. During the process in came Mrs. Hay, Alice and Helen, and I went back to the ball room with them. Mr. Carter [the second secretary of the American embassy] met us and told us that I could not sit with the daughters of Ambassadors, but at that moment dear old Sir William came up and squeezed me in beside Alice Hay.

"The ballroom is longer than square and absolutely magnificent, without a tinge of garishness. At one end were the musicians and at the other the platform for Royalties. On either side of this platform were tiers of seats, one for the diplomatic corps, the other for British Duchesses. At a quarter past eleven the Prince and Princess of Wales came in, and with them the Dukes of Cambridge and Connaught, The Princess Christian and their suites. Then the music began—a waltz. I danced first with Spencer then with Mr. Carter, with whom I later went to supper. In the Square dances Spencer was asked to dance with Alice Hay, but she did not want to try it for some reason. Three Americans were asked to dance and not a single Spaniard! While we were in the supper room (the famous room that contains the gold plate) I stood with Alice by Mrs. Hay. The princess of Wales came up and shook hands with us, and chatted for some time.... Coming out I met the Vicomte de Brier, who thought I was a Russian, and regretted he couldn't dance because his shoes didn't fit! I talked for some time with M'lle de Gana, and that's all I want to say about myself at the ball. As a spectacle, it was the most beautiful I have ever seen—an indescribable blending of gold and lights, uniforms, dresses and jewels. An emotion filled my heart and I longed to live that life I saw for a brief moment around me."

One afternoon I went to tea at the Embassy, and met Mr. Henry James. He took a fancy to me, and we had a little talk together. He said, "When will you be going out?"—meaning [to] the American colonies. But I, of course, did not understand and said, "Oh, I shan't be coming out for another two years." He was very amused. After tea he suggested that we take a

walk in the park. Helen went too, and I wish I
could remember our conversation. Afterward
Mr. Hay said that I was the original of the
young girl in The Awkward Age.[57]

*I was in an atmosphere extremely Anglophile.
An alliance of Great Britain and the United
States was the solution of all world problems.
The Spanish-American war was at its height.
Less than two weeks before my presentation
Dewey had won the battle of Manila Bay.
Imperialism was in the air. All young men read
Kipling to stir their hearts, and Swinburne in
their romantic moments…. While we were in
London Gladstone died, and I wrote in my diary,
"Gladstone is dead, and the war goes on."*

While in London, Catherine furtively consulted
a well-known fortune-teller, going off "secretly
as I knew my mother would disapprove." The
fortune-teller predicted that Catherine would
have a chance to marry at twenty-two but
advised her to forego the opportunity. Instead,
Catherine recalled, "I should wait until
between the ages of twenty-four and twenty-six
when I could make a brilliant match and be
happy." It proved to be an uncanny précis of
Catherine's romantic future.

In December 1900, Catherine was formally
introduced to Chicago society, after being feted
at one of her aunt's most sumptuous dinner
parties. Following her debut, Catherine found
a great world opening all about her. In 1901,
she spent New Year's at Cannes, where she
and Spencer were the guests of his great friend
the Grand Duke Michael of Russia, second
cousin to Czar Nicholas, and the duke's wife,
Countess Torby. Later that year Catherine

traveled to The Hague with her friend Elsie
Porter, daughter of Horace Porter, U.S. ambas-
sador to France, to witness the wedding of
Queen Wilhelmina to Hertzog Hendrick von
Mecklenburg.

Thus, on the eve of 1902, Catherine was a
beautiful twenty-one-year-old woman—at home
in many of the world's great cities, protected by
a loving brother, and in command of several
languages—who had yet to come to terms with
her marital future.

Notes

This essay draws on a wide range of materials,
including a collection of papers in the possession of the Beveridge family that will be
donated to Chicago's Newberry Library. The
Beveridge Family Papers consist of several types
of material. First, there are three large annotated
albums in which Catherine kept newspaper
clippings, photographs, letters, and other
ephemera pertaining to her family. In citing
from the albums' newspaper clippings, we have
offered the fullest possible citation, though in
some cases it has not been possible to determine
the name of the newspaper or date of publication. In such cases, the album number is given,
and publication details in brackets represent
our best guess at missing information.

In addition to the albums, Catherine preserved
her 1901 engagement book, a family register,
and a small body of correspondence, consisting
primarily of letters her mother wrote her.
A body of loose newspaper clippings, dealing
mainly with Catherine's engagement, is also
part of the collection and is cited here.

[57] In the manuscript Catherine added "but that was nonsense,
of course." On second thought she crossed the phrase out.

Catherine at age sixteen

DRAMATIS PERSONAE

Page references are in grey numerals.

d'Abruzzi, Duke Luigi Amadeo (1873–1933), cousin of the king of Italy. He was venturesome, brave, and good-looking. Born in Madrid, he was the third son of Amadeo, king of Spain (1870–73). By his early thirties, the Duke d'Abruzzi had earned a reputation as an explorer of Africa and the Arctic. In 1899, he and a team explored Franz Josef Land and set a new record for attaining a northernmost point. He was the first to ascend Africa's Mount Ruwenzori. He served as commander in chief of the Italian navy during World War I and died in Italian Somalia. 166

Adam, Robert (1728–92), and James (1758?–94), brothers, were famous for reintroducing classical motifs into furniture design in the late eighteenth century. Their work challenged the Chinese, Gothic, and Rococo elements of the Chippendale style and laid the ground for the work of Hepplewhite and Sheraton. 67, 131

Adams, Henry (1838–1918), one of the leading intellectuals of his time. The Hay-Adams house, a famous double house on Lafayette Square in Washington, D.C., designed by H. H. Richardson, was home to Adams and his friend John Hay. Catherine's brother was well acquainted with Adams, the two having traveled with the Hay family to Egypt several years earlier. 78–9, 138, 139

Aldis, Arthur Taylor (1861–1933), a dapper real estate developer, clubman, and arts patron. He was involved in the development of some of Chicago's earliest skyscrapers. He was also one of the guiding spirits of Lake Forest, which was just emerging as a leading haunt of the wealthy. He was instrumental in the design of the town center, and was active in its cultural life. He was not only involved with the hunt, but soon established and acclaimed playhouse, known as the Little Theater, with his wife Mary on their Lake Forest estate. He was known for his generosity toward artists, many of whom he aided personally. The Aldis's son Owen, became a leading civil-rights activist. 48

Aldrich, Nelson Wilmarth (1841–1915), of Rhode Island was one of the Senate's most powerful members, who seldom spoke on the floor. He was moved to speak out angrily against Beveridge's support of Roosevelt's request for four battleships instead of the two the GOP Republican leadership wanted. It was a speech "of studied insult," according to Beveridge's biographer Claude Bowers, behavior that to observers like Catherine betokened vulnerability. 170

Allerton, Robert (1873–1964), of Chicago, only son of Samuel Waters and Pamilla Thompson Allerton, was an influential patron of the Art Institute and the Lyric Opera. He lavished his attention on a ten-thousand-acre estate outside Champaign, about 150 miles south of Chicago, where he built a forty-room mansion and a magnificent landscaped park, with statuary and formal gardens. Deeply interested in sculpture and landscape design, Allerton later bought a large parcel of land on the Hawaiian island of Kauai, where he created the park that is now Pacific Tropical Botanical Garden. 68, 74, 98, 155

Allison, William Boyd (1829–1908), of Iowa was a leader of the conservative Republicans in the Senate. Elected partly because he satisfied the powerful railroad interests in his state, Allison was a genius at building and maintaining unity among Republicans during his long tenure, which stretched from 1873 to 1908. 74

Ames, Butler (1871–1954), of Massachusetts was just beginning the first of five terms in the U.S. House of Representatives at the time he appears in the diary. He was a grandson of Massachusetts congressman and civil war general Benjamin F. Butler and son of Adelbert Ames, who during Reconstruction had served as governor of and senator from Mississippi. Ames, who earned an engineering degree from MIT, was an officer and engineer in the Spanish-American War. 57, 117–8, 120, 138–9, 145, 163

Anderson, Larz (1866–1937), sometime diplomat and cosmopolite, was a great-grandson of Nicholas Longworth of Ohio. When not engaged in some diplomatic mission, Anderson devoted himself to the cause of civilization and culture. During World War I he was active in relief work, and in 1912–13 he was U.S. ambassador to Japan. His wife, Isabel Weld Perkins (1876–1948), of Boston, was a writer. They built an imposing house on Massachusetts Avenue — today the home of the Society of the Cincinnati. 117

Anderson, Mary (1859–1940), was one of the most celebrated actresses of her generation. Achieving fame for her portrayal of Shakespeare's Juliet when in her teens, she went on to perform a wide range of roles, winning acclaim in both America and England. At age thirty, she ended her career to marry Antonio de Navarro (1860–1932), a wealthy New Yorker of Spanish descent. The couple moved to Broadway, remaining there for the rest of their lives. Mary occasionally returned to the stage for the benefit of war relief during World War I. 36

Angell, James Burrill (1829–1916), a former diplomat, was president of the University of Michigan from 1871 to 1909. 172

d'Arcos, Duke, Jose Brunetti Gayoso and his wife, American-born Virginia Woodbury Lowery Brunetti (c1854–1934). Duchess d'Arcos was the daughter of A.H. Lowery and sister of Woodbury Lowery. She was a noted art collector and made significant gifts to the National Gallery of Art in Washington and the Prado in Madrid. 101

Armour, Allison Vincent (1863–1941), from Chicago, was a noted yachtsman and friend of scientific exploration. After graduating from Yale in 1884, he spent most of his time on his yacht, the *Utowana*, which he raced in transatlantic contests (he won the King Edward VII Coronation Cup), sailed to far-flung and inaccessible parts of the world, and placed at the service of scientific and archaeological teams. His enthusiasm for yachting was the basis of his friendship with the kaiser, who received him whenever Armour happened to be in Berlin. Armour was also recognized for his role in introducing new plant species into the United States. 37

Armour, George Allison (ca. 1856–1936), brother of Allison Vincent, was likewise a man of leisure, but his particular passion was book collecting. (He owned Keats's personally annotated copy of Shakespeare's works, among other gems.) An alumnus of Princeton and a long-time resident of the town, Armour left his library to that university. 37

Armour, Malvina Belle ("Belle") Ogden (1842–1927), was the widow of Philip Danforth Armour. In her day, she was a famous beauty. 114

Astor, Caroline Schermerhorn (1830–1908), wife of William B. Astor, dominated New York society in the final decades of the nineteenth century. With Ward McAllister, she determined who were the best people in society, the so-called 400. Mrs. Astor lived in a mansion on Fifth Avenue for many years, but in the 1890s she had built and moved to an opulent residence overlooking Central Park. This is the house to which Catherine refers. 95

Bacon, Robert (1860–1919), assistant secretary of state, and his wife, Martha Waldron Cowdin Bacon (d. 1940). A Harvard graduate and one of the outstanding college athletes of his time, Bacon was, before 1903, a partner of J. P. Morgan, on whose behalf he undertook large and sensitive dealings with the government and others. He was later acting secretary of state and ambassador to France (1909–12). 161, 172

Bailly-Blanchard, Arthur (1855–1925), of New Orleans was educated at Paris and Dresden. He dabbled in journalism before choosing diplomacy. In 1901 he was made second secretary of the American embassy in Paris, becoming secretary in 1909. He was later envoy extraordinary and minister plenipotentiary to Haiti. 121

Barker, Rear Admiral Albert Smith (1843–1916), prior to his retirement in 1905, was commander in chief of the North Atlantic fleet. His wife was Ellen (Blackmar) Maxwell, whom he married in 1894. 162

Barrymore, Ethyl (1878–1959), a member of the theatrical Barrymore/Drew families. She scored her first success in William Gillette's production of *Secret Service* (1897) . Her best known Broadway roles were in Somerset Maugham's *The Constant Wife* (1926)and Emlyn Williams's *The Corn is Green* (1940). She won the Academy award for supporting actress in *None But the Lonely Heart* (1944). 59, 67

Barth, Theodor (1849–1909), a German politician, was a liberal deputy in the Reichstag. 27

Bartlett, Adolphus Clay (1844–1922), of Chicago was a partner of Catherine's late grandfather, Franklin Spencer, in the hardware firm of Hibbard, Spencer & Bartlett; *see* "Catherine's family." His wealth enabled his children to study abroad and cultivate their interest in art. 40, 79, 86

Bartlett, Evelyn Fortune (1887–1997), of Indianapolis, whom Frederic Bartlett married in 1931. Frederic was twice a widower, his first wife, Dora Tripp, dying in 1913, his second, Helen Birch, dying in 1925. Evelyn was the ex-wife of pharmaceutical manufacturer Eli Lilly (1885–1977), from whom she was divorced around 1927. Catherine, who once described herself as "the best friend of each of Frederic Bartlett's three wives," had encouraged the match, admiring Evelyn's considerable artistic talents and realizing that Frederic was lonely after Helen's death. 83n

Bartlett, Florence Dibell (1881–1954), sister of Frederic, became an art collector. She founded the Museum of International Folk Art in Santa Fe, New Mexico, and contributed to the textile collections of the Art Institute, where she was an honorary governing member. Florence, who did not marry, remained very close to Frederic and committed suicide soon after his death. 87

Bartlett, Frederick Clay (1873–1953), was Catherine's closest life-long male friend and the son of Adolphus Bartlett. After receiving an education in preparatory schools through the age of eighteen, he left to study art in Europe, graduating from the Royal Academy of Art in Munich and completing his studies with James Abbott McNeill Whistler. He returned to Chicago and opened a studio specializing in murals. His works may be found in the Second and Fourth Presbyterian Churches, the University Club, City Council Chamber, and Burnham Library of the Art Institute, all in Chicago. His most enduring legacy is the Birch-Bartlett collection of post-Impressionist paintings that he and his second wife, Helen, gave to the Art Institute in 1925.

Frederic retired from accepting commissions in the early 1930s and devoted his talents and energies to his homes in Fort Lauderdale, Florida, and Beverly, Massachusetts. Bartlett's Fort Lauderdale residence, Bonnet House, is open to the public.

The home of Frederic and his first wife, Dora, which Catherine refers to in the diary, named Dorfred House, was considered rather un-American. It had no veranda, or flower beds. It did not open itself up to the public, but kept aloof from neighbors with a

wall that, while low, was definite. Inside the house was secretive, its peculiarly proportioned rooms and unexpected passageways creating many places to hide and be private, many routes to travel without being seen. The rooms were sparingly but gorgeously furnished, reflecting Frederic's passions and eccentricities. 40, 58–9, 74, 83, 87, 96, 98, 115, 131, 155, 163, 179, 181

Beale, William Gerrish (1854–1923), a prominent Chicago lawyer, was a principal in the firm of Isham, Lincoln, & Beale. His wife was the former Emily Caruthers, whom he married in 1904. Beale drafted Marshall Field's controversial will and, as a joint trustee of Joseph Medill's estate, controlled the *Chicago Tribune* with Medill's two daughters, Eleanor Medill Patterson and Katherine Medill. McCormick. 109

de Béarn, Prince Henri Galard, also prince of Chalais, was the son of Gaston de Galard de Béarn, a French nobleman. In 1902, Henri was attaché to the French embassy in Washington. Later in the year he was attached to the French embassy in St. Petersburg. He married Beatrice Winans of Baltimore. 89

Beatty, Ethel Field (1873–1932), Marshall Field's only daughter, was the wife of British naval officer David Beatty (1871–1936). She married Beatty in 1901 after her first marriage ended in divorce. At thirty-four, David Beatty was already recognized as a fearless and formidable naval officer. He had played a noteworthy part in Kitchener's expedition in the Sudan and fought courageously in the Boxer Rebellion. He attained the rank of captain in 1900 at age twenty-nine, when the average age at promotion to that rank was forty-three. He was a rear admiral by age thirty-nine and later achieved glory as the hero of Jutland. He and Ethel were popular in society and enjoyed the friendship of Edward VII. 104, 116, 121, 127–9, 144–5

Beaumont, Henry Hamond Dawson (1867–1949), later Sir Henry, was second secretary of the British legation at Petersburg from November 1900 until December 1905. He was later envoy extraordinary and minister plenipotentiary to Venezuela (1916–23). 100

Bebel, August (1840–1913), a leading German socialist, came from a modest background and for many years while sitting in the Reichstag supported himself by practicing his trade as a wood turner. 27

Bell, Brigadier General James Franklin, (1856–1919), army chief of staff (1906–19), and his wife, Sarah Buford Bell. Bell was known for introducing innovations into the army's organization and methods of training, as well as for his ruthless leadership of American antiguerrilla forces in the northern Philippines. 162

Bellas, Emma Foote, was Delia's close friend and neighbor. She was the widow of Thomas Huey Bellas (1845–1902) and sister of Mrs. George Allison Armour. Her brother, Erastus Foote, was an iron manufacturer. Her daughter, Emmeline, was Catherine's friend. 96

Belloselsky-Belozersky, Constanin Hespérovitch (1843–1920), whom Catherine refers to as the "old prince," was general aide-de-camp to the Czar Nicholas. 28

Belloselsky, Prince Serge (d. 1951) owned extensive land and factories and was a prominent member of the court. He lived with his wife, the former Susan Tucker Whittier, on Krestovsky Island. Princess Belloselsky (ca. 1872–1934) was a famous New York beauty, daughter of Brigadier General Charles Albert Whittier. 28, 99, 100

Bennett, Ira Elbert (1868–1957), a leading Washington journalist. After cutting his teeth on West Coast papers, he joined the staff of the *Washington Post* in 1905 as an editorial writer. He was editor in chief of the paper from 1908 to 1933. In the 1920s, he was a key witness in the Senate's Teapot Dome investigations and a founder of the National Press Club. 173

von Bernstorff, Count Johann Heinrich (1862–1939), was born in London and educated in Germany. Married to Jeanne Luckemeyer of New York, he was the recipient of many honorary degrees from U.S. universities in the years prior to World War I. He served as minister to Cairo from 1906 to 1908 and as German ambassador to the United States from 1908 to 1917. 117

Berry, Walter Van Rensselaer (1859–1927), an American born in Paris, was a prominent international lawyer who spent much of his life abroad. Forty-eight years old at the time Catherine met him, Berry was known for his looks, his uncommon literary knowledge, and his conversation. (Bernard Berenson deemed him "the most noted lady's man in America.") Berry was an intimate of Edith Wharton, whom he first met in 1883 at Bar Harbor, Maine. Their rapport was instantaneous, and by the end of the summer they were,

in the words of Wharton's biographer, "dreaming of the possibility of marriage, yet something held both of them back." They did not see each other for almost fourteen years but then renewed their relationship and from their middle age were steadily together for large parts of the year, their closeness broken only by Berry's death. They are buried in close proximity in the Cimetière des Gonards at Versailles. 140

Berryman, Clifford K. (1869–1949), a political cartoonist, was known for his insightful, often hilarious, yet unmalicious drawings. Berryman originated the teddy bear in a 1902 cartoon about Roosevelt's decision not to shoot a scrawny bear presented to him as a possible victim at the end of an unsuccessful hunting trip. Berryman's drawings were much admired and sought after by Washington insiders. He won the Pulitzer Prize in 1944. 173, 174

Beveridge, Albert J. (1862–1927), Catherine's husband; United States Senator (1899–1911) and author of *The Life of John Marshall* (1916, 1919) and *Abraham Lincoln* (1928). 74–5, 77–8, 94, 109, 117–8, 131–2, 139–46, 148, 150–1, 153, 155, 160–181

Beveridge, Frances Eleanor Parkinson (1824–1918), Albert's mother, endured great adversity in her lifetime. She was the second wife of Thomas Henry Beveridge, a farmer whose first wife's death left him with six children. At the time of the marriage, Frances was a widow of thirty-seven, married for thirteen years and alone for seven. Albert was the only child of her second union. Soon after she married Beveridge, the civil war broke out; Thomas went to fight and went bankrupt afterward, when he resumed farming. The remainder of his career was spent in unhappy farming efforts and desperate contract labor. Albert worked hard for his father for much of his adolescence. 171

Billings, Frank (1854–1932), one of Chicago's most distinguished physicians, internationally known for his dedication to the advancement of medicine. Dean of Rush Medical College at the University of Chicago, he was active in building up and modernizing the medical corps around the time of World War I. 114

The **Birch** family
See "Catherine's Family"

> **Hugh** (1848-1943)
> was a successful Chicago lawyer who became general counsel of Standard Oil. 38n, 153, 155

> **Maria Root Birch** ("Cousin Mollie" d. 1913), his wife. Her mother, Delia Spencer, was the sister of Catherine's grandfather, Franklin Spencer, the patriarch of the family. 40n, 41, 48, 84-5, 103, 107, 109, 121, 125-6, 145, 147, 149, 181

> **Hugo** (1878-1907),
> Hugh's son, graduated from Yale in 1900 and died suddenly in Mexico of unknown causes. 145

> **Helen** (1882-1925),
> Hugh's daughter and Catherine's closest friend; she became the second wife of Frederic Bartlett (see above). 22, 38, 48-9, 56-9, 67, 76, 84-7, 98, 103-7, 109, 114-5, 120-2, 125-7, 131, 140, 142, 145, 147-9, 181

Bismarck, Prince Herbert (1849–1904), eldest son of Otto Bismarck, the great German chancellor. 27

Blair, Edith (1883–1946), daughter of Edward Tyler Blair (1857–1939) and Ruby McCormick Blair (1860–1917), was the sister of Robert Sanderson McCormick. The Blairs were a leading Chicago banking family. 49, 58, 109

Bliss, Robert Woods (1875–1962), a career diplomat from St. Louis, became a noted art collector and philanthropist. In 1908, he married Mildred Barnes, an heiress who was his stepsister by his father's second marriage. Bliss was aide to the American embassy in Paris in 1905, having been a secretary at Petersburg with Spencer the year before. He was later posted to Buenos Aires. The Blisses were assiduous collectors of Byzantine and pre-Columbian art. They arranged for their Washington, D.C., estate, Dumbarton Oaks, to be open to the public and their magnificent collections and research library to be permanently housed there. 100

Blythe, Samuel G. (1868–1947), distinguished political journalist whose closeness to several presidents, from Harding to FDR, contributed to the acumen of his reporting. Originally from Geneseo, New York, where his father had edited a paper, Blythe covered the Washington scene for the *New York World* and wrote a weekly column for the *Saturday Evening Post* titled "Who's Who—and Why." 180

Boardman, Josephine Porter (1873–1972), daughter of Florence (Sheffield) and William Jarvis Boardman. Her father, a wealthy lawyer and philanthropist, was a friend of John Hay. Originally from Cleveland, the family moved to Washington in the 1880s. Both Josephine and her sister Mabel were philanthropists. Josephine married Winthrop Murray Crane of Massachusetts, whose father had founded Crane's stationery company; Crane became a governor and U.S. senator. After Crane's death in 1920, Josephine moved to New York City, where she helped in establishing the Museum of Modern Art and the Dalton School. 77, 94, 107

Boardman, Mabel Thorp (1860–1946), was the daughter of William Jarvis Boardman and sister of Josephine. She was a leading philanthropist whose main achievement was revitalizing the American Red Cross, which had fallen into desuetude under the leadership of its founder, Clara Barton. 107, 164

Bonaparte, Charles Joseph (1851–1921), of Maryland was the grandson of Napoleon's brother, Jerome Bonaparte, king of Westphalia. He was a prominent champion of civil service reform and became secretary of the navy in 1905 following the resignation of Paul Morton. Bonaparte was attorney general from 1906 to 1909. 94

Bone, Scott Cardell (1860–1936), was a journalist and principal owner of the *Washington Herald* from 1906 to 1911. He was later territorial governor of Alaska (1921–25). 172

Boni, Giacomo (Commendatore) (1859–1925), and **Lanciani**, Rololfo Amaeleo (1847–1919), were archaeologists famous for their contributions to the understanding of ancient Rome. Boni, a Roman senator, was director of excavations at the Forum and the Palatine. He discovered on the Palatine what is thought to be the original settlement of Rome, previously a matter of legend and controversy. His death was mourned by thousands of Italians, and he was buried with high pageantry and honor. Lanciani was a prolific writer whose works acquainted the public with dramatic advances in archeological knowledge. 44

le Bourgeois, Lucretia (1879–1971), later Lucy van Horn, was the niece of Mrs. Herbert Wadsworth. Her early life is obscure, but she may have been related to Adele le Bourgeois (Mrs. Robert Chapin), who came from a Louisiana planter family. Lucretia married Robert O. Van Horn (ca. 1877–1941), a distinguished military man who rose to the rank of brigadier general. She painted, and after her husband's death, moved to California and dedicated herself to her work. 138, 162, 171

Brandegee, Frank Bosworth (1864–1924), of Connecticut was in the early years of his senatorial career when he appears in the diary. Elected to the Senate to fill a vacancy in 1902, he became a leading Republican, most famous as a chief of "the irreconcilables," who in 1920 successfully blocked entry of the United States into the League of Nations. Bowed down by ill health and financial worry, Brandegee committed suicide while in office. 139

Brun, Constantin (1860–1945), British envoy extraordinary and minister plenipotentiary to the United States from 1895 to 1908 and from 1912 to 1930. 162

Bryan, William James (1876–1908), of Florida served in the Senate on from December 1907 until his death in March of the following year. 162

Bryce, James (1838–1922), was British ambassador to the United States from 1907 to 1913. An accomplished scholar and statesman, Bryce was the author of *The American Commonwealth* (1888), a penetrating analysis of American government. His wife was Elizabeth Marion Ashton Bryce (d. 1939). On his return to England, Bryce accepted the title of viscount and became an influential member of the House of Lords. 162

Buisseret-Steenbecque de Blarenghien, Count Conrad (1865–1927), a Belgian diplomat, entered the Belgian diplomatic corps in 1886 and was posted to Vienna between 1900 and 1902. During an earlier posting to Washington, in the mid-1890s, he had married Caroline Story (1870–1914), daughter of Major General John Patter Story, with whom he had six children. Buisseret was minister to Washington between 1907 and 1911. He was then made minister to St. Petersburg and was recalled suddenly to that city in July 1914 while vacationing with his family at home in Belgium. The following month, the Germans invaded Belgium, destroying his estate. The countess, who was ill from recent surgery, died before Buisseret could see her again. He managed to be reunited with two of his children and return with them to Russia, but the tragedy and subsequent difficulties robbed him of emotional balance, and in 1917 he was recalled. He retired in 1921. 169, 172

von Bülow, Bernhard Fürst (1849–1929), chancellor of Germany from 1900 to 1909. 27

Burne-Jones, Phillip (1861–1926), an English artist and son of Pre-Raphaelite painter Sir Edward Burne-Jones (1833–98), was in the States exhibiting his work when he appears in the diary. *Dollars and Democracy* (1904), a droll account of his travels that he wrote and illustrated, testifies to his personal charm. 56

Burrows, Julius (1837–1915), United States Senator from Michigan. 172n

Burton, Congressman Theodore Elijah (1851–1929) of Ohio tried to unseat Cleveland's idiosyncratic reform mayor, Tom Johnson, in 1907. Johnson, a streetcar company president, was Burton's nemesis, having deprived him of his House seat for a time in the 1890s. Burton nonetheless enjoyed a long career in both houses of Congress. 153

Busoni, Ferruccio Dante Michelangiolo Benvenuto (1866–1924), was an admired pianist and composer of Italian-German parentage. 74

Byard, Theodore (d. 1931), Ella Root's second husband, was an English baritone who was born in India. The Byards lived in London and Venice and were well known in music circles (see Hurst below). 63, 84

Byrne, Jenny (1942–1934), personal maid and companion to Catherine and her mother. 22–4, 32, 36, 41–7, 56, 61, 65–6, 76, 86, 89, 114–8, 122, 143, 164–9, 171, 181

Cable, Benjamin Stickney (1872–1915), was born in Rock Island, Illinois. His father was a president of the Chicago, Rock Island & Pacific Railway. Cable was educated at Yale and Columbia and practiced law in Chicago. He later became assistant secretary of commerce and labor under Taft. He died in a car crash. 108

Cameron, Martha (d. 1918), later Mrs. Ronald Lindsay, was the daughter of J. Donald Cameron, former senator of Pennsylvania, and his wife, Elizabeth. The Camerons resided on Lafayette Square and were very close to Henry Adams. 118, 138

Cannon, Joseph Gurney (1836–1926),was one of the most powerful Speakers in the House's history. A representative of Illinois, he served forty-six years in the House between 1872 and 1923. He became speaker in 1903 and held the position, despite challenges, until 1911. As Catherine suggests, he could be belligerent, highhanded, and profane. 164

Cantacuzene, Princess Julia (1876–1975), the daughter of Fred Dent Grant, was born in the White House during her grandfather Ulysses's presidency. As a child she witnessed the poignant events of his later life: his bankruptcy, the composition of his memoirs, his death from cancer. She also had strong Chicago ties. Her mother, Chicago-born Ida Honoré, was sister of Berthe (Mrs. Potter) Palmer. Following Ulysses Grant's death, Fred Grant was shipped off as a U.S. minister to Vienna, where his daughter mastered manners, languages, and

waltzing. She met her husband, a landed aristocrat, while traveling in Europe with her aunt and uncle Palmer. Later to witness and flee from the Russian Revolution, the princess lived long enough to lunch at the White House with JFK. 27, 30, 99, 100

Carter, John Ridgely (1864–1944), served in various capacities at the U.S. embassy in London between 1894 and 1909. In 1911, he was offered the post of envoy extraordinary and minister plenipotentiary to Argentina but instead resigned from the diplomatic corps, realizing that promotion would place him deeply in debt. He became a partner in the Paris branch of J. P. Morgan and Co. He was treasurer of the American Red Cross in Europe during World War I and was closely identified with the Lighthouse, founded in France to care for men blinded in the war. 104

Cary, Frank (b. 1857), was a well-known Chicago obstetrician. 155, 179

The **Catlins** were an old St. Louis family who also hosted Alice Roosevelt during her stay in the city. The patriarch of the family, Daniel Catlin (1837–1916), was a prominent tobacco merchant. Among his children were Irene Catlin Allen and Theron Catlin (1878–1961), later a congressman from Missouri. 79

Caton, Arthur J. (1851–1904), was Delia's first husband and a prominent Chicago sportsman and clubsman. *See* "Catherine's Family." 37, 40, 58, 60–1, 67–8, 79, 86

Caton, John Dean (1812–95), father of Delia's husband, Arthur J. Caton. He was one of Chicago's earliest settlers, and served on the state supreme court for twenty-two years, including six years as chief justice. He amassed a fortune from telegraphy. *See* "Catherine's Family." 59

Chalmers, Joan, was the daughter of William James Chalmers, a founder of Allis-Chalmers, the world's largest maker of mining machinery. Her maternal grandfather was the detective Allan Pinkerton. 49

Chamberlain, Houston Stewart (d. 1927), was the son-in-law of Richard Wagner and a race supremacist. English by birth, he was the son of Rear Admiral W. C. Chamberlain and nephew of future prime minister Neville Chamberlain. His work, which was a popular success, glorified Germany, winning him the favor of the kaiser. Chamberlain left Britain to live permanently in Bayreuth and sided with Germany against Britain in World War I. 96

de Chambrun, Count Charles (1873–1952), a descendant of Lafayette, was secretary of the French embassy in Washington. His brother Adelbert, also based in Washington, later married Clara, the sister of Nicholas Longworth. 94, 117–8

Clark, Bruce (b. 1875), of Chicago, son of John Marshall and Mary Louisa (Qua) Clark, grew up at 2000 Prairie Avenue and was a member of Catherine's circle. He went to St. Mark's and Yale before becoming a stockbroker. He later lived and worked in New York City. His wife was Nancy de Wolf (Pegram) Clark, of Providence, Rhode Island. 59

Clark, Mrs. John Marshall, born Mary Louise Qua, was a Chicago neighbor of the Eddys and mother of Bruce Clark (see above). Raised in New York City, she married, in 1873, a peripatetic civil engineer who was one of the original proprietors of Denver. Mr. Clark was active in Republican politics in Chicago. Their daughter, Cecil Clark Davis, was a painter. 104

Cockran, William Bourke (1854–1923), a New York lawyer, was eloquent, erudite, and aristocratic in manner. Born in Ireland, he was a brilliant public speaker. At the time he is mentioned in the diary he was a sitting congressman; he is one of few Democrats Catherine reports meeting socially. His wife, Anne Ide, grew up in the Pacific, where her father was governor-general of Samoa and the Philippines. While a girl on Samoa, she met Robert Louis Stevenson, who, learning that she had a Christmas birthday, deeded his own birthday on November 13 to her. 165

Colburn, Alice D., was the daughter of Frances Draper Colburn, widow of the late Charles H. Colburn, of Washington. 67

Coleman, Joseph Griswold, Jr., was the son of a prominent Chicago hardware merchant. His wife was Agnes Almy Coleman, formerly of Philadelphia, whom he married in 1903. 96

Coleman, "Nancy," was either Anna W. Coleman (Mrs. Joseph Griswold Sr.) or Agnes Almy Coleman (Mrs. Joseph Griswold Jr.). The Colemans' fortune, like the Spencers', came from hardware. 59

Collier, Robert Alfred Hardcastle (1875–1964), a British diplomat, later became 3rd Baron of Monkswell. 77

Colloredo-Mannsfeld, Count Hieronymus Hubertus Frans Alfred Ernst Maria, was an Austrian nobleman and diplomat. 46

Coolidge, Bertha (d. 1933), later Mrs. Marshall Perry Slade, was the daughter of Mr. and Mrs. Albert Leighton Coolidge of Boston and niece of children's authoress Kate Douglas Wiggin. She went to college in Constantinople before settling in New York, where she worked as a painter of miniatures. She served in the Red Cross in World War I. 67

Crafts, Clemence, was the daughter of Clemence Haggerty Crafts and James Mason Crafts, an outstanding chemist and briefly president of MIT (1898–1900). 57

Craigie, Pearl Mary Teresa (1867–1906), was an authoress who wrote under the name John Oliver Hobbes. Though American-born, she settled in England at age nineteen, having married an Englishman, from whom she obtained a divorce in 1890. She was a successful novelist and playwright. 109

Cranley, Lord Richard William Alan Onslow (1876–1945), was the 5th Earl of Onslow and a dedicated public servant. In 1905—then Viscount Cranley—he was third secretary of the British legation at St. Petersburg and private secretary to the ambassador. He later rose to become undersecretary of war (1924–28) and served on numerous government boards. 100

The **Creeds** were an English family of tailors who established a firm in Paris in 1850. The younger Henry Creed (b. 1863) presided over the firm circa 1900, producing an immensely popular line of women's tailored suits, cut with a basque jacket and a full skirt flaring over the hips. 148

Crossley, Florence Josephine Field, later Lady Crossley (d. 1954), a niece and heir of Marshall Field. She was Stanley Field's sister and the daughter of Joseph N. Field (see below). Like Stanley, she was raised principally in England. Her husband, Kenneth Irwin Crossley (1877–1957), later Sir Crossley, was chairman of Crossley Bros., Ltd., and Crossley Motors. He was an avid big game hunter. 104

Crowninshield, Louise du Pont (1877–1958), married Francis Boardman Crowninshield (b. 1869) in 1900. As a wedding gift, they were given Eleutherian Mills, the first home of the Du Pont family in America, which they restored and which later became part of the Hagley Museum. Mrs. Crowninshield was greatly respected for her work as a preservationist, while her husband wrote and edited several charming books documenting the history of his illustrious family. The couple lived mainly in Boston and on the North Shore. 164, 166

Cullom, Shelby (1829–1913), of Illinois, was one of the most senior members of the Senate, a self-effacing yet dedicated legislator who authored the landmark Interstate Commerce Act (1887) and was chair of the Senate Foreign Relations Committee. 162

Cyril, Grand Duke (1876–1938), son of the Grand Duke Vladimir and his wife Maria Pavlovna. In 1924, Cyril tried to claim the title of czar. 78

Davis, Sarah Helen Frelinghuysen, was the widow of Judge John Davis of Washington, D.C., who died in 1902. She married Charles Laurie McCawley in 1906. 117

Day, William Rufus (1849–1923), an associate justice of the Supreme Court, was appointed to the bench in 1903. Prior to his appointment, he was known for his important role in the State Department during the Spanish-American War (he was assistant secretary under the senescent secretary, John Sherman) and for his close friendship with McKinley. 160

Deering, Barbara, was the daughter of Charles Deering and niece of James Deering of Evanston, Illinois. In 1910, she married Richard Ely Danielson (1885–1957), an editor who became president of *Atlantic Monthly* and earned a distinguished military record in World War I. 164

Deering, James (1859–1925), was one of Delia's closest friends. He and his half-brother owned Deering Harvester, the Chicago reaper company that their father founded. At the time of Deering's appearance in the diary, the merger of the Deerings' firm with that of the McCormicks had just resulted in the creation of International Harvester. James, though an active vice president of the new firm, continued to spend much of his time abroad. Like his brother, who counted Whistler and Anders Zorn among his friends, James had a deep passion for art. His principal achievement was the

building and furnishing of Viscaya, his Florida estate, an eighty-two-room baroque mansion on Biscayne Bay. 42–3, 58, 108, 144

Depew, Chauncey Mitchell (1834–1928), senator from New York, a charming man who throughout his time in the Senate remained chairman of the New York Central Railroad. In 1901, Depew married May Palmer, a woman many years his junior. 160, 164

Dexter, Gordon (1864–1937), was the son of Franklin Gordon and Susan Greene Amory Dexter. He married Annie Linzee Amory in 1906; she died in 1916. The Dexters and Amorys were old Boston families. 102, 104–5

Dexter, Josephine (1846–1937), was the wife of Wirt Dexter (1832–90), a prominent Chicago lawyer and the father of Katherine Dexter. 56–7, 76, 84–5,104–5, 169–70

Dexter, Katherine (1825–1967), a close friend of Catherine, was a remarkable woman. She was one of the early graduates of MIT, where she began her career as a reformer by refusing to follow the school's rule that women wear hats at all times, including in chemistry laboratories. Subsequently, she became a leader of the National American Woman Suffrage Alliance and a major supporter of Margaret Sanger and birth control. Katherine was married to Stanley McCormick (1874–1947), a tragic liaison that was never consummated because of Stanley's breakdown immediately after the wedding. 56–7, 68, 84–5, 109, 169–70, 177

Dibblee, Laura Field (1850–1921), the sister of Marshall and Joseph

Field (see below) and her husband, Henry (1842–1907), lived on Calumet Avenue near the Catons. Originally from New York, Henry Dibblee was a successful merchant who, as president of the Chicago Auditorium Association, was behind the construction of one of Chicago's most significant buildings. 79, 104, 106

Dillingham, William Paul (1843–1923), Republican of Vermont. A former governor, he was senator from 1900 until 1923. 153, 164

Dodge, Henry Percival (1870–1936), second secretary to Berlin; later minister to Honduras and Salvador (1907–8), chief of the State Department's Division of Latin-American Affairs (1910–11), and minister to the kingdom of the Serbs, Croats, and Slovenes (1919–26). 24

Dohna, Alfred Burggraf (1849–1907), father of Alfred zu Dohna-Mallmitz (see below). 99

Dohna, Alfred Klemens Sylvius Fabian (1875–1914), became Catherine's suitor in 1905. He was killed in action near Kalisch on August 9, 1914. The *New York Times* identified the Dohna family as among the German noble families hardest hit by the war. They had lost four members by the end of 1915. 96–9, 101–4

Dolliver, Jonathan Prentiss (1858–1910), of Iowa spent eleven years in the House prior to his elevation to the Senate in 1901, where he remained until his early death of a heart attack. The son of a circuit preacher, he was one of the most gifted Republican orators. Though able to work with the powerful conservatives in his party (including his senior colleague Senator Allison), Dolliver led the insurgent movement against the tariff in 1908. 164

Doucet, Jacques (1853–1929), a leading couturier, was also an outstanding collector of art and a powerful patron of artists and writers. He joined his family's clothing firm in 1875 and helped develop it into one of Paris's leading houses of haute couture. 68

Dugdale, Frank (1857–1925), became an honorary colonel and equerry-in-waiting to the Queen England. His attractive wife, Lady Eva Sarah Louisa Greville, daughter of the 4th Earl of Warwick, was Lord Warwick's sister. 145

du Pont, Senator Henry Algernon (1838–1926), of Delaware. As Catherine notes, he was a military man, a West Point graduate, who served in the army from 1861 to 1875. He attained the rank of lieutenant general and won a Congressional Medal of Honor for his valor during the Civil War. 166

Dyer, Elisha (1862–1917), a leader of Newport society, was the son and grandson of Rhode Island governors. His obituary identified him as an expert on the cotillion and the choice of favors for party functions. 121

Eames, Mrs. Frederic Sherrill, born Isabel Porter, was related by marriage to the Catons. Her late husband was the brother of Emily (Eames) MacVeagh. Their mother, Emily Sherrill Eames, was the sister of Laura Sherrill (Mrs. John Dean) Caton. 87–8, 96

The **Eddy** family
See "Catherine's Family"

Augustus (1848-1921), Catherine's father. 22, 37, 48, 58, 67, 76, 79-80, 85-6, 88-9, 95, 103-6, 109, 114, 120-1, 130, 138, 142-3, 145-7, 151, 165, 176

Abby Spencer Eddy (1850-1909), his wife.

Catherine (1881-1970), his daughter. No page citations are given to the text for Abby or Catherine as they appear on virtually every page of the diary.

Spencer (1873-1939), his son, Catherine's older brother. 24, 29, 33, 35-7, 43, 45, 47, 59, 65, 67, 79, 95, 99-104, 109, 117-8, 121, 130, 138, 142-3, 145-7, 151, 165, 176

Delia Spencer (1853-1937), Abby's sister first married to Arthur Caton then to Marshall Field. 37-8, 40-3, 48, 56, 58-62, 67-8, 74, 76, 78, 80, 82-3, 86-8, 95-8, 103-9, 114-5, 118, 121-2, 128-30, 151, 153, 176-6, 179-80

Elcho, Lady Mary (1862–1937), was witty, affectionate, beautiful, and radiated glamour when the occasion required. Lady Elcho was a principal in the social circle known as the Souls, who united aristocratic birth, cleverness, and fashion. Among the Souls were Arthur Balfour, George Curzon, George Wyndham and his wife, and the young Winston Churchill. Some saw the Souls as representing an alternative to the artificiality of "the Prince of Wales set," though the simplicity and rusticity the Souls affected was often equally costly. As Catherine suggests, Lady Elcho held an important place

in the affections of Arthur J. Balfour (1848–1930), whose philosophizing bent, impeccable manners, and love of society made him one of the most stylish of prime ministers (a post he held from 1902 to 1905). The absence of physical passion in Balfour's life was much remarked, both at the time and subsequently.

Lady Elcho and her family, like many others, suffered greatly in World War I. Two of the Elchos' sons were killed. In 1910, Cynthia, a daughter, married Herbert (Bebs) Asquith, whose father, H. H. Asquith, had become prime minister in 1908. During the war, Bebs suffered shell shock and was incapacitated. Cynthia turned to writing, publishing biographies, anthologies of children's tales and ghost stories, two novels, and three volumes of reminiscences. She became private secretary to playwright J. M. Barrie, who so valued her that he left her his estate when he died. 35–7, 121

Elkins, Katherine (ca. 1886–1936), was the daughter of Senator Stephen B. Elkins of West Virginia. As Catherine notes in her diary, she carried on a highly publicized romance with the Duke d'Abruzzi before marrying William F. R. Hitt. 94, 118, 139, 166, 171–2

The **Emmet** family produced a number of female painters, including three sisters—Lydia Field Emmet, Rosina Emmet Sherwood, and Jane Emmet de Glehn—friends of Robert Allerton. Catherine, however, most likely refers to their cousin **Ellen Gertrude Emmet** (1875–1941), a San Francisco–born artist who was becoming known as a portraitist of leading men. Having settled in New York, where in 1902 she was given a one-woman show at the Durand-Ruel Galleries, Emmet was commissioned to paint portraits of John Hay, Elihu Root, and, later, Theodore Roosevelt. She was a cousin of Henry James and had studied in France with Frederic MacMonnies. She became the wife of William Blanchard Rand. 153

Ernst, Oswald Herbert (1842–1926), a retired brigadier-general, was a distinguished military engineer. He had been a superintendent of the U.S. Military Academy and served on the Isthmian Canal Commission (1898–1904), which oversaw the construction of the Panama Canal. His projects included deepening the entrance to Galveston Harbor, harbor improvements to the coast of Texas, and fortification of the Pacific Coast. Helen Amory Ernst was his daughter, and Elizabeth Amory Lee, his wife. 161–2, 165

Ewart, William Herbert Lee (1881–1953), was honorary attaché to the British embassy in Washington. 94

Fairbanks, Charles Warren (1852–1918), of Indiana, was Albert's senior colleague in the Senate before he assumed the vice presidency in 1905, the office having been vacant for several years after the death of McKinley. His wife, Cornelia Cole Fairbanks (d. 1913), was the daughter of an Ohio judge. She attended Ohio Wesleyan University (graduating in 1872) and met her husband while working on the college paper. At the time of his election to the vice presidency, she was president of the Daughters of the American Revolution. 160–2

de Faramond de Lafajole, a lieutenant commander of the French navy who in 1905 was the French naval attaché in Washington. 94

Farquhar, William, a native of Scotland, was the husband of Marian Peck, member of a large and wealthy Chicago family. After the Farquhars' marriage in 1901, Scotland became their permanent home. 38, 40, 96

The **Field** family
See "Catherine's Family"

> **Marshall Field** (1834-1906), the "merchant prince" of Chicago and Delia Caton's long-time friend and second husband. 58, 62–5, 79, 83, 86, 96, 103–9, 114–6, 141–5

> **Marshall Jr.** (1863–1905), his son and **Albertine** (1872-1915) his daughter-in-law. Marshall, Jr., the only son of the mercantile giant, was a man of leisure who took no part in his father's business enterprise. He was raised mostly in Europe, where he spent much of his life with his mother. Marshall Jr.'s wife, Albertine Huck Field, whom he married in 1890, was the daughter of a wealthy Chicago brewer. Her mother was an accomplished singer. Albertine was a wonderful beauty. She and Marshall had had three children: Marshall Field III (1893), Henry (1895), and Gwendolyn (1902). 58, 62–5, 79, 83, 86, 96, 103–9, 114–6, 141–5

> **Joseph Nash Field** (ca. 1831–1914), Marshall Field's brother, was born in Massachusetts but had lived in England since the 1850s, having moved there to oversee the flow of goods to his brother's Chicago firm. He was the father of Stanley Field. 104

Stanley Field, (1875–1964), was the son of Joseph Field and nephew of Marshall. After Marshall Field's death, Stanley ran Marshall Field & Co. with John G. Shedd and James Simpson. His greatest achievement, however, was the development of the Field Museum of Natural History. President of its board from 1908 until 1962, Field endowed the museum with many of the features that made it an institution of international renown. His wife, Sarah Carroll Brown Field, originally of Baltimore, was the sister of Mrs. Honoré Palmer. 114

Flint, Frank Putnam (1862–1929), of California, a former superior court judge and U.S. district attorney who served a single term in the Senate. He did not seek reelection. 162

Foley, Lady Mary Adelaide Agar (d. 1921), was the youngest daughter of the 3rd Earl of Normanton and wife of Henry Foley, secretary to the Earl of Kimberley. Their son became the 7th Baron Foley. 127

Foraker, Louise, was the daughter of Senator Joseph Benson Foraker of Ohio. 139

Francis, David Rowland (1850–1927), was governor of Missouri from 1889 to 1893. A grain broker and former mayor of St. Louis, he owned the *St. Louis Republic* and was active in banking and philanthropy. He was briefly secretary of the interior in 1897–98 and between 1916 and 1918 was ambassador to Russia. He was one of the original proponents of the Louisiana Purchase Exposition. 79

Frewen, Clara Jerome (1850–1935), was a daughter of Leonard Jerome, a prominent New York speculator. She and her two sisters grew up mostly abroad and married into the English aristocracy. Clara's husband was a lesser nobleman who dabbled in currency manipulation and Wyoming cattle ranching. Her sister Jennie (1854–1921) became Lady Randolph Churchill and was the mother of Winston Churchill. 37

Frothingham, Paul Revere (1864–1926), belonged to one of New England's famous ministerial families. He was an overseer of Harvard, a fellow of the American Academy of Arts and Sciences, and a trustee of the Perkins Institute and the Massachusetts School for the Blind. 84

Frye, William Pierce (1831–1911), a quiet power in the Senate. A conservative from Maine, he shared Albert's keen interest in the acquisition of the Philippines and was a member of the negotiating team that obtained the archipelago through the Treaty of Paris. Although president of the Senate, he appears in the diary as a rather forlorn yet likable man. 153, 161–2

von Fürstenberg, Baron Max Egon II, was the son of Prince Maximilian Egon von Fürstenberg, intimate friend of the kaiser. 30, 46

Gallinger, Jacob Harold (1837–1918), was a U.S. Senator from New Hampshire. 153

Garden, Mary (1874–1967), lyric soprano, was one of the most colorful opera stars of her generation. Born in Aberdeen, Scotland, she was the daughter of an engineer. The family moved to the United States when she was a young girl, eventually settling in Chicago about 1888. Her talent was recognized early by her teacher, Mrs. Robinson Duff, who convinced her family that she should study in Paris, then the center of vocal instruction, and took the lead in raising the necessary funds from Chicago supporters. Gardner never revealed the names of her benefactors, whom she distained because they withdrew their aid on hearing reports that she was leading an immoral life in Paris. If Catherine's Aunt Mollie (Maria Root Birch) was a supporter, as she probably was, she obviously was not lumped together with other Chicago patrons. Mary Gardner's career took off when Debussy, over Maeterlinck's strong objections, chose her as the first Mélisande when *Pelleas and Mélisande* made its debut in 1902. Massenet wrote *Cherubin* for her, and she introduced *Thais* to American audiences in 1907. Garden eventually returned to the States and had a lengthy career. She was a mainstay of Chicago's Lyric Opera and served as its director during the 1921–22 season. 41

Gardner, Isabella Stewart (1840–1924), a patron of the arts and museum founder. She befriended among others James McNeill Whistler and John Singer Sargent; the latter painted a stunning portrait of her. She was also a friend of Bernard Berenson who was one of her principal artistic advisors. She was the guiding sprit behind the Isabella Stewart Gardner Museum in Boston. 40, 57, 74

Garfield, James Rudolph (1865–1950), the son of the assassinated president James A. Garfield and his wife Lucretia. The younger Garfield served on the U.S. Civil Service Commission (1902–3) prior to becoming Roosevelt's secretary of the interior (1907–9). His wife was Helen Newel, whom he had married in 1890. 161–2, 172

Garrett, John Work (1872–1942), diplomat and scion of a wealthy Baltimore railroad family. His grandfather was president of the B & O Railroad, and management of the company passed down through the family. During World War I, he was given responsibility for the care of civilian prisoners in France. He was minister to the Netherlands and Luxembourg (1917–19) and later ambassador to Italy (1929–33). 84

Gaylord, Louise, of Chicago, married Walter Francis Dillingham (1875–1963) in 1910. Dillingham's father built the first railroad on Hawaii and owned thousands of acres of its land. Walter Dillingham had already assumed direction of his ailing father's enterprises, which became highly lucrative only in the twentieth century. Louise and her husband settled in Hawaii. 108

Gayoso, Jose Brunetti, Duke d'Arcos, was married to the American-born Virginia Woodbury Lowery (ca. 1854–1934), the daughter of A. H. Lowery and sister of Woodbury Lowery. She was related to Montgomery Blair and Woodbury Blair. The duchess owned a valuable art collection, which she left to the National Gallery of Art in Washington and to the Prado in Madrid. 101

Gillett, Frederick Huntington (1851–1935), represented Massachusetts in the House from 1893 to 1925. He was Speaker from 1919 to 1925. 153

Gillette, Howard Frank (1872–1943), Chicago-born son of James F. and Jennie (Parker) Gillette. His father was one of the leading grain and provision brokers in Chicago. Howard attended private schools in Chicago, Lake Forest, and Berlin; attended Harvard briefly; and then graduated from Northwestern University Law School and practiced law for a few years before becoming involved in wholesale trade. He was the head of Chase National Bank's Chicago office from 1916–1939. From c1919 until the end of his life, Gillette was involved in the Boy Scouts movement, founding the Sea Scouts, and serving on the Scouts' national board. 58–9, 108, 114

Gillette, William (1855–1937), an American actor and playwright, was the first to popularize Sherlock Holmes as a theatrical character. Catherine failed to mention in her diary that the play she viewed marked the stage debut of Charlie Chaplin. 37

Gilmore, General John Curtis (1857–1922), and his son, Captain John C. Gilmore Jr. (1869–1934), were both officers of the U.S. Army. 94

Gizycki, Count Josef (ca. 1860–1926), was a wastrel and abusive husband. He met his future bride, Cissy Patterson, when she was presented to the Austro-Hungarian court in 1902, the same year Catherine was presented to the courts of Berlin and St. Petersburg. 178

Glyn, Elinor (1864–1943), was a novelist. Her novel *Three Weeks* (1907), which portrayed, as she put it, a "certain type of Russian woman who openly throws off the marriage tie," was a best seller. Mrs. Glyn, who once referred to herself as "the high priestess of the God of Love," made her reputation writing risqué novels. *Three Weeks* sold as many as fifty thousand copies a month but was banned in Canada and angered American clergymen. Her other notable success was the 1927 novel *It*, which gave Americans a new shorthand for sex appeal. 160

Goelet, Robert Walton (1880–1941), a few years before he appears in the diary had inherited an estate worth an estimated $60 million from his father, making him one of the wealthiest New Yorkers. The Goelets owned extensive real estate in New York City, including the Ritz-Carlton; there is some chance that Catherine is referring to Goelet's cousin, also named Robert Goelet, son of Ogden Goelet. The latter was called Robert, the former Bertie. 89

Grant, Ulysses S., III, son of Frederick Grant and grandson of the late president, served as a lieutenant in the Philippines. 118

Greville, Francis Richard Charles Guy, Lord Brooke, 5th Earl of Warwick (1853–1924). His wife, Frances Evelyn Maynard ("Daisy"), Countess of Warwick (1861–1938), was one of the most captivating women of her time. An intimate of Edward VII, she was an outspoken critic of British society, eventually allying herself with the socialist cause. 122, 129, 144–5

Gurney, Hugh (1878–1968), was third secretary at the British embassy in Washington from November 1903 until December 1905. 94

Gwynn, Miss Mary, was the friend and traveling companion of Hope Gammell Slater. 43, 59, 84–6, 122, 129–30, 153, 161

Hale, Chandler (1873–1951), son of Senator Eugene Hale of Maine and brother of Frederick Hale. He married Rachel Cameron and was later assistant secretary of state (1909–13). 117, 161

Hale, Frederick (1874–1963), son of Senator Eugene Hale of Maine and brother of Chandler. Frederick had just been elected to the Maine legislature at the time he appears in the diary. He followed in the footsteps of his father, becoming a U.S. senator. 117, 138

Hall, Dr. Thomas Cuming (1858–1936), mentioned frequently in the diary, was professor of Christian ethics at New York's Union Theological Seminary from 1898 to 1917. His father, John Hall, a leader of Orthodox Presbyterianism, was pastor of the Fifth Avenue Presbyterian Church in New York. His brother, Bolton Hall, was an advocate of the flat tax and a founder of the American Longshoremen's Union. The Eddys probably came to know Dr. Hall during his tenure in Chicago in the late 1880s and 1890s, when he was pastor of the First and Fourth Presbyterian Churches. Though of Irish descent, Hall had strong German sympathies and later brought suspicion on himself by criticizing the Triple Entente during World War I. In 1915, he exiled himself to Germany, where he did relief work and held a professorship at the University of Göttingen. He was married to Jennie L. E. Bartling Hall. 86, 96–7, 145–8

Hamid, Sultan Abdul II (1848–1918), ruled Turkey from 1876 until he was deposed in 1909 following the revolt of the Young Turks. He died in prison. 46

Hamilton, Adelaide, later Mrs. Edwin Warner Ryerson, was one of Catherine's closest friends. She was the daughter of David G. and Mary Jane (Kendall) Hamilton. Her father was a lawyer deeply involved in railroads and real estate. Her mother was from one of Chicago's oldest families. 38, 48–9, 56–8, 67, 80, 85–9, 96, 109, 142, 153, 163, 179–81

Hanna, Charlotte Augusta Rhodes, was the widow of Mark Hanna and mother of Ruth Hanna McCormick. Her father, Daniel P. Rhodes, had been a coal and iron mine operator. Her brother was historian James Ford Rhodes.

Hanna, Marcus Alonzo ("Mark") (1837–1904), Ruth Hanna McCormick's father, was one of the most powerful men in politics, regarded as "unquestionably the foremost man in his party after President Roosevelt." Hanna, who was credited with putting McKinley in the White House, struggled unsuccessfully against Roosevelt to regain preeminence in the party after McKinley died. Hanna's death on February 15, 1904, symbolized the declining power of Old Guard Republicans of the civil war generation, encouraging new power struggles within the party. 162

Hanna, Ruth (1880–1945), was the only daughter of Senator Marcus Alonzo Hanna (see above). A political maverick, she went into politics after the death of her husband,

Medill McCormick. She won a seat in the U.S. House in 1928, an accomplishment that landed her on the cover of Time. She also ran unsuccessfully for the Senate. Her second husband was U.S. congressman Albert Gallatin Simms of New Mexico. 48–9, 108

Hanly, James Franklin (1863–1920), of Indiana was a man of modest circumstances and education. The son of a cooper, he had attended rural schools and worked as a seasonal laborer and schoolteacher before passing the bar and practicing law. He served two terms in Congress and was governor of Indiana from 1905 to 1909. He was the Prohibition Party's presidential candidate in 1916. 172

Hansborough, Henry Clay (1848–1933), was elected to Congress from North Dakota on its admission as a state in 1889 and was senator from 1891 to 1909. 153

Hardin, Dr B. Lauriston (1870–1936), was a prominent Washington physician. 160, 181

Hardinge, Lord Charles, (d. 1944), later 1st Baron of Penhurst, was British ambassador to Russia from 1904 to 1906. Between 1910 and 1916 he was viceroy of India. 100

Hardinge, Lady (d. 1914), born Winifred Selina Sturt, was the daughter of the 1st Baron Alington. At the time of her marriage, she was bedchamber-woman to Princess (later Queen) Alexandra and afterward became her lady-in-waiting. Musically gifted, Lady Hardinge owned a Stradivarius and was considered one of the finest amateur violinists in England. 99

Harlan, Justice John Marshall (1833–1911), associate justice of the Supreme Court, was a Kentuckian who had had a tumultuous career in politics from the 1850s through Reconstruction before being appointed to the bench when in his mid-forties. A large and oddly unruly man, he was one of the longest sitting justices, participating in more than fourteen thousand cases over thirty-four years. 161–2

von Hatzfeldt-Wildenburg, Count Hermann (b. 1867), was counselor of the legation and first secretary of the German embassy at Washington. 138–9, 173

Hay, Alice (1880–1960), was the daughter of secretary of state John Milton Hay and the sister of Helen Hay Whitney. 47–8, 76–7, 94

Hay, John (1838–1905), litterateur, journalist, and diplomat, was secretary of state from 1898 to 1905. He began his career as secretary to President Abraham Lincoln. He and John Nicolay wrote an influential biography of the president. He helped negotiate the Treaty of Paris (1898) ending the Spanish-American War, and the Hay-Pauncefote Treaty (1901), authorizing construction of the Panama Canal, and was credited with authoring the open-door policy toward China. He was an intimate friend of Henry Adams (see above) and a patron of Catherine's brother, Spencer. 76–7, 79, 94, 100

von Heidenstam, Carl Gerhard (1876–1939), of a noble and distinguished Swedish family; later envoy to Moscow (1924–30). His relative, Werner von Heidenstam (1859–1940), was awarded the Nobel Prize for Literature in 1916. 32n, 33–4

Hemenway, James Alexander (1860–1923), of Indiana was elected to Fairbanks's Senate seat when Fairbanks resigned to become vice president. Before that he had served a decade in the House. He failed to win reelection to the Senate. 162, 172

von Hengelmüller von Hengervár, Baron Ladislaus (1845–1917), was the Austro-Hungarian ambassador. 161

Henry, Prince (1862–1929), was the only brother of the kaiser. Though loyal to his brother, Henry was more liberal, easygoing, and unassuming. He loved racing automobiles and yachting. His visit to the States elicited frenzied attention and a flood of press coverage. Though intended to warm relations with the United States, Henry's visit also created anxiety, underscoring the problematic nature of patriotism in an era when many Americans had a German background. The booster-ism, provinciality, and conflicting allegiances that Henry's visit brought out were skewered in the cartoons of John McCutcheon. 37–8

Herbert, Lady, born Helen L. Gammell, was the sister of Hope Gammell Slater and the wife of Sir Arthur James Herbert (1855–1921), who was minister at Christiania from 1905 to 1910. 123

Herrick, Robert Welch (1868–1938), was from an impoverished but old and genteel New England family. With help from an uncle, he attended Harvard. He then built up a successful career as a novelist and teacher. He taught literature and composition at the University of Chicago from soon after its found-ing until 1923. Considered an expert on race relations in the

Caribbean, he was government sec-retary of the Virgin Islands in his final years. 96

Hertling, Wilhelm Jakob (1849–1926), Austrian painter known for his landscapes of Munich and the Taunus region. 65

Hibbard, William Gold, Jr., son of Franklin Spencer's business partner; *see* "Catherine's Family." 155

Hibben, Paxton (1880–1928) was a graduate of Princeton and Harvard law school and had just begun his diplomatic career when he appears in the diary. He was third secretary at St. Petersburg. He continued in diplomatic service until the outbreak of WWI, when he became a journal-ist, covering the war in Europe first for *Collier's*, then for the *Associated Press*. After the war, he remained in Europe on various military and humanitarian missions, developing a strong interest in eastern Europe. He was an early advocate for recog-nition of the Soviet Union, a position that brought suspicion on him. Hibben continued throughout his life to write for newspapers and magazines. Before his early death from flu and pneumonia, he wrote biographies of Henry Ward Beecher and William Jennings Bryan. 121

Higgins, Cecil M. S., was second secretary of the British embassy in Washington in 1907. 138, 140, 144

Higinbotham, Alice (1879–1966), was daughter of Harlow Niles Higinbotham (1838–1919), presi-dent of Marshall Field & Co. (1881–1901); as president of the World's Columbian Exposition Association, which sponsored the 1893 world's fair, he was a nationally known figure. In 1902, Alice became the wife of newspaperman Joseph

Patterson. Before their divorce in 1938, they had four children, among them Alicia Higinbotham Patterson (1906–63), who with her third husband, Harry F. Guggenheim, founded the Long Island newspaper *Newsday*. 38, 48, 56

Hitchcock, Frank Harris (1867–1935), civil servant and Taft's campaign manager. His reward was the position of postmaster general, which he held from 1908 to 1913. 175

Hitt, Robert Stockwell Reynolds (1876–1938), third secretary of the United States Embassy at Paris, later minister to Panama (1909–10) and Guatemala (1910–13). 24, 30, 32, 41, 117, 166

Hitt, William F. R. (ca. 1880–1961), brother of Reynolds Hitt, was later to marry Katherine Elkins. The son of a congressman, Billy Hitt graduated from Yale but had no occupation. He was a sportsman. He was devoted to Miss Elkins, courting her before and after the appearance of the Duke d'Abruzzi, and finally marrying her in 1913. The couple, who had no children, divorced in 1921, then remarried in 1923.

Holmes, Oliver Wendell, Jr. (1841–1935), a Supreme Court justice from 1902 to 1932. 76, 161, 172

Hooper, Louisa C. ("Looly") (1874–1975), niece of Henry Adams, later the second wife of Ward Thoron. Adams, being both a widower and childless, was close to his niece. His late wife, Marian ("Clover") Hooper (1843–85), a charming, independent-minded woman, who among her other gifts was an accomplished photographer, committed suicide at age forty-two. 120

Houghteling, Laura, daughter of James Lawrence Houghteling (1855–1910) and his wife, Lucretia Ten-Broeck Peabody. Laura's father was a banker, a native Chicagoan, later a resident of Winnetka, and a principal in the firm of Peabody Houghteling & Co. He founded the Brotherhood of St. Andrew, a principal male lay order of the Episcopal Church. Her sister married into the Aldis family. 141

Howard, Esme (1863–1939), later 1st Baron of Penrith, was councillor of the British embassy at Washington from 1906 to 1908. He was a member of the British delegation to the Paris Peace Convention in 1919 and ambassador to the United States (1924–30). 161, 165

Howlett, Morris E. (ca. 1874–1939), one of the foremost professional whips of his time. Born and raised in Paris, he became an instant sensation in 1900 when he won the international coach-and-four competition at the National Horse Show in New York City. After that, he lived in the States and taught socialites the art of coaching. With Alfred G. Vanderbilt, James Hazen Hyde, and Rodman Wanamaker, he engaged in many races and equestrian escapades around Manhattan, Long Island, and New Jersey. 61

Hoyos, Count Frederick, was attaché of the Austro-Hungarian embassy in Washington in 1904. 77, 94

Hunt, Richard Morris (1828–95), a prominent American architect, designed Marshall Field Sr.'s mansion, which was built in the Prairie Avenue district of Chicago in the early 1870s. 107

Hurst, Ella Root (Cousin Ella), was the sister of Maria Root Birch (Cousin Molly) and a cousin of Delia. Her first marriage was to a prominent Methodist bishop, John Fletcher Hurst (1834–1903), a German-trained theologian who was chancellor of the fledgling American University in Washington. The marriage was unhappy and Ella lived mostly abroad. After his death she married Theodore Byard, an English singer who had been born in India. The couple lived in London and Venice and were prominent in music circles. She died in 1937. 40n, 63, 84, 86, 121

von Hutten, Baroness, was probably the widow of Baron Klemens August von Ketteler (b. 1853), who was killed in Beijing on June 20, 1900, as Boxers attacked members of the diplomatic community, creating siege conditions that lasted until mid-August, when Western forces entered the city. Like so many other titled women of the time, she was an American, born Matilda Cass Ledyard, daughter of Henry B. Ledyard of Detroit, president of the Michigan Central Railroad. 102

Huysmans, Jaris Karl (1848–1907), a French writer of Dutch descent who wrote novels in a decadent vein. His writing had a sensationalist quality and toward the end of his life explored the aesthetic and emotional aspects of the struggle toward religious faith. Part autobiography, part esoteric treatise, *The Cathedral* (1898) describes the medieval symbolism of Chartres, where Huysmans experienced a conversion that led him into the Benedictine order. 67, 106

Hyde, Lord Henry Molyneux Paget Howard (1877–1917), Viscount Andover and Baron Howard, Earl of Suffolk and Berkshire. In 1904, he married Margaret Leiter (d. 1968) of Chicago, known as "Daisy," youngest daughter of the late Levi Leiter and sister of Lady Mary Curzon. Lord Hyde owned ten thousand acres and had a celebrated picture gallery with a fine collection of Old Masters. 127

Imperiali, Guglielmo Giovanna Maria colonna di Paliano, wife of the Italian ambassador Guglielmo Imperiale (1858–1944), who remained ambassador in Berlin until 1903, and subsequently became ambassador to London (1910–20) and a member of the Italian delegation to the Paris Peace Conference of 1919. 26

Innes-Kerr, Robert Edward (1885–1958), Major Lord, younger brother of Henry John Innes-Kerr, the 8th Duke of Roxburghe. The duke was married to May, daughter of Ogden Goelet and cousin of Robert Goelet. The Innes-Kerrs' mother was Lady Anne Emily Spencer Churchill, a daughter of the 7th Duke of Marlborough. 144–5

Jackson, John Brinckerhoff (1862–1920), was secretary to the American embassy in Berlin; in 1902, he was named ambassador to Greece; and later became minister to Cuba (1909) and the Balkan States (1911). His wife was Florence Baird Jackson. 24, 26–7

James, Henry (1843–1916), the noted author whom Catherine had met when she was presented at the Court of St. James. 57, 96

Jameson, Mrs. Ovid B., was Booth Tarkington's younger sister. 155

Johnson, Robert Underwood (1853–1937), associated with *Century* for several decades, was instrumental in making it a foremost periodical of its day. He was the first to encourage Grant to write about his wartime experiences and materially aided him as he struggled to complete his memoirs. Johnson battled unsuccessfully to prevent San Francisco from buying the beautiful Hetch-Hetchy Valley, which was submerged under a reservoir, and, with John Muir, originated the proposal to preserve Yosemite as a national park. He was an active proponent of the international copyright law and a founder of the American Academy of Arts and Letters. 172

Jusserand, Jean Jules (1855–1932), at the time of Catherine's mention of him, had just taken up his post as ambassador to Washington, a position he held with distinction from 1902 to 1925. A learned yet endearing man with a deep love of the United States, he wrote numerous books and won the Pulitzer Prize in 1916. He was a great friend of Theodore Roosevelt, with whom he regularly walked and played tennis. 58, 79, 153, 172

Jusserand, Elise Richards (d. 1948), a French-born American, married Jean Jules Jusserand in 1895. The daughter of a Paris-based banker, she was raised in France and at the time of her marriage had never seen the United States.

Kean, John (1852–1914), was senator from New Jersey from 1899 to 1911. He was from an old and well-known New Jersey family descended from Governor Livingston. Senator Kean was unmarried. His mother, Lucy (ca. 1825–1912), lived in Washington and acted as his hostess. 77, 161

Keep, Frederick A. (ca. 1858–1911), was prominent in the lumber business in the West before moving to Washington, D.C. in 1900. He was married to Florence Sheffield Boardman Keep (ca. 1864–1954), sister of Mabel and Josephine Boardman. 107, 131, 153, 163–4

Kelly, Howard Atwood (1858–89), one of the nation's leading gynecologists, was a tireless man who published voluminously and maintained a large clinical practice. He attended Mrs. Eddy during her long illness. Prior to his appointment at Johns Hopkins, he had established a hospital of his own in Philadelphia, known as Kensington Hospital. 179

Kohlsaat, Pauline, daughter of powerful Chicago newspaperman Herman Kohlsaat; later the wife of Potter Palmer Jr. 108

La Follette, Robert Marion (1860–1919), senator from Wisconsin. He and his wife, Belle Case La Follette (1859–1931), were a recognizably modern political couple and partners in public life. Mrs. La Follette, the first woman to graduate from the University of Wisconsin Law School, helped write her husband's legal briefs and was active in his political career. She coedited *La Follette's* magazine and campaigned tirelessly for social justice.

Her husband was one of the earliest political leaders to articulate and unite the themes that characterized Progressivism. 162, 173

Lathrop, Mrs. Bryan, born Helen Lynde Aldis (1849–1935), was the sister of Arthur Aldis and Mrs. Thomas Nelson Page. Her husband, Bryan Lathrop (1844–1916), who was born in Virginia, was a Chicago real estate investor whose signature project was the fashionable Graceland Cemetery. He had a background in trust management as well. The couple owned a magnificent home on Chicago's near north side that became the home of the Fortnightly Club. The Lathrops were benefactors of many Chicago cultural enterprises, especially the Chicago Symphony. 97, 109

Leishman, John G. A. (1857–1924), ambassador to Switzerland, Turkey, and Germany. Orphaned at an early age, he grew up in a Pittsburgh orphan asylum and went to work in the steel mills as a boy. He became the first president of Carnegie Steel when it was organized in 1886, a position he held until 1897. He was married to Julia Crawford of Pittsburgh. 45, 65

Leishman, Marthe (ca. 1881–1944), eldest daughter of John Leishman, became the wife of Count Louis de Gontaut-Biron. Divorce proceedings were under way when he died. She then married James Hazen Hyde (1876–1959), son of Henry Baldwin Hyde, founder of Equitable Life Assurance Society. The Hydes were divorced in 1918 on grounds of conflicting sympathies for Germany and France during World War I. 45–7, 67

Leiter, Mrs. Levi (1844–1913). Her husband, Levi (1834–1904), was an early partner of Marshall Field. The Leiters built a large house on DuPont Circle in Washington, D.C. (since demolished), and Mrs. Leiter married her three daughters to English aristocrats. The eldest, Mary Victoria, married George, Lord Curzon, who became viceroy of India; the middle daughter, Daisy, married the Earl of Suffolk; and the youngest, Nancy, married Colin Campbell, an army officer. She seems to have been a sort of model for Delia and Abby. 44, 164

Lenbach, Franz von (1836–1904), important Munich portraitist who painted Abby shortly before his death. 63–5

de Ligne Prince Albert, of Belgium, a descendant of Eugene Lamoral, Prince de Ligne (1804–80), a statesman revered for his role in establishing an independent Belgium. 26

Lincoln, Robert Todd (1843–1926), a lawyer, diplomat, and neighbor of the Catons, was the son of Abraham and Mary Todd Lincoln. Settling in Chicago with his mother after his father's assassination, he gained admission to the bar and became partner in the firm of Isham, Lincoln, and Beale. He was secretary of war under Garfield and Arthur (1881–85) and ambassador to Great Britain (1889–93). Between 1897 and 1911 he was general counsel and then president of the Pullman Company. His wife was Mary Harlan, daughter of Senator James Harlan of Iowa. 86

Lindsay, Ronald Charles (1877–1945), was in 1904 second secretary of the British embassy in Washington. He had a distinguished diplomatic career, later serving as ambassador to Berlin (1926–28), undersecretary of war, and ambassador to the United States (1930–39). 118, 138–9

Little, Arthur (1852–1925), was a prominent Boston-born architect who specialized in residential work. He was interested in colonial architecture and designed a house in the Federal style for Mrs. Wirt Dexter. His masterpiece was the Larz Anderson house in Washington, D.C. 57

Littleton, Alice, was the daughter of William Edmund and Anne Semple Littleton of Philadelphia. Mr. Littleton (1838–1903) was a lawyer active in Philadelphia politics. He was a councilman and selectman of the city and a delegate to the convention that revised Pennsylvania's constitution. Mrs. Littleton was the daughter of Matthew Semple, a physician. Alice later married Frank Tracy Griswold. Her grandson, Frank T. Griswold III, became presiding archbishop of the Episcopal Church. 42, 47, 58, 62, 67, 95

Lockwood, George Roe (1861–1931), a New York physician who was an authority on diseases of the stomach. He was an attending physician at Bellevue and professor of clinical medicine at Columbia. 86

Lodge, John Ellerton (1878–1942), son of Henry Cabot and Anna Cabot Mills Davis Lodge and brother of George Cabot ("Bay"). An expert on oriental art and languages, he became curator of Asiatic art at the Boston Museum of Fine Arts (1910–31) and later director of the Freer Gallery of Art in Washington. 77–8, 94

Lodge, Matilda Elizabeth Frelinghuysen Davis (d. 1960), was the wife of George Cabot ("Bay") Lodge (1873–1909). Bay Lodge was a poet who served in the Spanish-American War and was his father's private secretary before an early death from heart failure. Elizabeth Lodge was, according to Edmund Wilson, a "survival of rare American stock… with the usual leash of Senators, Cabinet officers, and other such ornaments in her ancestry." One of her sons became a U.S. senator; the other, governor of Connecticut. 117

Longworth, Nicholas (1869–1931), scion of one of Cincinnati's wealthiest families, was just wrapping up his first term as a congressman at the time of his mention in the diary. A charming man, with a great love of society and of music, he later proved himself one of the House's most effective Speakers. In 1906 he married Alice Roosevelt. 94, 117, 162

Lorimer, George Horace (1867–1937), was in the early stages of his illustrious career at *The Saturday Evening Post* when Catherine mentions him in her diary. A native Kentuckian with strong Chicago ties, Lorimer had joined the moribund magazine as its literary editor in 1898. Founded by Benjamin Franklin in 1728, the periodical had reached a nadir after flourishing during the civil war. After Lorimer's promotion to editor in 1899, the *Post* became the era's most widely read magazine, with a circulation of 3.1 million. 173, 180

Lowther, Lancelot Edward (1867–1953), later the 6th Earl of Lonsdale. His brother, Hugh Cecil Lowther (1857–1944), the 5th Earl, an outstanding sportsman, was proprietor of some sixty-eight thousand acres and patron of fifty-nine livings. Both brothers served in World War I. Lancelot, a captain, was decorated for his services and mentioned in dispatches from the war. 127

von Luttwitz, Baroness, born Mary Cary of Cleveland, was wife of Baron Arthur von Luttwitz, German military attaché at Petersburg. He was later governor of Belgium for three months after the German invasion in 1914. Princess Cantacuzène disliked the baroness as one who, despite having bad manners, put on airs. 28, 32

MacGregor, Alexander, one of Delia's most trusted menservants, was often delegated to help Abby and Catherine. His daughter, Catherine MacGregor, was later in Catherine's service as well. Delia left Alexander MacGregor $12,000 in her will. 77, 95, 109, 131, 142, 153, 175–6

MacVeagh, Eames (1871–1958), was the son of Emily and Franklin MacVeagh; the only one of their five children to reach adulthood. At one point, he was a suitor of Catherine. 56, 59, 108, 114, 139

MacVeagh, Emily Eames (1844–1916), was born into a leading Chicago banking family. She was a prominent socialite and wife of Franklin MacVeagh (1837–1934), who later served as U.S. secretary of the treasury (1909–13). 38, 89, 96, 163

MacVeagh, Isaac Wayne (1833–1917), of Pennsylvania was a former U.S. attorney general and ambassador to Italy (1893–97). His brother,

Franklin MacVeagh of Chicago, and Franklin's wife, Emily, were close friends of the Catons and Eddys. The MacVeaghs and Catons were related; *see* "Catherine's Family." Wayne MacVeagh's wife, born Virginia Rolette Cameron, was the daughter of Simon Cameron (1799–1889) and sister of J. Donald Cameron(1833–1918), both former senators. 76, 118

MacVeagh, Margaretta Cameron (d. 1938), daughter of Wayne and Virginia (Cameron) MacVeagh. She later married naval officer Stuart Farrar Smith and settled permanently in Washington. 77–8, 94, 114–8, 172

Marlborough, Duchess of; *see* Consuelo Vanderbilt.

Martyn, Hazel (1880–1935), the daughter of Mr. & Mrs. Edward Jenner. Martyn was recognized as one of the great beauties of her day. She married Ned Trudeau in 1903, but he died shortly thereafter of tuberculosis. She then married Sir John Lavery, a well-known English portraitist, and became one of his favorite subjects; he painted some 20–30 portraits of her. According to the Oxford Dictionary of National Biography she "became one of the great society hostesses of her day— the friend, confidante, and occasionally lover to many powerful social and political figures. Her close friendship with Michael Collins was crucial in his negotiations with the British government over the future of the Irish Free State in 1920–21." She is the subject of a 1996 biography *Hazel: A Life of Lady Lavery, 1880–1935* by Sinead McCoole. 68

McClain, Edward Lee (1861–1934), was a successful textile manufacturer and lifelong resident of Greenfield, Ohio. 143, 152, 162

McCawley, Charles Laurie (1865–1935), a high-ranking Marine Corps officer, eventually brigadier general, who between 1902 and 1910 was on duty with the president. He held high-ranking positions during the Spanish-American War. In 1906, he married Sarah Davis. 94

McCormick, Robert Rutherford ("Bertie") (1880–1955), a Chicago friend of Catherine, was the son of diplomat Robert Sanderson McCormick, ambassador to Austria-Hungary. Bertie, who had been educated in Britain and was even as a boy remarkable for his intense patriotism, became one of the most powerful newspaper publishers of the century, editing the *Chicago Tribune* for five decades. 46

McCormick, Cyrus Hall, II (1859–1936), was president of International Harvester and son of Cyrus Hall McCormick I (1809–84), inventor of the McCormick reaper. Stanley McCormick was his younger brother. 58

McCormick, Joseph Medill ("Medill") (1877–1925), son of Katherine Medill and Robert Sanderson McCormick, was a politician through and through. After his marriage to Ruth Hanna, daughter of Republican power broker Marc Hanna, he became a U.S. congressman (1917–19) and senator (1919–25). Failing to retain his Senate seat, he committed suicide, a fact concealed from the public for many years. 38, 40, 48–9, 59, 68, 74, 78

McCormick, Robert Hall ("Hall") (b. 1847), son of Leander J. McCormick and cousin of William and Robert Sanderson McCormick. Hall and his father were active in developing the McCormick Harvester but were ousted from the company by other members of the family in 1880. This branch of the family had large Chicago real estate holdings. Hall was devoted to art collecting and coaching. 107

McCormick, Robert Sanderson (1849–1918), was a diplomat who served as secretary to the United States legation to Great Britain under Robert T. Lincoln and then as minister-ambassador to Austria-Hungary (1901–2), where Cissy Patterson (see below) met Count Gizyck, and later as ambassador to Russia (1902–5) and France (1905–7). Spencer Eddy served under him at the last two posts. He was married to Katherine Medill (1853–1932), the daughter of Joseph Medill, owner and editor of the *Chicago Tribune*. 46, 74, 78, 121

McCormick, Stanley F. (1874–1947), son of Cyrus and Nettie Fowler McCormick and brother of Harold McCormick. Educated at Princeton and Northwestern, Stanley helped run International Harvester before the onset of profound mental illness. In the years following his 1904 marriage his mental condition deteriorated. He was declared mentally incompetent in 1909 and lived the remainder of his years under close supervision. 56, 68, 84–5, 109, 114, 169

McCormick, William Grigsby (1851–1941), brother of Robert Sanderson McCormick and father of Catherine's friend Mary Grigsby McCormick (Mrs. Herbert S. Stone). He was the first of the McCormicks to be born in Chicago, after the family brought its reaper business there. He attended the University of Virginia and founded the Kappa Sigma fraternity. He was a banker by profession. 86

McCoy, Frank Ross (1874–1954), at the time that Catherine's mentions him in her diary, had just returned from a tour of duty in Cuba, where he had assisted his mentor, Military Governor General Leonard Wood, and Wood's successor, William Taft. McCoy eagerly participated in the army's strenuous efforts to put down Muslim insurgents in the Moros Province, leading the party that killed rebel leader Datto Ali. He was regarded as an exceptionally able soldier. His military ability, combined with a capacity for friendship, brought him military distinction and a career embracing diplomacy, politics, and colonial administration. 139

McCutcheon, John Tinney (1870–1949), a leading cartoonist who drew for the *Chicago Tribune*. A native of Indiana, McCutcheon was and would remain one of Albert's closest friends. The two men first met during Albert's trip to the Philippines. McCutcheon knew Catherine from Chicago as well. 142–5, 153, 173, 180

McLean, Edward Beale ("Ned") (1886–1941), John and Emily McLean's only child, was known for his weak chin and even weaker character. His chief talent was spending money. In 1908, he mar-

ried Evalyn Walsh (1887–1947), the daughter of Thomas Walsh, Colorado gold miner. The couple reportedly spent $200,000 honeymooning. Evalyn later owned the Hope diamond, which had the reputation of bringing bad luck. Evalyn never believed it and wrote, "As a matter of fact, the luckiest thing about it is that, if I even have to, I could hock it," which she did several times. 140

McLean, Mrs. John R. (d. 1912), born Emily Beale, was a reigning Washington social leader. She was a daughter of civil war–era general Edward [F.] Beale and came of age in the famous Decatur house on Lafayette Square. Her husband, John R. McLean (1848–1916), a native of Cincinnati, was a true maverick, commanding a huge fortune (estimated at $100 million) in coal mines, railroads, and Cincinnati and Washington real estate. He owned two major newspapers, the *Cincinnati Enquirer* and the *Washington Post*, and was actively interested in Ohio politics. The McLeans' Washington residence, at 1500 I Street, was one of the showplaces of the city. 89, 94, 139, 161

Meeker, Arthur, a friend of the Caton family and a chronicler of Chicago society. His best known work is the roman a clef, Prairie Avenue (1949). 109

Meynell, Alice (1850–1922), noted English poet and beloved of her compatriots, author of *Coventry Patmore*. She raised eight children in addition to having a productive literary career. 38

Meyer, George von Lengerke (1858–1918), at the time of Catherine's writing, had returned to the United States from several important diplomatic appointments and had been made postmaster general. A Boston patrician involved in politics since the 1880s, Meyer was ambassador to Italy (1900–1905) and Russia (1905–7). He had strong relationships with Kaiser Wilhelm and the czar and helped negotiate the treaty that ended the Russo-Japanese War. He later became Taft's naval secretary. His daughter, Julia, a great friend of Catherine in later years, married an Italian, Count Brambilla. Widowed early, she settled in Washington and devoted her considerable energies to introducing young diplomats to American contemporaries in the city, including Catherine's grandchildren. 99, 166

Meyer, Marion Appleton, wife of George von Lengerke Meyer. A Bostonian, of one of the oldest and wealthiest mercantile families, she married Meyer in 1885.

Michael, Grand Duke Michael Michaelovich (1861–1929) was the grandson of Czar Nicholas I and a first cousin of Czar Alexander III. He was educated as a military officer but as the result of his 1891 morganatic marriage to Countess Torby (d. 1927), a granddaughter of the poet Pushkin, was banished from Russia by Alexander, whom Michael had defied. The marriage had further consequences; when his mother, the Grand Duchess Olga, learned of it she had a heart attack and died. The Grand Duke and the Countess split their time between Cannes and London; he was a close friend of Edward VII and a friend of Spencer who visited him frequently. Michael suffered a substantial financial loss when banished from Russia, but he was able to maintain a comfortable lifestyle until 1917 when the Russian Revolution completely impoverished him. Faced at the age of 56 with the necessity to work for the first time, he accepted a position in the British civil service.

He had a son, Count Michael Torby and two daughters, Nada, the Marchioness of Milford Haven and Zia, wife of Colonel Harold Wernher. 24, 33–5

Milburn, John George (1851–1930), a prominent New York lawyer who was host to McKinley on his fatal visit to Buffalo and at whose home the president died. He was a founding partner of the New York firm Carter, Ledyard & Milburn LLP. 114, 116

Milburn, Rev. Joseph Anthony (b. 1858), and his wife, writer and lecturer Lucy Fitch McDowell Milburn (b. 1863). Mrs. Milburn was a spiritualist. Rev. Milburn was pastor of the Plymouth Congregational Church. The Eddys were close to the Milburns and saw them often. 155

Millet, Francis Davis (1846–1912), a well-known American-born muralist, was director of decoration for the 1893 World's Columbian Exposition in Chicago. Catherine reports seeing his painting of Edward's coronation during her visit to England in 1902, which is puzzling. At the time, Edward was still Prince of Wales, though plans were being made for his coronation. It is possible that the painting she saw was the work of Edwin Austin Abbey, Millet's friend and fellow-painter, who had been chosen to paint the coronation. His wife, Lily, and his friends Edwin A. Abbey and John Singer Sargent were among the most prominent members of the artist colony in the English town of Broadway, where Millet lived and had his studio. 36–7

Mitchell, James, was a socially prominent Washington physician. 94

de Montebello, Madame, was the wife of Count Julien de Montebello, whom von Bülow described as "one of the most brilliant French diplomats." 28, 30–1

Moewis, Elise von Roche; familiarly known as "Frudy" (see Remington below). 43–7, 66

Moody, William Henry (1853–1917), appointed to the Supreme Court in 1906, had previously been Roosevelt's attorney general and, before that, his secretary of the navy. Moody had had an important role in Roosevelt's handling of trust issues, and it was hoped that he would continue to assert from the nation's highest bench a vision of judicial progressivism. Painfully afflicted with rheumatism, however, Moody served only a few years, retiring in 1910. 164

Morgan, Edwin Vernon (1865–1934), later ambassador to Brazil (1912–33). 27–8, 31–4

Morton, Paul (1857–1911), was the son of Julius Sterling Morton of Nebraska, who was agriculture secretary under Grover Cleveland. Paul had gravitated to Chicago as a young man and worked his way up in railroads, becoming a vice president of the Atchison, Topeka, and Santa Fe. Having become Secretary of the Navy in July 1904, he resigned a bare year later when the ICC found the Atchison, Topeka to have granted illegal rebates to a fuel company in which Morton was also involved. The episode did not harm Morton's reputation among businessmen, and he was later made president of the ailing Equitable Life Insurance Company, which he was credited with helping to save. 94

Morton Pauline, of Chicago, daughter of Paul Morton. She later married J. Hopkinson Smith Jr. 94–5

Muck, Karl (1859–1940), a former director of the Berlin State Opera, made his debut as conductor of the Boston Symphony Orchestra in 1906. He was one of the most acclaimed conductors in Europe, known for his searching and fastidiously prepared performances. A leading interpreter of Wagner, he conducted regularly at Bayreuth between 1901 and 1931. His affiliation with the Boston Symphony came to an end during World War I, when he was jailed and finally deported because of his sympathy for his native land. 144

The **Munn** family

The Munns were close friends and traveling companions of the Eddys. The family consisted of **Charles Alexander Munn** (1852–1903), his wife, **Carrie Louise (Gurnee) Munn** (1853–1922) and five children: Charles Alexander (d. 1955), who was about to enter Harvard when he appears in the diary; Carrie Louise (1889–1979), who married Reginald Boardman in 1911, divorced him in 1932, and married Lawrence Waterbury that same year; Ector, about whom there is little information; Gladys Mildred (1899–1975), who first married Charles Minot Amory and after a divorce in 1924 married Herbert Pulitzer, youngest son of Joseph Pulitzer; and Gurnee, who married Maria Louise Wanamaker, granddaughter of John Wanamaker, the founder of Wanamaker and Company, the great department store. The family had Chicago connections but made their home in Washington, D.C. Mrs. Munn was independently wealthy, as she owned Chicago's Wellington Hotel. 41–2, 47, 61–2, 67–8, 76–7, 80–6, 95, 116–8, 130, 140, 147–9, 151, 160, 177–8, 181

Munsey, Frank (1854–1925), maverick publisher, the Rupert Murdoch of his time. From the outset of his career, Munsey was a shameless tinkerer and risk taker, running newspapers on a shoestring and experimenting in farseeing ways with modes of distribution, price, and format. In time, his strange, fluctuating empire flourished. At any given moment he owned several major metropolitan dailies and the popular *Munsey's* magazine. By 1907 he claimed to have earned $9 million from publishing. 153, 172

Myer, Walden (d1926), an Oxford-educated Episcopal clergyman, was the son of General Albert James Myer (1829–80) of Washington. His father, an army surgeon in the civil war, was famous for founding the signal corps. Walden, a canon of the Cathedral of Saints Peter and Paul in Washington, was traveling in Europe with his sister Gertrude at the time he is mentioned in the diary. 83, 94, 107

Newbold, Mary (1870–1905), born Mary Dickinson Scott, was the daughter of Thomas A. Scott (1823–81), president of the Pennsylvania Railroad. The Scotts had an estate in Hyde Park, New York. Mary became the wife of Clement Buckley Newbold, scion of a prominent Philadelphia family. She died young, following an appendectomy. 60

Newell, Franklin Spilman (1871–1949), a leading Boston obstetrician; at the time he is mentioned in the diary he is professor of obstetrics at Harvard. He pioneered advances in cesarean section deliveries and in caring for pregnant women with heart disease. 170, 177–8, 180

Nicholas II (1868–1918) became emperor of Russia in 1894 on the death of his father, Alexander III. In the same year Nicholas married Alexandra (1872–1918), a princess of Hesse-Darmstadt. Alexandra's mother was Princess Alice of Britain, one of Queen Victoria's children. Like his wife, Nicholas was related to the British royal family. His mother, Empress Dowager Maria

Fedorovna, and Alexandra, Princess of Wales (later Queen Alexandra), were sisters. Nicholas was thus nephew of Edward VII and cousin of George V. 30–1, 34, 101

Northrup, Cyrus (1834–1922), though trained as a lawyer, was a professor of rhetoric and English literature at Yale from 1863 until 1884, when he became president of the University of Minnesota, continuing in the office until 1911. 172

Norton, Lillian (1859–1914), known as Nordica, was a famous American-born prima donna. She created a sensation with her performances of Wagner in the late 1890s. 62

Nott, Marjorie (1876–1957), was the daughter of Alice (Hopkins) and Charles Cooper Nott. Her father was the chief justice of the U.S. Court of Claims. She later married Victor Morawetz, a railroad lawyer and financier. She was very active in relief to the French during the world wars and was decorated by the French government four times. She was also director of the American Association of Indian Affairs. 77, 117

O'Connell, Monsignor Dennis Joseph (1849–1927), rector of Catholic University in Washington. 162, 171

Odell, John Johnson Peavey (b. 1847), with his wife Emma Talbot Odell, was prominent in Chicago society. Their son, George Talbot Odell, was about Catherine's age. William Rice Odell, a real estate broker who belonged to all the right clubs and lived on Lincoln Park Boulevard, may have been J. J. P. Odell's brother; his wife was Laura V. Johnson Odell. 59

O'Laughlin, John Callan (1873–1949), a reporter on Washington and international affairs for the Associated Press and later the *Chicago Tribune*. He was a close friend of Theodore Roosevelt, whom he had accompanied on his travels in Africa. Later in life, O'Laughlin published the influential *Army and Navy Journal*. 173

Orloff, Princess Olga Constantinovna née Princess Belloselsky-Belozersky (1874–1923), was generally considered the most beautiful woman in the Russian court. She was the sister-in-law of Princess Susan Belloselsky (see above). 100–1

Osborn, Chase Salmon (1860–1949), a crusading midwestern newspaperman who in 1910 became governor of Michigan. 172

Paderewski, Ignacy (1860–1941), probably the foremost pianist of his age and prime minister of Poland (1919), was also a noted wit, which made him a social lion in wealthy American salons. At one party, a hostess confused him with a well-known polo player who was also expected as a guest. When she greet Paderewski and enthused over his polo playing, he is reported to have replied, "No, Madame, he is a rich soul who plays polo; I am a poor Pole who plays solo." 38

Page, Thomas Nelson (1853–1922), a Southern writer. In 1893 he married Florence Lathrop Field (d. 1921), the widow of Marshall Field's brother Henry. Florence was the sister of Bryan Lathrop and mother of Minna Field, who was around Catherine's age. Thomas

Page later became increasingly involved in politics, rallying support for Wilson in 1912 and serving as ambassador to Italy (1913–19). 122

Palmer, Bertha Honoré (1849–1918), widow of Potter Palmer (1826–1902). 114

Palmer, Honoré (1874–1964), son of Potter and Berthe (Honoré) Palmer, graduated from Harvard in 1898 and, at the time he is mentioned in the diary, was helping to run the Palmer House, his family's famous hotel. Like Joe Patterson, he had an interest in politics. In 1901, he was elected Democratic alderman of Chicago's twenty-first ward; he won reelection in 1903. He was married to Grace Greenaway Brown, of a prominent Baltimore family. Her sisters, in turn, were married to Walter Keith and Stanley Field. Like other wealthy Chicagoans of the time, Palmer invested extensively in Florida, founding the Palmer National Bank and Trust Company of Sarasota and becoming involved in real estate and citrus. 59, 114

Parsons, Herbert (1869–1925), at the time he is mentioned in the diary a congressman from New York. His wife was Elsie Clew Parsons (1874–1941), a feminist and later a noted anthropologist. The couple married in 1900. Elsie Parsons was a friend of Katherine Dexter, Stanford White, Robert Herrick, and George Young. 153

Patterson, Elinor Medill ("Cissy") (1884–1948), daughter of Robert W. Patterson and Eleanor Medill Patterson (see below), had a vibrant and rambunctious personality. After travels abroad and a disastrous marriage to the impecunious Count Gizycki, whom she divorced in 1911, she settled down in the States, married Elmer Schlesinger, a lawyer, wrote a few novels, and became the editor of the *Washington Herald*, one of William Randolph Hearst's newspapers. 35, 43, 49, 67, 78

Patterson, Joe (Joseph Medill) (1879–1946), had just graduated from Yale at the time he is mentioned in the diary. After his father's death, in 1910, he ran the *Tribune* with his cousin Bertie McCormick. The two then founded the *New York Daily News*, which under Joe's leadership became the country's most widely read newspaper. Joe had a socialist streak and wrote several didactic novels and plays. 22, 38, 48, 78

Patterson, Mrs. Robert, and her family were members of the *Chicago Tribune* dynasty. Born Eleanor Medill, she was the daughter of former Chicago mayor Joseph Medill, the paper's founder. On his death, control passed to her husband, Roger W. Patterson Jr., who had worked his way up through the ranks and married the boss's daughter. Eleanor and her sister, Katherine Medill McCormick, between them had four extraordinary children, all of whom became prominent in politics and journalism. All were near Catherine's age and among her close friends. They were Robert Rutherford McCormick ("Bertie"),

Elinor Medill Patterson ("Cissy"), Joseph Medill McCormick ("Medill"), and Joseph Medill Patterson ("Joe"). 22

Pavlovna, Maria Grand Duchess Vladimir (1854–1920). Catherine succinctly identifies the characteristics that made the grand duchess a force unto herself: her German birth, immense personal dignity, and maturity relative to the empress. In 1902, Nicholas and Alexandra were in their mid-thirties. Surrounding them were older figures of Alexander III's generation, notably the Grand Duke and Duchess Vladimir and Alexander's widow, Maria Fedorovna, the empress dowager. Unlike the czarina, who shrank from the public eye, Maria Pavlovna was attentive to foreigners and cultivated their good opinion. Bismarck had thought her the "cleverest girl in Germany." 28, 31–4

Peck, Josephine, of Chicago was the daughter of Annah Luther Peck and Harold S. Peck. With her mother and sisters—Annah, Haroldine, and Marion (Mrs. William R. Farquhar)—she spent much of her time abroad. Her uncle Ferdinand Wythe Peck was a Chicago real estate magnate. 78

Percy, Lord Eustace (1887–1958), later 1st Baron Percy of Newcastle, youngest son of the 7th Duke of Northumberland. After some early years in the diplomatic service—he served at the British embassy in Washington from 1910 to 1914, Percy returned to England where he became a member of Parliament, an author, and a cabinet member. He was for five years president of the Board of Education (1920–25)

and minister without portfolio (1935–36). Retiring from politics, he was, it appears, rector of the Newcastle Division of the University of Durham (1937–52). 118

Perkins, Janet Russell (1853–1933), Catherine's former tutor, was an American-born scientist resident in Berlin. An extremely learned women for her time, she was born in Indiana and educated at the University of Wisconsin, Paris, and Heidelberg. She traveled widely and was an expert on plants of the Philippines. 25–6, 144

Perkins, George Walbridge (1862–1920), a partner of J. P. Morgan and vice president of the New York Life Insurance Company. A successful businessman with a keen interest in politics, Perkins had taken an early interest in Albert's career and frequently offered him political advice. Perkins retired from business in 1910 to devote all his time to political activities. He was a staunch supporter of Roosevelt, following him out of the Republican fold and into the Progressive Party. Perkins was married to Evelyn Ball, whom Catherine found uninteresting. 143, 153, 165–6, 170

Pettit, Henry (1863–1913), a lawyer, was a former speaker of the Indiana House of Representatives. In 1901, he was appointed U.S. marshal for the district of Indiana, a position he held until 1911. Pettit was a graduate of the U.S. Naval Academy and came from a family prominent in Indiana politics. His wife was Eva Stitt Pettit. 163, 180

Phillips, David Graham (1867–1911), was perhaps Albert's closest friend. The two met while students at DePauw, though Phillips later graduated from Princeton. Beveridge's drive and impoverished family history fascinated the well-to-do Phillips, whose fiction and journalism often dealt with just such themes. His flare for exploring the seamier side of American life found expression in a 1906 essay, "The Treason of the Senate," whose nasty and irreverent tone shook the political community when it ran in *Cosmopolitan*. The piece is understood to have inspired President Theodore Roosevelt's characterization of "The Man with a Muck-Rake" at a Gridiron dinner, giving a name to an emerging style of journalism. Phillips was shot and killed by a man who mistakenly thought that one of Phillips's novels was about his sister. 153

Pinchot, Gifford (1865–1946), a pioneering figure in forestry and conservation, was later a powerful figure in the Progressive Party. Raised in Connecticut in a family of French descent, Pinchot studied forestry in Western Europe and first applied what he had learned to the development of the Vanderbilts' Biltmore estate. Pinchot was an early proponent of the nation's forest system, heading up the new forest service under several administrations. In 1902, he issued recommendations regarding husbanding the natural resources of the Philippines. He was twice governor of Pennsylvania. 140–1, 172

Platt, Jeannie, twice widowed, was born Jeannie P. Smith, the daughter of Senator Truman Smith of Connecticut. After the death of her first husband, a Mr. Hoyt, she married Orville Hitchcock Platt (1827–1905), an elderly widower who lived only a few years subsequently. Platt was a highly regarded figure in the Senate, of which he was a member from 1879 until his death. He was the author of the Platt Amendment making Cuba a U.S. protectorate. 151

Platt, Charles Adams (1861–1933), at the time he is mentioned in the diary, was beginning to make his reputation as an architect of country homes, after beginning his career as a landscape architect. 172

Porter, George French (1881–1927), who in 1903 graduated from Yale, was the son of Henry Holmes Porter and Eliza French Porter. His father made a large fortune through speculative investment in railroads, lumber, and coal and steel. Freed of the need to work, George Porter became active in politics and remained active in business and as a trustee. In 1912 he was the western treasurer of the Progressive National Committee. Suffering from mental illness, he fatally shot himself in 1927. 96, 108

The **Porter** family

Horace (1837–1921), a graduate of Harvard and West Point, was a famed raconteur whose civil war memoir, *Campaigning with Grant* (1897), admiringly captured Grant's genius in action. He was close to McKinley, having served as one of his principal political fund-raisers. His daughter and Catherine's friend wrote a biography of her father, *An American Solider and Diplomat*, in 1927. As ambassador, Porter lived in grand style, turning up his nose, Henry Adams wrote, at the hotel that had served Whitelaw Reid, his predecessor. The house he took instead was, in the words of his daughter Elsie, "filled with the most magnificent works of art, old armor, tapestries, pictures, carving, inlaid work, marble, stained glass and everything that is old and beautiful." Many of the objects were the legacy of Austrian-born Friedrich **Spitzer** (1815–1890), a famed collector of medieval and Renaissance art who had previously occupied the house. 22, 24, 27, 30, 32–3, 61–2

Sophie McHaig Porter (d 1903), his wife. 22, 24–5, 27–8, 30, 32–3, 35, 96

Elsie (1879-1933), his daughter and one of Catherine's closest friends; married Edwin Mende and lived in Berne, Switzerland. 22, 24–8, 30–3, 35, 41, 61–2, 67, 80, 96, 106, 146–7, 149–50

Price, Bruce (1845–1903), was a sought-after architect who designed a variety of buildings in Canada and the United States. He designed the Alberta Hotel in Banff and the Hotel Frontenac in Quebec. In addition to building churches, railroad termini, city houses, and resort homes, he designed innovative railroad cars. He was the author of *The Large Country House* and the father of etiquette maven Emily Post. 122

Proctor, George (1896–1915), a concert pianist, at the time he is mentioned in the diary was in town to play Liszt's Piano Concerto in E-Flat with the Chicago Symphony. The concert was performed on January 1, 1904, but because of the December 30, 1903, Iroquois Theater fire the audience was small and even Proctor's excellent performance could not pierce the city's mourning. Proctor was affiliated with the New England Conservatory of Music in Boston. 74

Reid, Whitelaw (1837–1912), a newspaperman turned diplomat, was nearing the end of an eventful career that stretched back to the civil war. He first came to wide attention for his reporting of civil war battles. In the 1860s, he went to work for Horace Greeley at the *New York Tribune*. He became editor and, after Greeley's death, bought the paper. He was a Republican from his earliest days. In 1881 he married Elizabeth Mills (1825–1931), the only daughter of Darius Ogden Mills. At her father's death in 1910, she and her brother inherited his estate of between $60 million and $100 million. Reid was appointed ambassador to the Court of St. James in 1905, holding the post until 1912. During his ambassadorship, the couple lived at Dorchester House and entertained on a royal scale. Mrs. Reid was chair of the American Red Cross in Britain during World War I. 104

Reilly, Emma Pauline Tower, was an heiress. A daughter of coal and iron magnate Charlemagne Tower Sr., she inherited a fifth of his large fortune. Ruth Snyder was her daughter by her first marriage, which presumably ended with Mr.

Snyder's death. Her second husband, Thomas Reilly (ca. 1855–1916), was a leather merchant in New York City. In 1926, she married George Smith Downing, a prominent banker. In 1907, her daughter, Ruth, married a Belgian nobleman, becoming Countess Camille de Borchgrave d'Altena. 24–7, 30, 32, 40–1

The **Remington** and **Leiter** families were patrons of Frudy Moewis. **Flora Carver Remington** and her husband, **Samuel Remington** (ca. 1827–82), scion of the Remington Arms Company of New York, went abroad after the civil war when domestic sales of weapons fell off. From roughly 1866 to 1877, the Remingtons lived in Paris, where Samuel became one of the era's most prominent arms dealers, selling arms throughout Europe, Asia, and the Middle East. In gratitude for his "services" to Egypt, Khedive Ismael Pasha gave Remington a parcel of land in one of the most desirable sections of Cairo. Toward the end of his life, Remington built a small marble palace on the property, which the family sometimes occupied. It was eventually sold to the British government, which used it for diplomatic purposes until the 1950s.

Jennie (b. ca. 1863), the Remingtons' daughter, grew up mostly abroad. Like a heroine out of a James novel, she married not an aristocrat but a painter, William Pretyman of England. Though her 1883 wedding was minutely described in the papers (an attention unusual for the time), little was heard of her subsequently.

The case was otherwise with the Leiters. Flora Remington's sister, Mary Carter Leiter (Mrs. Levi Z. Leiter), was matriarch of one of Chicago's wealthiest families (see Leiter above). 44

Remsen, Ira (1846–1927), a distinguished chemist, was from an old New York family. He served as president of Johns Hopkins University from 1901 to 1913. 172

Riddle, John Wallace (1864–1941), ambassador to Russia (1906–9) and Argentina (1921–25). 27

Rodenbach, Georges (1855–98), was a symbolist novelist and poet whose work was inspired by Belgium, his native land. He was a friend of Stephen Mallarmé. Catherine indirectly alludes to Rodenbach's *Musée de Béguines*, which she may have read after its publication in 1906. 79

Rogers, Emily, and her brother Nathaniel Pendleton Rogers lived near the Frederick Vanderbilts in Dutchess County, New York. They were likely the children of Nathaniel Pendleton Rogers and Emily Moulton. The younger Nathaniel, who joined the military during World War I, died of typhoid in 1916. 60, 77, 85, 95

Roosevelt, Alice (1884–1980), the headstrong daughter of Theodore Roosevelt by his first wife, Alice Higginson Lee (1861–84), was nineteen when her father became president. By her own account, she felt herself an "orphan" in her own family, causing her to act out by smoking, driving fast cars, and otherwise attracting attention, which she did brilliantly. She was the subject of popular songs including "Alice Blue Gown" and "Alice, Where Art Thou?" She possessed great star power. Alice married the congressman Nicholas Longworth in a dazzling White House ceremony in 1906. The couple had one child, Pauline (1925–57). During her long life, Alice remained a luminary of the Washington social scene; her attitude was probably best described by a pillow on which she embroidered "If you can't say something nice, then sit next to me." 77–8, 94–5, 117, 161

Roosevelt, Theodore (1858–1919), 26th President of the United States. 74, 160–1

Root, Edith, was the daughter of Elihu Root. She later became the wife of U. S. Grant III. 118, 138–9

Root, Elihu (1845–1937), a New York lawyer, was secretary of war beginning in 1899. He resigned partly to recover from overwork (he had overseen the American military effort in the Spanish-American War) and partly to please his wife, Clara Frances Wales Root (1853–1928), who did not like Washington. Ironically, the Roots soon returned to Washington after John Hay's death in 1905, yielding to Roosevelt's desire that Root become secretary of state. Root later represented New York in the Senate from 1909 to 1915. He was president of the Carnegie Endowment for International Peace (1910–25) and was awarded the Nobel Peace Prize in 1912. 76, 139, 161

Rosen, Baron Roman Romanovitch (1847–1922), Russian ambassador to the United States from 1905 to 1911. He was from a wealthy family of Swedish descent that owned extensive lands in Lithuania. Baron Rosen was highly cultivated, and fluent in English, Italian, French, German, and Japanese. He had a distinct social presence and was described by the *New York Times* as being as well known personally to Americans "as any Russian of his generation." He fled Russia during the 1918 revolution, eventually settling in New York City. Having lost his wealth, he supported himself in his last years by writing. 161

Rothschild, Leopold G. (d. 1924), Albert's trusted political aide. 180

Royaards, W. A., was a member of the Netherlands legation. 162

von Rubido-Zichy, Baron Ivan (b. 1874), was secretary of the Austro-Hungarian embassy at Washington in 1904. He was later minister at Bucharest and London. 117

Runnells, Clive (1877–1935), was son of the president of the Pullman Company. 38, 49, 58, 114

Ryerson, Edwin Warner (1872–1961), was born in New York City. He was trained as a physician at Harvard and abroad. In 1899, he moved to Chicago with his mother and only brother after his father, George W. Ryerson, died. Ned had a brilliant career as an orthopedic surgeon, introducing a number of innovations especially as related to the clubfoot. He taught at Northwestern University. He married Catherine's close friend Adelaide Hamilton; the couple remained intimates of Catherine their entire lives. 58, 85

Sala, Count Antoine (d. 1946), attaché to the French embassy in Washington. 94

Santos-Dumont, Alberto (1873–1932), dapper Brazilian-born aviation pioneer. 61

Sears, Eleonora Randolph (1881–1968), daughter of Frederick Richard and Eleon Randolph Coolidge Sears of Boston, was one of the great female athletes of her time. In addition to being a pioneering sportswoman, she was a fashion plate and prominent socialite. She was a great-great-granddaughter of Thomas Jefferson. She had a residence at Pride's Crossing, Massachusetts, where Delia Field died, in 1937. 57, 77

Sears, Joseph Hamblen (ca. 1865–1946), was president of the publishing house D. Appleton & Co. He met Albert while working at Harper & Brothers, when that press published *The Russian Advance*. Boston-born and well educated, Sears was a sophisticated, unsentimental man. The Sears and Albert were close friends, and Albert would often visit Sears and his wife, Anna Wentworth Caldwell Sears (d. 1937), at their home on Oyster Bay. 143, 172

Sears, Sarah Choate (1858–1935), an artist, was wife of Joshua Montgomery Sears and the daughter of Elizabeth (Carlile) and Charles Francis Choate of Boston. Her uncle, Joseph Hodges Choate, was ambassador to Great Britain (1899–1905). At the time she is mentioned in the diary, Sarah was reaching her prime as an artist, winning medals at several international expositions. 57

Seeds, William (1882–1973), later Sir William, was attaché to the British embassy in Washington. Son of the queen's advocate, Robert Seeds, and Lady Kaye of Dublin, he became a high-ranking diplomat, serving as British high commissioner to the Rhineland (1928–30) and ambassador to Brazil (1930–35) and to the USSR (1939–40). 118

Shaw, Albert (1857–1947), founding editor of the *Review of Reviews*, an American monthly modeled on the venerable British periodical. Shaw held a doctorate in history and political economy from Johns Hopkins and early on had written several studies of municipal government, being one of a number of young reformers to take an interest in urban problems. Commenting monthly on the American scene in the *Review of Reviews*, he exercised considerable influence over thinking Americans. 165–6, 170, 172

Siam, Crown Prince of (1881–1925), later King Vajiravudh (Rama IV), was one of the many sons of King Chulalungkorn, admired in the West as one of the most "progressive" rulers of Asia. King Chulalungkorn was a pupil of Anna Leonowens, whose 1870 account of her experience as *The English Governess at the Siamese Court* would later be popularized in *The King and I*. The crown prince, who like his father had received a Western education, was on an extensive tour of Europe and the United States at the time he appears in the diary. 27

de Sibour, Jules Henri (1872–1938), a young Beaux Arts graduate who had become Bruce Price's associate, (see above). A viscount, born in Paris, de Sibour was brought to the United States as a

child and raised as an American. De Sibour went to Yale, where he was a star football player. His first success as an architect was as consulting architect of New York's Hudson Terminal. He designed Bancroft Hall at the Annapolis Naval Academy. 122

von Siebert, Benno (1876?–1926), an admirer of Catherine whom she refers to both as de Siebert and von Siebert. He was attached to the Russian Embassy. In all likelihood, the reference is to Benno Aleksandrovich Fon Ziebert who was the author of several books on diplomacy written in German. The only work that appears to have been translated into English is *Entente Diplomacy* and *The World: Matrix of the History of Europe 1909–1914* (1921). 98, 109, 117–8, 138, 140

Simmons, Furnifold McLendel (1854–1940), a Democratic senator from North Carolina. He took his seat in 1901 and remained in the Senate until 1931. 78

Slater, Elizabeth Hope Gammell ("Hope") (1854–1994), of Newport and Washington, one of Delia Caton's closest friends. She and her husband, John Whipple Slater, lived apart. 43, 59, 61, 67, 74–7, 84–7, 94–5, 109, 116–8, 122, 129–30, 139, 141, 153, 161, 164, 172

Slocum, Luna Garrison(d 1928), was from St. Louis. Her husband, Colonel Stephen L'Hommedieu Slocum (1859–1933) was nephew of New York financier Russell Sage. A cavalry officer formerly active in the Indian wars in the American West, he was military attaché at Lisbon, London, and St. Petersburg. 27–8, 32–4

Smalley, George Washburn (1833–1916), an American-born journalist, had nearly completed his apotheosis at the time he appears in the diary. He had begun his career in the 1860s as European correspondent for the *New York Tribune*; in 1895, he became the American correspondent for the London *Times*. 118

Smith, Joseph Lindon (1863–1950), was an artist whose work included murals, paintings, and the design of masques and pageants. Several of Smith's pageants were performed in Chicago, and one such event may have brought him to the city at the time he appears in the diary. Smith was deeply interested in archeology and ancient art and was considered an authority in fields such as Egyptology and Cambodian art. 109

Smith, William Alden (1859–1932), was a U.S. senator from Michigan. 170

Somers, Elizabeth Jane (1837–1924), Catherine's great-aunt on her father's side, was the sister of Thomas Mears Eddy. She was founder of the Mount Vernon Seminary for Girls, subsequently Mount Vernon College, a two-year female junior college in Washington, D.C. The school closed in the 1990s and the property is now owned by George Washington University. 162

Spreckels, Claus August ("Gus") (ca. 1858–1946), learned the sugar-refining business from his father and became the secretary of all the Spreckels companies. He spent a good deal of time on the east coast, first managing one of the family's refineries near Philadelphia and later organizing the Federal Sugar

Refinery Company in Yonkers, which he ran from 1901 until the 1920s. In 1883, Spreckels married Oroville Dore (ca. 1866–1933) of San Mateo, California, who was known as a beauty. The couple were drawn to France, which they made their home for long periods of time, maintaining a Paris residence on the Avenue Foch and a villa in Monte Carlo. They amassed a notable collection of paintings and decorative art, which they were forced to auction when their fortune shrank in the 1920s. 120–1, 143

Spreckels, Lurline Elizabeth (1885–1969), was a California heiress, the member of a contentious dynasty headed by her grandfather, Claus Spreckels (1826–1908), who had amassed a fortune in sugar. The grandfather Spreckels was a consummate innovator, creating and bringing together the elements necessary for sugar refining, in the process becoming, for a time, de facto ruler of the kingdom of Hawaii. He also owned railroads and gas companies. Lurline's father, Claus August (see above), was one of Spreckels's four sons. In the 1890s he and another brother pitted themselves against their father and siblings in a bitter attempt to gain control of the family's estate. In 1906, Lurline, an only child, married Catherine's brother, Spencer Eddy; the couple divorced in 1923. 105, 107, 121–2, 125, 143, 173, 175

Stephens, Redmond Davis (1874–1931), was a lawyer and vice president of the Chicago and Oak Park Elevated Railroad. 38

von Sternburg, Baron Hermann Speck (1852–1908), was born in England of a German father and an English mother. He was a naturalized British citizen. His grandfather was a landed German nobleman who had made his fortune in England, trading in beef. Young von Sternburg went to Germany and became a German subject at age eighteen in order to take part in the Franco-Prussian War. In 1895 he became military attaché to the German legation in Washington. He rose in the ranks and was ambassador to the United States from 1903 until his comparatively early death in 1908. In this time he became a close friend of Teddy Roosevelt and was considered a popular and effective ambassador, personally credited with creating warm feelings between the United States and Germany. His success was aided by his American wife, Baroness von Sternburg (d. 1959), born Lillian May Langham, of Louisville, Kentucky. Her sister, a famous beauty, was the model for "the Gibson girl." After the baron's death, his wife resided permanently in Germany, remaining loyal to that country during the early years of World War I. 138–9, 160, 162, 172

The **Stone** case held the attention of the American media, Congress, and Protestant religious groups for several months. In Turkey, on September 4, 1901, American Ellen Stone (1846–1927), a fifty-five-year-old Protestant missionary, was kidnapped by members of the International Revolutionary Organization of Macedonia and Adrianople (IMRO). The group's motive was to pressure Turkey, which remained in charge of Macedonia after the 1878 Treaty of Berlin, to implement certain "reforms" the treaty required. The group, chronically short of cash, decided to fill its treasury by holding a missionary for ransom. Miss Stone was an available victim. Sensitive to the morality of the time, the kidnappers decided she should have a companion to preserve her reputation, so they also kidnapped a thirty-five-year-old Albanian, Katerina Tsilka (1866–1952), who was five months pregnant. For six months the women were held in captivity, shuttled among primitive hiding spots in the mountainous region dividing Bulgaria and Turkey. Katerina give birth to a baby girl, Elena, who survived.

At his post in Istanbul, Spencer was right in the middle of the case. He was closely involved in the rescue efforts, which were hampered by bureaucratic infighting and lack of cooperation from Turkey and Bulgaria. These governments, determined to avoid reparation claims, were interested only in tracking down and killing the kidnappers without regard to the victims. At first, the United States declared it would not pay a ransom (a position that predictably changed), although the ransom—$66,000, then a large sum—was raised by public subscription. Also detrimental to the rescue efforts was the existence of two U.S. negotiating teams, neither appearing to recognize the other.

But all ended well. Ellen Stone and Katerina Tsilka were ransomed. Each lived into her eighties and profited from the experience through magazine articles and lecture tours, where baby Elena appeared to tumultuous applause at the climax of the talks. The U.S. government reimbursed subscribers to the ransom fund in 1912. The only participant to fare badly was IMRO, which frittered away the ransom money, lost most of its leaders, and saw its movement effectively suppressed. 35, 47

Stone, Herbert Stuart, and his wife, Mary, were among Catherine's most cherished friends. Herbert (1871–1915) was the son of renowned journalist Melville E. Stone, who founded the *Chicago Daily News* and was a force behind the creation of the Associated Press. Herbert received his early education in Switzerland before attending Harvard, where his first publication, *The Chap-Book*, gave early evidence of a sophisticated sensibility. Returning to Chicago, he and a classmate founded Stone & Kimball Publishing Co., which published an astonishing list of avant-garde works by such authors as Yeats, Ibsen, Maeterlinck, Anatole France, Stephen Crane, Rimbaud, Verlaine, and Mallarmé. *The Chap-Book* and the lithographic posters Stone & Kimball commissioned to advertise their books have been credited with bringing the art nouveau tradition of graphic design to the States. After 1901, Stone also owned and edited the periodical *House Beautiful*. He died aboard the Luisitania in 1915. 38, 58–9, 96, 98, 108–9, 114, 179

Stone, Mary Grigsby McCormick (1878–1955), daughter of William G. McCormick, was the wife of Herbert Stone. She was yet another member of the numerous Patterson-McCormick clan.

Stuck, Franz von (1863–1928), a leading artist, illustrator, and designer, was one of the founders of the Munich Secession. His large villa, built in 1897–98, reflected his preoccupation with linking works of art to their setting. The house was decorated in a sort of "Pompeian style" with "unusual and sumptuous materials." 40, 63

The **Duchess of Sutherland** (1867–1955), born Lady Millicent Fanny St. Clair-Erskine, was a daughter of the 4th Earl of Rosslyn. Both she and her half-sister Frances Maynard, Countess of Warwick, known as "Daisy," were famous for their charm and beauty. 31–2, 165

Tarkington, Booth (1869–1946), not yet forty when he appears in the diary, had achieved celebrity with his novels *The Gentleman from Indiana*, *Monsieur Beaucaire*, and *The Conquest of Canaan* and with the hit play *The Man from Home*. A true local hero, who would win the Pulitzer Prize twice, he scarcely needed brushes of East Coast and European sophistication to render him glamorous. Tarkington was representative of the creative talent then emerging from the Midwest. 155

Taylor, Hannis (1851–1922), a lawyer and diplomat, was minister to Spain from 1893 to 1897, just prior to the Spanish-American War. He served as special counsel to the government before the Spanish Treaty Claims Commission of 1902 and the Alaska Boundary Commission in 1903. 172

Thorndike, Olivia (1877–1968), daughter of John Larkin and Florence Greenough Thorndike of Boston. Her father was a founding partner in the firm of Storey, Thorndike, Palmer, & Dodge, which handled the legal affairs of the Union Pacific Railroad. In 1911, Olivia became the wife of Nathaniel Stone Simpkins Jr.; he died in 1918 in the battle of Verdun. The Simpkinses, though a Boston family, were involved in mining in Michigan's upper peninsula. They had a residence at Beverly Farms,

Massachusetts, and Olivia remained a lifelong friend of Catherine. 57, 117

Thoron, Ward (b. 1867), grandson of humanist Samuel Gray Ward, was a banker, scholar and friend of Henry Adams. Thoron married Ellen Warder in 1893; they later divorced. He then wed Adam's niece, Looly Hooper. Thoron, who was a Francophile and lived much in France, provided the research Adams needed to revise his book on Chartres, which was first printed and circulated in 1904–5. Thoron also edited a volume of letters by Mrs. Henry Adams. 139

Tillman, Benjamin Ryan (1847–1918), Democratic senator from South Carolina. Prior to holding public office, Tillman led a campaign of violence against African Americans in his state that had as its object driving Republicans and people of color from power. He was a fierce opponent of Roosevelt. 166

Tower, Charlemagne, Jr. (1848–1923), and his sister Mrs. Reilly (see above) were beneficiaries of the wealth their brilliant father, Charlemagne Tower Sr. (1809–89), had accumulated. The senior Tower was a lawyer whose first fortune came from his involvement in a suit concerning the title to rich coal lands in Schuylkill County, Pennsylvania, which he won after laboring twenty-five years. In the 1870s, he demonstrated his boldness in his determination to open Minnesota's Vermilion iron range, then a forbiddingly remote territory. 24, 27–8, 30, 143–4, 148

Townsend, Mary Matilde Scott (d. 1949), was a young heiress prominent in Washington society. She was the daughter of Mrs. Richard H. Townsend (born Mary T. Scott) and granddaughter of William Lawrence Scott of Erie, Pennsylvania, a coal, railroad, and shipping baron who endowed her with a large fortune. It was rumored in 1908 that she was to marry the highly eligible Duke of Alba of Spain, but in 1910 she married Senator Peter Goelet Gerry of Rhode Island. They divorced in 1924; shortly thereafter, she married high-ranking but mercurial diplomat Sumner Welles (1892–1961). The Welleses' extravagant lifestyle and sexual mores scandalized official Washington and affected Sumner Welles's already tempestuous political career. The Welleses' residence at 2121 Massachusetts Avenue is now the Cosmos Club. 94, 117

Trudeau, Edward Livingston, Jr. ("Ned") (ca. 1873–1904), was a young physician who went to college at Yale, where he played on the baseball team and belonged to the Skull and Bones. His father, Edward Livingston Trudeau Sr. (1848–1915), also a physician, was regarded as a pioneer in the treatment of tuberculosis. Suffering from the disease himself, the elder Trudeau founded a famous sanatorium at Saranac, New York, believing the air of the Adirondacks to have therapeutic qualities. The Trudeaus figure in the E. L. Doctorow novel *The Waterworks* (1994). In 1903, Ned married the beautiful Hazel Martyn (1880-1935) of Chicago. Their marriage was cut short by Ned's death from pneumonia the following year. Hazel subsequently

married the Irish-born painter John Lavery, who immortalized her in many of his works.(see Martyn, above). 68, 107

Tuttle, George Montgomery (1856–1912), was a prominent New York gynecologist. He taught at Columbia University and was attending gynecologist at Roosevelt Hospital from 1888 until his retirement. 74, 76, 86, 152

van Tuyll, Baron E. L. L. van Serooskerken, was the secretary of the Netherlands legation at Washington (and interim chargé d'affaires) in 1904. 94

Tyson, Russell (ca. 1868–1963), was born in Shanghai. He attended Harvard and became a partner in the Chicago real estate firm of Aldis & Co., a position he held until his retirement. He lived in Lake Forest, Illinois, and became a noted collector of Chinese and Korean art, which he donated to the Art Institute. 107

Upjohn, Richard (1802–78), and his son Richard Mitchell Upjohn (1828–1903) were leading exponents of Gothic Revival architecture in the United States. Walden Myer's father, General Albert Myer, built the house that Catherine refers to in the diary. The Myers were apparently devotees of the Gothic style, both Albert and Walden ardently supporting the building of the National Cathedral. Walden and his sister, Gertrude, are buried within its precincts. 94

Vanderbilt, Consuelo (1877–1964), was the Duchess of Marlborough. Under pressure from her ambitious

mother, she had married the 9th Duke of Marlborough, becoming mistress of Blenheim at age seventeen. In 1902, when Consuelo was to be presented at the Russian imperial court, the prospect made even her high-born husband jumpy. The Romanov Russian court was renowned for its opulence, particularly in the years prior to the Sino-Russian War. Few Europeans could compete with the Russians when it came to jewels: many ladies wore different jewels for every entertainment. The Duke of Marlborough therefore anxiously invested in new diamonds for Consuelo and invited along Milicent, Duchess of Sutherland, to make sure theirs would be an impressive party.

Throughout her life, Consuelo was a celebrity, radiating fragility and a defiant intelligence. After bearing two sons, she and her husband ended their loveless marriage, incurring publicity and disapproval. She later married a man she loved, Jacques Balsan, and became an unpretentious but determined advocate of humanitarian causes. 31–3

Vanderbilt, Mrs. Frederick W. (1844–1926), a tireless philanthropist with a particular interest in young people, was born Louise Holmes Anthony. She had been married to Albert Torrance, Mr. Vanderbilt's nephew, whom she divorced before marrying Mr. Vanderbilt. 44, 60, 76, 79, 95, 97, 140, 161

Vladimir, Grand Duchess Maria Pavlovna (1854–1920), was an influential member of the Russian court who befriended Catherine during her 1902 visit to St. Petersburg. 28, 31–4

Wadsworth, Craig Wharton (1872–1960), American diplomat. He was second secretary at London from 1905 to 1909. He was a Rough Rider and a member of Roosevelt's staff when the latter was governor of New York. 144, 161

Wadsworth, James (1877–1952), though later to become a U.S. senator, had mainly distinguished himself, at the time he appears in the diary, as a Yale first baseman, qualifying for the 1898 All-American team. The son of Congressman James Wolcott Wadsworth Sr. of New York, Jimmie spent the rest of his life alternating between service in the House or Senate and running the ancestral farm in Genesco. 47–8, 76

Wadsworth, Martha Blow (ca. 1862–1934), was the wife of Herbert W. Wadsworth of Maine, cousin of James W. Wadsworth Jr. She was born in Missouri and was the sister of Susan Blow, who was famous as a promoter of kindergarten. Mrs. Wadsworth was an outstanding horsewoman, noted for her daring. She was instrumental in establishing the Geneseo region of New York as an important center of horse breeding. The Wadsworths' Washington residence, at 1801 Massachusetts Avenue, occupied the whole block. It is now the Sulgrave Club. 138

Walker, Charles Cobb (1871–1950), a Chicago friend of Catherine, affluent, carefree, and cosmopolitan, who joined the Boston law firm of Story, Thorndike, Palmer, and Thayer. In Boston he lived in a mansion built by Peter Charndon Brooks;

he also had a large estate at Manchester, Massachusetts. 41

Wallace, Sir Richard (1818–90), the natural son of Richard Seymour-Conway, the 4th Marquis of Hertford (1800–1870), was a racy character whose genius as a collector he shared with his father. Both men lived substantial portions of their lives in Paris, successively amassing a tremendous collection of European art, which on the death of Sir Richard's widow in 1897, was bequeathed to the British nation. 42

Walls, Frank Xavier (b. 1869), a Chicagoan, was an attending physician at Cook County, St. Luke's, and Wesley hospitals and professor of pediatrics at Northwestern Medical School. 179

Warder, Ellen, born Ellen N. Ormsbee (d. 1928), was the widow of Benjamin Head Warder (1824–94). Her husband had beena leading citizen of Springfield, Ohio, where his firm, the Warder-Bushnell-Glessner Company, manufactured reapers. The family moved to Washington in 1887, where Mr. Warder built several hundred buildings and held stock in several banks and financial institutions. He died in Egypt while traveling. Mrs. Warder had three daughters, two of whom, Ellen (later Mrs. Ward Thoron) and Alice (later Mrs. John Work Garrett), Catherine saw socially while in Washington. 76, 84, 118

Washburn, George Hamlin (1860–1933), was a Boston-area physician specializing in obstetrics and gynecology. 178

Wetmore, George Peabody (1846–1921), former governor of Rhode Island, was a U.S. senator from 1895 to 1913. 94

Whigham, Henry James (1869–1954), a Scottish-born journalist who, as correspondent for the London *Morning Post*, had covered the Boxer Rebellion and the Russo-Japanese War. In 1906–7 he was foreign editor of the London *Standard*. Whigham spent several years in the United States lecturing and writing. In 1896 he lectured on political economy at the University of Chicago and worked as drama critic for the *Chicago Tribune*. In 1908, he became editor of *Metropolitan Magazine* (later *Town & Country*), a position he held until 1935. 121

White, Andrew Dickson (1832–1918), historian and educator turned diplomat, served the U.S. as ambassador to Russia and to Germany. He was known as a champion of science and objectivity. He not only presided over the formation of Cornell (1867–85) but was the first president of the American Historical Association. In his scholarship, he lauded the ascendancy of scientific knowledge over religious superstitions of the past. Ironically, the death of White's first wife and his subsequent marriage to the much younger Helen Magill (1853–1944) stimulated his interest in spiritualism. Helen, who was the daughter of Edward Hicks Magill, longtime president of Swarthmore, was one of the first American women to earn a PhD. She had been raised a Quaker and sought to kindle in her skeptical husband a religious faith that seemed natural to her. 24–5, 27

White, Stanford (1853–1906), a prominent architect, was a principal in the New York firm McKim, Mead & White. He was killed by Harry K. Thaw, the jealous millionaire husband of actress Evelyn Nesbit, whom White had seduced when she was sixteen. The murder dominated the tabloids for months. 60

Whitney, Helen Hay (1875–1944), was the daughter of U.S. secretary of state John Milton Hay (see above); her husband, Payne Whitney (1876–1927), was one of the country's wealthiest men. 41

zu Wied, Prince (dates unknown), was a member of one of the oldest noble families in Germany. In 1898, he had married the daughter of the Duke of Wurtemberg. 26

Wilhelm II (1859–1941), who ruled Germany from 1888–1918, had many fervent admirers in the English-speaking world prior to the outbreak of World War I. In 1902 when Catherine was presented at court, the Kaiser was fourteen years into his reign, but he was a relatively young man, having come to the throne when just twenty-nine. Wilhelm was ambitious for himself and his nation; he was determined to lead the world. Though injured at birth, with impaired hearing and balance and an impaired arm, he rode and was regarded as an excellent marksman—qualities valued in a "strenuous age." In 1881, Wilhelm married Auguste Vikotira (1858-1921), princess of Schleswig-Holstein-Sonderburg-Augustenburg. He and the empress had a large family: six boys and a girl. Wilhelm's partly English identity

(he was Queen Victoria's eldest grandchild) and his membership in the "family" of sovereigns somewhat mitigated the anxiety that his aggressiveness aroused.

Following Germany's defeat in World War I and the outbreak of a civilian revolution, the kaiser abdicated the throne and spent the rest of his life in exile in the Netherlands at Huis Doorn. During the Nazi period, Wilhelm's unaltered chauvinism expressed itself in a telegram he sent Hitler congratulating him on the occupation of Paris in June 1940. Wilhelm died the following year. 25–6, 66

Williams, Caroline Caton (1844–1927), was the widow of Norman Williams (1835–1899), a prominent Chicago lawyer. The sister of Arthur Caton, she was Delia's sister-in-law. Catherine Williams had two children, Norman Jr., and Laura, who became the wife of General Wesley Merritt in 1898. Sometime after 1902, Mrs. Williams moved from Chicago to Washington, D.C., where she continued to be well known in society. 49, 86, 102, 164

Wilson, James (1835–1920), Scottish by birth, emigrated to the United States in 1852 and eventually settled in Iowa. In the 1890s, he became a professor of agriculture at the Iowa Agricultural College. He was secretary of agriculture from 1897 to 1913. During his tenure, agricultural stations were set up all over the United States, demonstration projects were begun in the South, and expert advice on farming was sought from all over the world. 161, 164

Woods, Adeline Percy (d. 1927), later Mrs. George Sherwin Hooke Pearson. Her father was Admiral Sir Henry Woods Pasha, one of two imperial aides-de-camp attached by the British government to the the staff of the Turkish sultan Abdul Hamid II. 46–7

Wyndham, George (1863–1913), an English author and politician, was known for his efforts to implement moderate and humane policies in Ireland. Handsome and of a literary bent, he was married to Sibyl Grosvenor, one of the most admired women of her generation. 36

Young, Sir George (1837–1930), 3rd baronet, was an English civil servant known for his administrative talents and longevity. He was descended from British naval officers and inherited from them a distinctive country house in Berkshire, England, called Formosa Place, that was built to resemble the admiral's quarters on a man-of-war. 45

Young, George (1872–1952), son of the above and later 4th baronet was a young diplomat attached to the British embassy in Constantinople. He later became secretary to the British embassy in Washington. Young was both dashing and intellectual. In addition to being the first Westerner to codify Turkish law, he helped draft the Weimar Constitution and organized and led rescue and relief missions during the Spanish Civil War. 45–7, 173

CHANGES MADE TO
THE MANUSCRIPT

Page Change

65 Changed Inferno to *Inferno*

65 Changed "Glyptotek" to "Glyptothek"

65 Changed "Bocticelli" to "Botticelli"

65 Changed "landeau" to "landau"

66 Changed "Karrersee" to "Karersee"

66 Changed "Walschhofen" to "Welschnofen"

74 Changed "entre act" to "entr'acte"

79 Changed "Belle Allience" to "Belle Alliance"

85 Changed "Elysee Place" to "Elysée Palace" Hotel

85 Changed "Devé" to "Dévie," to accord with spelling in 1902

85 Changed "Fontainbleau" to "Fontainebleau"

86 Changed "preceeded" to "preceded"

88 Changed "nothing to eat by corn husks" to nothing to eat but corn husks"

89 Changed "accoustics" to "acoustics"

94 Changed "Farramond" to Faramond"

94 Changed "Boardman's" to "Boardmans'"

94 Changed "Gurnee" to "Gurney"

95 Changed "boullion" to "bouillon"

96 Changed "occulist" to "oculist"

99 Changed "Beloselsky" to "Belloselsky" to accord with earlier message

101 Changed "Riesemuelle" to 'Riesemuhle" to agree with earlier message

104 Changed "Crosleys" to "Crossleys"

105 Throughout—changed "Spreckles" to "Spreckels"

105 Changed "Lenotre" to Le Nôtre"

106 Changed "Huysman's " to "Huysmans'"

108 Changed "Kohlstaat" to "Kohlsaat"

108 Capitalized Sunday in "my mother's sunday lunches"

109 Changed "suger" to "sugar"

117 Changed "Bernsdorf" to "Bernstorff"

117 Changed "I went with . . . others for tea on the Mayflower" to "I went . . . for tea at the Mayflower"

118 Changed "Eustice" to "Eustace" Percy

118 Changed "lillies" to "lilies"

122 Changed "Kennilworth" to Kenilworth"

Page Change

123 Changed "Barocque" to "Baroque"

127 Changed "Landsdowne" to "Lonsdale" per WBI entries for the Lowthers

127 Changed "Edinborough" to "Edinburgh"

128 Changed "Albergeldie" to "Abergeldie" per typescript

138 Throughout—changed "Sternberg" to "Sternburg"

139 Changed "Brandigee" to "Brandegee"

143 Changed "the Goerge Perkins'" to "the George Perkinses"

144 Changed "Wahnsee" to "Wannsee"

145 Changed "Contrexeville" to "Contrexéville"

146 Following—changed "Domrémy" to "Domremy," per Baedeker

146 Added close-quote after the phrase, 'is a quaint village.' Based on the tenses, that is probably where the quotation ends.

147 Added close quote after the phrase, 'and to Spencer's'

149 Changed "Maestro" to "Mestre" per usage on page

151 Changed "Bahnhof Strasse" to "Bahnhofstrasse"

153 Changed "Gillette" to "Gillett" per BDAC

153 Changed "enceinte" to "enceinte"

153 Joined the two-sentence paragraph, beginning with the sentence, "I began to think I was enceinte," to the previous paragraph.

155 Changed "Carey" to "Cary"

155 Changed "at my mothers" to "at my mother's"

160 Changed "Glynn" to "Glyn"

162 Changed "Collom" to "Cullom"

162 Throughout—changed "LaFollette" to "La Follette"

162 Changed "Hemmingway" to "Hemenway" per BDAC

165 Changed "Bourke-Cochrans'" to "Bourke Cockrans'" per BDAC

168 Changed "duane" to "douane"

169 Changed "Beverely" to "Beverly"

170 Added close quote after *La Boheme*

171 Changed "O'Connor" to "O'Connell"

172 Changed "a dull, old, dry-as-dust." to "a dull, old, dry-as-dust man."

The book was designed and produced
by Salsgiver Coveney Associates, Inc.
in Westport, Connecticut.

It is set in the typeface Electra. Designed
in 1935 by William Addison Dwiggins,
Electra has been a standard book typeface
since its release because of its evenness of
design and high legibility. In the specimen
book for Electra, Dwiggins himself points out
the types identifying characteristics: The
weighted top serifs of the straight letters of the
lower case: that is a thing that occurs when you
are making formal letters with a pen, writing
quickly. And the flat way the curves get away
from the straight stems: that is a speed
product. Electra is not only a fine text face
but is equally responsive when set at display
sizes, realizing Dwiggins intent when he set
about the design: "... if you dont get your type
warm it will be just a smooth, commonplace,
third-rate piece of good machine technique,
no use at all for setting down warm human
ideas, just a box full of rivets....I'd like to make
it warm, so full of blood and personality that
it would jump at you."

The book was printed and bound in an
edition of 1000 copies by Edwards Brothers,
Incorporated in Ann Arbor, Michigan.